T0302140

Base of the Pyramid Markets in Affluent Countries

This book focusses on the Base of the Pyramid (BOP) in affluent countries and examines the challenge of how to address the needs of deprived population groups in wealthy societies.

The BOP concept was originally developed for the situation of the bottom-tier of societies in developing and emerging countries. It presents an avenue for businesses and other organisations to develop opportunities and new business models that enable and empower those at the BOP. This book adapts BOP models to the context of affluent countries. BOP projects present also in affluent countries promising avenues for businesses, entrepreneurs and civil society actors to become agents of change through value creation and business models that enable the BOP population to raise their socio-economic welfare and well-being. This book thus furthers our understanding of the characteristics of BOP markets (BOPMs) and BOP initiatives in affluent countries, an area widely ignored by BOP scholars so far. It discusses challenges and opportunities of how to mitigate poverty and increase welfare in a sustainable manner while protecting vulnerable groups, and describes several instances of the lives of those affected. The different chapters employ a variety of theoretical and methodological approaches to lay a first foundation for BOP research in affluent countries.

This book is recommended reading for managers and policy makers, as well as students and academics interested in the Base of the Pyramid.

Stefan Gold is Professor and Holder of the Chair for Business Management with focus on Corporate Sustainability at the University of Kassel, Germany.

Marlen Gabriele Arnold is a Professor in the field of Sustainability. Currently, she holds the Chair for Corporate Environmental Management and Sustainability at the Chemnitz University of Technology, Germany.

Judy N. Muthuri is Associate Professor of Corporate Social Responsibility at Nottingham University Business School (NUBS), UK, and chairs the Social and Environmental Responsibility Group leading the School's UN Principles for Responsible Management Education work.

Ximena Rueda is Associate Professor at the School of Management at the Universidad de los Andes, Colombia.

Innovation and Sustainability in Base of the Pyramid Markets

Series Editors:

Marlen Gabriele Arnold
Chemnitz University of Technology, Germany

Stefan Gold
University of Kassel, Germany

Judy N. Muthuri
Nottingham University Business School, UK

Ximena Rueda
Universidad de los Andes, Colombia

Base of the Pyramid Markets in Asia
Innovation and challenges to sustainability
Edited by Marlen Gabriele Arnold, Stefan Gold, Judy N. Muthuri and Ximena Rueda

Base of the Pyramid Markets in Africa
Innovation and challenges to sustainability
Edited by Judy N. Muthuri, Marlen Gabriele Arnold, Stefan Gold and Ximena Rueda

Base of the Pyramid Markets in Affluent Countries
Innovation and challenges to sustainability
Edited by Stefan Gold, Marlen Gabriele Arnold, Judy N. Muthuri and Ximena Rueda

For more information about this series, please visit https://www.routledge.com/Frugal-Innovation-in-Base-of-the-Pyramid-Markets/book-series/FINNBOP

Base of the Pyramid Markets in Affluent Countries

Innovation and Challenges to Sustainability

Edited by Stefan Gold, Marlen Gabriele Arnold, Judy N. Muthuri and Ximena Rueda

LONDON AND NEW YORK

First published 2021
by Routledge
2 Park Square, Milton Park, Abingdon, Oxon OX14 4RN

and by Routledge
605 Third Avenue, New York, NY 10158

Routledge is an imprint of the Taylor & Francis Group, an informa business

British Library Cataloguing-in-Publication Data
A catalogue record for this book is available from the British Library

Library of Congress Cataloging-in-Publication Data
Names: Gold, Stefan, editor. | Arnold, Marlen Gabriele, editor. | Muthuri, Judy N., editor. | Rueda, Ximena, editor.
Title: Base of the pyramid markets in affluent countries : innovation and challenges to sustainability / edited by Stefan Gold, Marlen Gabriele Arnold, Judy N. Muthuri and Ximena Rueda.
Description: 1 Edition. | New York : Routledge, 2021. |
Series: Innovation and sustainability in base of the pyramid markets | Includes bibliographical references and index.
Identifiers: LCCN 2020054836 (print) | LCCN 2020054837 (ebook) | ISBN 9781138390119 (hardcover) | ISBN 9781032008790 (paperback) | ISBN 9780429423512 (ebook)
Subjects: LCSH: Poor--Developed countries. | Business planning. | Poverty--Prevention. | Sustainable development. | Social change.
Classification: LCC HC79.P6 .B3547 2021 (print) | LCC HC79.P6 (ebook) | DDC 658.4/063091722--dc23
LC record available at https://lccn.loc.gov/2020054836
LC ebook record available at https://lccn.loc.gov/2020054837

ISBN: 978-1-138-39011-9 (hbk)
ISBN: 978-1-032-00879-0 (pbk)
ISBN: 978-0-429-42351-2 (ebk)

Typeset in Times New Roman
by MPS Limited, Dehradun

Contents

Preface

The edition on *affluent countries* concludes the Base of the Pyramid (BOP) book series that discusses BOP markets (BOPMs) around the globe, following the Asia, Africa and the South America & the Caribbean editions. The BOP affluent countries edition is important in a number of ways. First, the Base of the Pyramid population segment in affluent countries in Europe, America and Asia has barely received attention from BOP scholars so far, thus vastly neglecting challenges and opportunities of business for the resource-poor people of wealthy nations. Second, the United Nations have strived for *inclusive* development, production and well-being through the Sustainable Development Goals (SDGs), which makes the base part of national income pyramids primary target groups for policy-making (and business-activities). Despite the SDGs' aim to enhance societal equality, inclusive value creation, and development, there is a growing divide in many affluent economies between poor and wealthy population groups. Third, the BOP in affluent countries – both as producers, entrepreneurs, distributors, employees and consumers – may serve as a joint for transferring innovations and business models devised in a developing and emerging country context to the industrialised world, and vice versa. Hence, exchange and mutual learning may be fostered across world regions regarding how to better the standard of living of the bottom tier. After the financial crisis in 2008 there were attempts to transfer innovations from BOP projects in Asia and Africa (e.g. regarding low cost production of products with satisficing quality) to Europe which faced increased low-income consumer groups, but fortunate (though unexpected) fast recovery of affluent economies in the aftermath of the crisis has largely halted those endeavours. Analysts say that the economic recovery from the current COVID-19 crisis will probably take more time, and may thus increase the importance of business approaches and policy-making that address the societal bottom tier in affluent countries.

Although affluent economies are largely situated within rather well-functioning state authorities, private sector actors, such as multinational organisations, small and medium enterprises and entrepreneurs, together with civil society actors, have an important role to play in addressing the socio-economic and development challenges experienced by the bottom tier of the income pyramid. Although income is not always a reliable indicator for the participation opportunities of people within society, lack of income and lack of participation appear to be highly correlated, in particular if low income is linked with low education, isolation, diseases, handicaps etc. The BOP as an important market-based approach to poverty presents also in affluent countries promising avenues for business and entrepreneurs to become agents of change through value creation and business models that enable the BOP population to raise their socio-economic welfare and well-being. Thereby, businesses have to collaborate with other stakeholders to address the needs and tap the potentials of the BOP population to lift them out of poverty and empower them economically as well as socially and culturally. For example, traditional corporate social responsibility (CSR) activities of businesses addressing poor communities may switch to inclusive multi-stakeholder approaches that see the communities not as objects of development but as agents of their own development. At the same time, governments are called for to create institutional structures and regulation that protects vulnerable population groups and hence establishes a level playing field that elicits the potential of all societal members for the benefit of the entire society.

The BOPMs book series is organised into four main sections:

A BOP markets

BOP markets have specific characteristics: core innovations, inclusive business models, main stakeholders and actors involved. BOPMs are related to frugal, reverse and inclusive innovations that can foster a (sustainable) development and initiate new business models and value streams from which other countries can profit as well. Still, the sustainability of related performance is not always clear and warrants critical reflection.

B Drivers and barriers of BOP markets

Institutional voids and mechanisms strongly influence BOPMs, both positively and negatively. Moreover, governmental and international interventions play pivotal roles in progressing BOPMs. Often, business models fill in institutional gaps as strategies to scaling social and economic impact, trade-offs and unanticipated outcomes.

C Roles, cooperation and structure in BOP markets

The configuration of BOPMs is closely linked to cooperation, structure, roles, relations and patterns. Inclusive approaches, for instance, aim at participation, involvement or cooperation between various market actors along the entire value chain. Hence, analysis of (frugal) innovation networks, consumer behaviour, value co-creation and cross-sector collaboration, the role of multinationals, innovation and knowledge capabilities and empowerment of women is pivotal for an understanding of BOPMs.

D Design, integration, innovation and change of BOP markets

The capabilities of BOPMs aim at the differences of key success factors of networks, the interactions concerning the management of design, production, procurement and logistics, sustainable supply chains and integration. The transformation of BOPMs is often accompanied by renewal, innovation, learning, intellectual property and global standards, social business, inclusive corporate social responsibility, circular business models and approaches integrating sustainability.

As evident in the chapters in this book, scholarly interest in the BOP in affluent countries is awakening. This book examines the characteristics of BOPMs and BOP population in affluent countries, focussing on challenges and opportunities to address poverty and development in a sustainable manner while protecting vulnerable groups. The book covers various themes such as modern slavery, new business models, bottle collecting as societal inclusion mechanism and entrepreneurship at the BOPMs. The chapters reflect different socio-economic and national backgrounds, comprising Germany, UK, Ireland and Scandinavian countries, and various sectors such as hand car washes, housing and construction and agriculture. All chapters yield valuable recommendations for researchers, managers and policy-makers.

The first chapter – ***The Base of the Pyramid markets in affluent countries: Opportunities and challenges*** – by Stefan Gold and Wolfgang Bichler-Riedl provides background details on the bottom tier of societies in affluent countries, which helps understanding the opportunities and challenges linked to this population segment and how it links to the BOP in other world regions. It features three interviews – one verbatim and two analogous – with experts on BOPMs in affluent countries, who provide great insights into the drivers, barriers and future of BOP enterprises in the so-called industrialised world.

Andrew Phillips and Alexander Trautrims in the second chapter – ***Feeding a rich nation: Modern slavery reporting in UK agriculture*** – investigate compliance of the UK agricultural sector with reporting obligation on modern slavery as stipulated by the Modern Slavery Act.

The third chapter – ***Bottle collectors between societal exclusion and inclusion in affluent countries*** – by Wolfgang Bichler-Riedl, Annika Mies and Stefan Gold, shows how bottle collecting in Germany may serve as a mechanism of societal inclusion, while society tends to see bottle collecting as outcast activity.

Ahmad Arslan, Asif Ruman, Pia Hurmelinna-Laukkanen and Tahir Ali present in chapter four – ***Varieties of capitalism and the Base of the Pyramid population segment in affluent economies: Discussion on entrepreneurship***

financing and skills development – a comparison of the current BOP situation in selected coordinated and liberal market economies, with focus on entrepreneurship financing and skills development dynamics.

The fifth chapter – ***Tiny Houses as innovations for the Base of Pyramid markets in Germany: A critical perspective under the lens of sustainability*** – by Anne Fischer and Marlen Gabriele Arnold, points to the impact of Tiny Houses as a BOP innovation for the German market, particularly regarding its potential to reduce inequalities by offering shelter to homeless people, providing an affordable alternative for people with low incomes or reintegrating people into society.

In chapter six – ***Far from clean: Labour exploitation in the UK's hand car wash sector*** – Akilah Jardine, Alexander Trautrims and Alison Gardner examine labour exploitation in the hand car wash sector in the UK and expose its threats to workers, the environment and the public.

September 2020

Acknowledgements

The editors would like to express their sincere gratitude to all those who contributed, in one way or another, to the development of this edited collection on the BOPMs in affluent countries. Special thanks go to Simon Probst who helped a lot with proofreading and layout, and facilitated overall success. The book relies essentially on the scholarly input of the chapter contributors to whom we are indebted. Moreover, we appreciate the time and efforts of the voluntary reviewers whose constructive comments and feedback was invaluable for developing each chapter. Finally, we would like to thank the team at Routledge for their support at various stages of the book development and its publishing.

Acknowledgements

[illegible]

Part I

BOP markets

1 The Base of the Pyramid markets in affluent countries

Opportunities and challenges

Stefan Gold and Wolfgang Bichler-Riedl

Introduction: Economic development in affluent countries and BOP

With globalisation, average income has been increasing steadily for developed nations with the exception of the global financial crisis of 2008. This is shown in Figure 1.1 for OECD countries. Other indicators monitoring differing forms of wealth also illustrate that the industrialised world provides opportunities and financial possibilities. For example, gross domestic products (GDPs) have been rising continuously, except during the financial crisis (OECD, 2019a), and graduation rates for upper, secondary education has been steadily growing within the OECD region towards an average of 86% in 2017 (OECD, 2018).

However, not every individual partakes in this development in the same manner. For years, the percentage of income of the richest parts of society has been increasing – especially since the 1960s – which has been decoupled from the general GDP growth (Andrews et al., 2010). Several more instances of inequality are prevalent and often stir hot debates in contemporary societies; for example, precarious working conditions have been rising across developed countries (Kalleberg, 2009), or increasing income inequality leaves workers, who are fully dependent on their salaries, persistently decoupled from decent economic situations (Möller, 2016). These developments ultimately result in a stratum of the population that has been called 'precarity', which consists of people living in uncertainty and instability (Campbell and Price, 2016). However, at least most OECD nations have implemented some sort of a welfare state protecting their citizens from worst deprivation (Bergh et al., 2016).

Since developing nations on the one hand face more severe forms of poverty, and on the other hand lack regulatory programmes protecting their poor, a special focus in business and management research was put upon BOP markets (Prahalad and Lieberthal, 1998). Individuals within these were first addressed by President Roosevelt in 1932 who spoke about 'the forgotten, the unorganized but indispensable units of economic power [...], the forgotten man at the bottom of the economic pyramid' (quoted in Mason

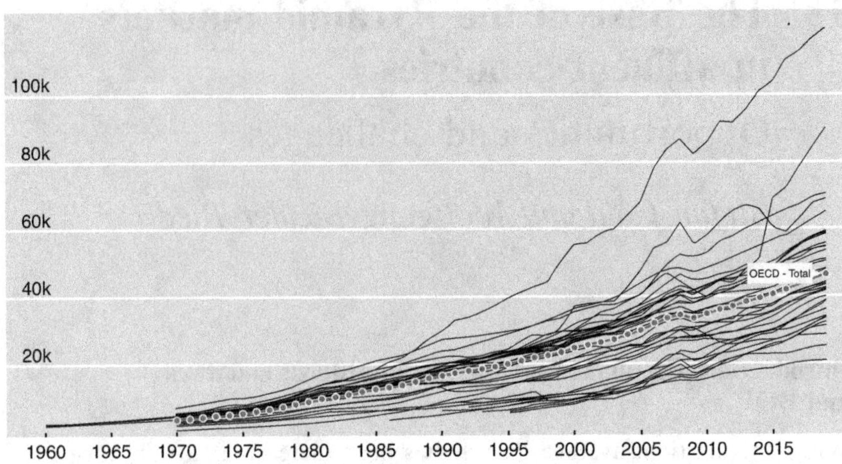

Figure 1.1 Development of GDPs in OECD countries.
Source: OECD (2019a).

et al., 2013, p. 402). Hammond et al. (2008) estimate the size of BOP markets to roughly 4 billion people mostly located in the developing world, based on an often monetary threshold, which is usually used in BOP definitions (Hammond et al., 2008; Kolk et al., 2014; Muthuri and Farhoud, 2021). However, profound differences to the BOP in developing nations require definitions of the BOP in affluent countries to reach beyond exclusively financial characterisations.

Developing nations often lack effective governmental and public programmes aiming at individuals at the base of the (income) pyramid. There are instances of social security systems, 'but large population groups are not covered' (Dethier, 2007, p. 280). Historically, developed nations invested into their social security after World War II, although this depends on the respective national business system (e.g. liberal market economies tend to have less extensive social security programmes). Still this helped to 'reduce poverty drastically, by at least 40% in Europe - in heavily [sic] insured countries such as Belgium and Sweden by more than 70% - and by 28% in the United States' (Dethier, 2007, p. 281).

More recently, however, social security, welfare states and organisations (such as unions) dedicated to vulnerable groups of affluent countries are failing to reach certain groups of the population. To name a few instances, (a) one-in-three workers in the UK fall into the category of 'vulnerable workers' which includes low pay and lack of representation by for example a union, as illustrated by Pollert and Charlwood (2009). Furthermore, (b) increasing total numbers of homelessness in the UK (Terry, 2019), of elderly homeless individuals in Canada (Gaetz et al., 2016), or an increase of 50% of total homeless people in France since 2001 (Yaouancq et al., 2013) show similar tendencies around differing affluent countries. These more frequently missed groups face constant psychological distress concerning (socioeconomic) anxiety and security. Furthermore, depending on an individual's background, such institutions may fail affected people in several manners: due to the erosion of social security and welfare systems, more and more people fall through the social net of benefits, oftentimes minorities. Martin (2012) describes how unions, despite their best intentions, increase the social split between migrant workers and natives, ultimately resulting in even less coverage. Such lack of security from governmental organisations combined with the inability of non-governmental organisations (NGOs) and unions to fully substitute their services constitute a crucial component of BOP membership.

Poverty in developing nations is not congruent to poverty in developed nations. However, both become somewhat comparable using the concept of relative poverty, which is widely defined as having less than 50% of the median household income in a certain country. Applying this threshold for OECD countries, 11.7% of the population were (relatively) poor on average in 2016 (OECD, 2019b). However, not all (relatively) poor individuals are also members of the BOP: for example for Germany, the threshold for relative poverty is determined at 781€/month (Statista, 2008), an income level that more than one in four university students does not reach during their studies (Statista, 2019). Due to education, family background and only temporarily low standards of living, most university students would not consider themselves as part of the BOP in affluent countries. Hence, a combination with other types of handicaps is needed.

BOP members in general operate and act mostly in the informal market sector (London, 2008), a market sector which is characterised by 'small-scale, semi-legal, often low-productivity, frequently family-based, perhaps pre-capitalistic' enterprises (Maloney, 2004, p. 1). Compared to developing countries, where the informal sector sometimes represents the main economic market for a significant part of society – for example, 90% of 15–24-year-old Egyptian workers fall into the segment of informal work (Tansel and Ozdemir, 2019) – such markets are less salient in developed countries. Renooy (1990) states that the most crucial characteristic distinguishing the informal sector from the formal sector is a lack of governmental control. It thus seems plausible that the prevalence of informal sectors depends on a government's ability to monitor and regulate (all) sectors of the economy, resulting most likely in smaller and less salient informal markets in developed countries. It is worth noting that evidence suggests that not every individual operating in informal markets is '[…] disadvantaged, precarious, or underpaid' (Maloney, 2004, p. 2), not even in developing countries.

Summarising, we propose that the BOP in affluent countries may be defined by the simultaneous existence of three conditions as illustrated in Figure 1.2: (relative) poverty, membership in informal markets, and a lack of public protection, for example, by welfare or social security systems, unions or similar. Furthermore, it is worth noting that *individuals within the*

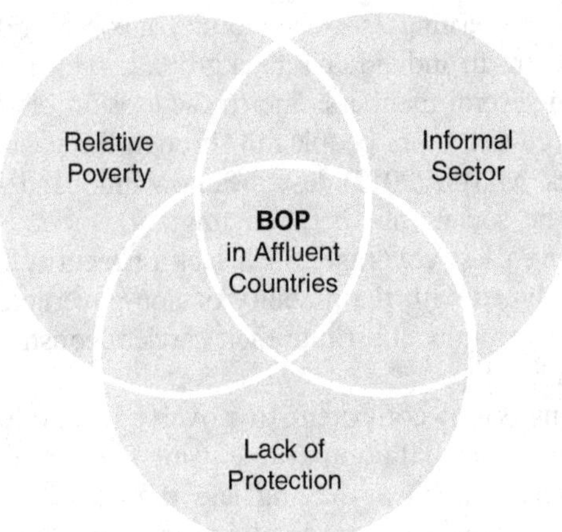

Figure 1.2 Conceptualisation of BOP in affluent countries.
Sources: Own work based on concept of relative poverty, London (2008), and Maloney (2004).

BOP in affluent countries are most likely not a well-defined category but comprise a range of stratums within society.

BOP markets (BOPMs)

In 2015, the United Nations passed the Sustainable Development Goals (SDGs); several of which focus on issues mostly prevalent to BOP members in developing countries (United Nations, 2015). However, the SDGs apply to BOP individuals in the industrialised world as well. For example, Goal 10 'Reduce inequality *within* and *among* countries' [emphasis added] has a direct aim to reduce inequalities not only between richer and poorer nations but also within (rich) nations (United Nations, 2015).

There are several possible avenues for reducing such inequalities which will be discussed within the expert interviews in this chapter. Concerning BOP research in developing nations, scholars argue for businesses to expand their economic activities beyond their core markets and integrate Base of the Pyramid *Market* (BOPM) activities into their portfolio (London, 2008). However, the BOPM perspective in general must be understood in a more nuanced manner than 'large companies selling smaller sizes or easier-to-afford versions of their existing products to respond to the limited purchasing power and investment capabilities of those at the BOP' (Hammond, Kramer, Katz, Tran, and Walker 2008, p. 2). We thus base our understanding of BOPM on the six principles of London (2008) as illustrated in Figure 1.3 and apply these to affluent countries based on our findings of BOP in affluent countries as shown in Table 1.1.

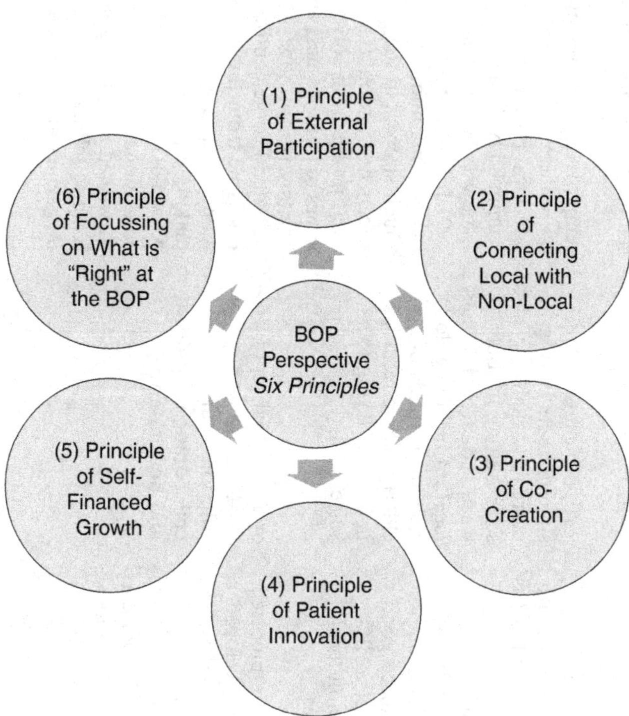

Figure 1.3 Six principles of the BOP perspective according to London (2008).
Sources: Own work based on London (2008), Hammond Kramer Katz Tran and Walker (2008), and London and Hart (2004).

First, the Principle of External Participation emphasises the need of an (external) organisation to enter and participate in the informal market system. Instances of such organisations in affluent countries are ecclesiastical or private organisations, often acting outside of profitability constraints and rather trying to *enable* individual capabilities. Second, local must be connected with non-local (Principle of Connecting Local with Non-Local). In developing countries, non-local institutions are often multinational corporations or NGOs which use resources (e.g. knowledge) from their domestic origin and apply these to local conditions. In developed countries, this connection often means that a *local problem* (e.g. food waste of large supermarket chains and resulting Food Banks) is tied to a *non-local problem* (e.g. poverty among the elderly and resulting hunger), trying to tackle or diminish both. Third, there is the Principle of Co-Creation, which argues that *knowledge* obtained by the (external) organisation is combined with the *wisdom* of BOP individuals, resulting in value or opportunities. Papaoikonomou et al. (2009), for instance, evaluated social enterprises collecting and recycling electronic and electric waste owned by Roma people in Greece. They illustrate that crucial benefits arise from forming an

Table 1.1 Exemplary application of the six principles to affluent countries

BOPM principle	*Definition (London, 2008)*	*Developing countries*	*Affluent countries*	*Example affluent countries: The Big Issue*
External Participation	'Requires the entry of an exogenous, or external, venture or entrepreneur into the informal economy'	multinational corporations, domestic firms, NGOs, non-native individuals, …	Mostly NGOs and ecclesiastical organisations as well as former BOP-firms	The Big Issue Foundation cooperates with homeless people, allowing them to sell their paper for a profit
Connecting Local with Non-Local	'Either bringing non-locally produced products to BOP markets [BOP as consumer], or by taking BOP-produced goods or services to non-local markets [BOP as producer]'	BOP as consumer: providing goods and services not currently offered in local markets; BOP as producer: taking locally produced goods and selling them in other (e.g. affluent country); marketsCombination: take a locally produced good and sell this product to BOP markets in other (non-local) regions or countries	*Local* problem (e.g. supermarkets buying more food than they can sell resulting in food waste) connected to *non-local* problem (e.g. low retirement funds of elderly people resulting in hunger) trying to solve both	Unemployed people reliant on welfare or NGOs (i.e. non-local problem) combined with 'The Big Issue was launched in 1991 […] in response to the growing number of rough sleepers in the streets of London' (i.e. local problem) to solve issues of homelessness and creating (social) jobs
Co-Creation	'Allows these ventures to combine knowledge developed at the top of the pyramid with the wisdom and expertise found at the bottom'	Rather than relying on imported solutions from the developed world, the business model of the BOP venture and any associated technological solution is co-created among a diversity of partners, with local ownership and involvement	Not an application of pre-existing business solutions, but a collaboration top-down and bottom-up	Originally: People can buy Big Issue from their own money and re-sell it, making a profit. Nowadays: Additional, educational programmes (if wished for), trying to balance selling of magazines and providing

				income opportunity (bottom-up creation) with personal development through training (top-down)
Patient Innovation	'Firms attempting to enter these markets must develop new problem-solving approaches, rely on different evaluation metrics, and find a structure that provides some level of isolation from the influence of existing organisational routines[, which takes time]'	Patient Innovation: Innovation just as important as in mainstream business research, but due to lower funds more patiently. No real try-and-error possible. Patient Capital: investments start small and are then potentially scalable	BOP individuals facing handicaps (e.g. illiteracy, addictions, etc.) are reliant on knowledgeable organisations further developing individual capabilities towards a suitable(!) ideal	The Big Issue Foundation reinvests funds into workshops for their sales personnel tackling (1) personal sale goals, (2) financial handlings, (3) housing, (4) obtaining ID, (5) health and well-being, (6) addiction treatment, (7) employment, (8) education, (9) personal aspirations -> innovation through education
Self-Financed Growth	'Competitive advantage and the associated long term sustainability of the venture will most likely emerge from establishing a set of mutually beneficial partnerships with local organisations and entrepreneurs currently operating at the BOP'	Meeting the needs of the poor creates competitive advantage, that does not raise the overall playing field within the sector. Maximising the benefit of the poor = competitive advantage, that allows for slow, but self-financed growth	Organisations aiming to support BOP individuals grow through increased capabilities of its members and resulting profit; only exceptions are donations from outside that are reinvested into the cause	The Big Issue itself grows through increased sales of BOP individuals, which is achieved through learning processes and teachings (self induced growth). The Big Issue Foundation is open for external donations and reinvests its income into educational programmes for its employees, not market share growth

(*Continued*)

Table 1.1 (Continued)

BOPM principle	*Definition (London, 2008)*	*Developing countries*	*Affluent countries*	*Example affluent countries: The Big Issue*
Focussing on What Is 'Right' at the BOP	'This means that the BOP venture, be it a for-profit business or a non-profit initiative, ought to focus on leveraging what is "right" in BOP markets'	The BOP perspective enhances what already exists and builds from the bottom-up. This distinguishes it from poverty alleviation approaches emphasising the development of an enabling environment. These latter efforts are more policy oriented and stress the benefits of moving informal business activities to the formal economy	Support for BOP individuals trying to enhance individual capabilities. However, for affluent countries, this means formalisation to a certain degree, otherwise the organisations might act illegally	Individuals selling street papers of The Big Issue can get educational workshops, can work for the Social Enterprise as long as they want, etc. However, since income from selling papers is fiscally relevant, they somewhat 'loose' their informal nature (i.e. employment) while still working in an informal market (i.e. small-scale, semi-legal [depending on the selling location], low productivity)

Source: Definitions from London (2008); peculiarities of developing nations from London (2008); information concerning The Big Issue derived from The Big Issue (2019a, 2019b)

organisation and incorporating further 'employees', thus co-creating value *from the bottom* while using knowledge *from the top*. As a fourth principle, innovation occurs more patiently due to sparse resources on the BOP side (Principle of Patient Innovation). Reconsidering habits and developing new business models takes time, but once implemented it is expected to be (slowly) scalable. In affluent countries, educational programmes of charitable organisations often lead to such innovations. Using the aforementioned Roma people in Greece as an illustration, the organisation itself spreads knowledge about differing peculiarities of various recycling programmes. Due to illiteracy for roughly half the participating individuals, such information 'taught' participants *which* container and material could be recycled in a specific manner, ultimately increasing their income (Papaoikonomou et al., 2009). Fifth, growth must be financed by the project itself (Principle of Self-Financed Growth). For developing countries, this often means mutually beneficial partnerships and cooperation between (local) organisations and individuals. However, this is not applicable for non-profit organisations in affluent countries enabling BOP individuals through educational or practical support, since the mission of such organisations is *support within financial constraints* rather than *profit*. Nevertheless, growth is (mostly) not occurring within the NGO's scope of supporting individuals but happens on the individual's level. Instances of street papers depict this crucial difference: The Big Issue, one of the largest street papers in the UK, works like a non-profit-organisation (NPO): all income is reinvested in individual sellers of the paper, mostly homeless people, to provide an alternative to criminal activities or begging (Hanks and Swithinbank, 1997). The sole reason for growing number of sales and hence the street paper itself are growing sales of *individual sellers*, who *are* making a profit and reinvest it into their 'business'. The organisation itself mostly provides, for example, information on how to increase sales and other educational programmes (The Big Issue Foundation, n.d.). The last principle is the ethical component of BOPMs (Principle of Focussing What Is 'Right' at the BOP). Such initiatives are supposed to mainly benefit BOP individuals. The core implication according to London (2008) is that BOP initiatives focus on an *enabling environment* for such individuals rather than just lifting them out of poverty. This is also expected to be the main goal of most charitable and ecclesiastical organisations in affluent countries.

Groups of the BOP in affluent countries

A representative example of BOP individuals in affluent countries are (homeless/stigmatised) individuals selling street papers in European cities, as illustrated in the last column of Table 1.1 using The Big Issue from the UK. There are several other examples of BOP groups in affluent countries that are within the BOP boundaries or at least checkmark certain characteristics of BOPMs. In the following, two of such instances will be illustrated: the so-called 'working poor' as well as (illegal) migrant workers.

Working poor

Being employed and earning income regularly is a major factor in poverty reduction (OECD, 2009). However, for households in the OECD area where at least one individual works, poverty is still occurring for 7% of people on average (OECD, 2009). Reportedly, these numbers have been increasing for affluent and non-affluent countries (Brady et al., 2010; Levanon, 2018). The OECD (2009) further discusses the role of net social transfers, minimum wage and other governmental programmes providing security and emphasise the beneficial role of such systems for reducing poverty. In the sense of our definition, missing security and (relative) poverty are thus checkmarked for the working poor.

However, since they *are* legally employed per definition, their operations and informality must be discussed. The key decisive factor here is whether affected individuals try to find alternative income options: as shown in chapter 3, there are instances of regularly employed individuals starting to collect deposit containers to improve their income. In a similar fashion, Marina (2018) reports that many 'busker' (i.e. street musicians) in New Orleans entertain pedestrians for a tip 'to supplement their meager [sic] wages earned working in the New Orleans service industry' (p. 307). We thus argue that not all working poor in affluent countries belong to the BOP, but individuals affected by poverty although employed might start earning extra income in the informal sector, hence approaching their situation in a BOPM manner.

Migrant workers

Immigration and adjacently the necessity for foreign workers are constantly discussed issues in developed countries. During the COVID-19 pandemic, these discussions became especially apparent for migrant workers in agriculture who used to conduct harvest for various agricultural businesses but were no longer allowed to enter (e.g. Jacobs, 2020). For the UK, Rogaly (2006) describes business rationales in agriculture towards workers who 'are willing to work hard to close, detailed instructions, and are available for the amount of time required and no more' (p. 14). This rationale reportedly originates from increasing requirements towards growers, for example quality, volume and low margins on the grower's side. Furthermore, many of these workers either work illegally or legally, are subject to UK's minimum wage (if working legally), and are either paid a time or a piece rate (i.e. for the latter, salary per unit of e.g. fruit picked). This leaves several workers operating in an informal sector (i.e. working illegally in the shadow economy), sometimes receiving salaries below the minimum wage (i.e. (relative) poverty), and facing worse insecurity than their domestic counterparts: beyond socio-economic and employment insecurity, such workers also face residency insecurity (lack of protection). In chapter 6 within this book, migrant workers in the UK will be discussed concerning hand car washes, and chapter 2 illustrates the case of modern slavery within the UK agricultural sector.

Both working poor and migrant workers thus have important interfaces with the BOP concept, but not all individuals within either are necessarily part of the BOP. Individual characteristics must be evaluated, and individuals within such groups most likely populate different facets of the BOP-spectrum.

Expert views on BOPMs in affluent countries

As a concept that was only recently adopted to affluent countries, BOP individuals and markets in the developed world face different challenges and possibilities compared to their developing-world counterparts. To enrich our understanding of these markets and individuals, three interviews with experts were conducted in spring and summer of 2020: a verbatim interview with Professor Steffen Boehm and two written interviews with Professor Alexander Dietz and Reverent Wolfgang Gern. Answers of Alexander Dietz and Steffen Boehm are printed in the following, while the statements of Wolfgang Gern are aiming to support and further illustrate the discussed issues. All three experts come from differing backgrounds revolving around poverty, (public) institutions and international development. In the following, their wealth of knowledge and expertise will provide a fuller understanding of the BOP in affluent countries.

Steffen Boehm

Steffen Boehm is professor of Organisation and Sustainability at the Department of Science, Innovation, Technology, and Entrepreneurship (SITE) at the Business School, University of Exeter, UK. His research focusses on studying grand social and planetary challenges, interrogating the role of management and organisation within business-society-ecology dynamics. He has published five books: Repositioning Organization Theory (Palgrave), Against Automobility (Blackwell), Upsetting the Offset: The Political Economy of Carbon Markets (Mayfly), The Atmosphere Business (Mayfly) and Ecocultures: Blueprints for Sustainable Communities (Routledge). A new book, Climate Activism, is forthcoming with Cambridge.

Alexander Dietz

Prof. Dr. Alexander Dietz is professor for Studies of Christian Social Services and Systematic Theology at the Hannover University of Applied Sciences and Arts. Academic studies in Theology, Philosophy and Business Administration, doctorate on business ethics, postdoctoral lecture qualification on medical ethics. He has long-standing work experience within church welfare organisations specialising on poverty and is a member of the scientific advisory council of the German Tafel [food banks]. Several publications revolving around Political Poverty Reduction, Food Banks, as well as poverty and community.

Wolfgang Gern

Reverent Dr. Wolfgang Gern is a retired, ordained protestant minister. Currently, he is a visiting professor/senior lecturer at the Protestant University of Rwanda in Butare (Huye) and senior lecturer at Mainz University. Studied Protestant Theology and History of Religions at Berlin and Heidelberg University, doctorate in Theology at Heidelberg University. He was president of Diaconia Hessen (39,000 co-workers) from 2000 to 2016 and speaker of the German Anti-Poverty Conference. He has long-standing experience in several socially relevant areas such as Social Work Assistant in refugee work during the Vietnam War in Laos and Cambodia; membership of Governmental Boards on Social Politics, Migration and Integration; and educational occupations such as his contemporary professorship in Rwanda. Wolfgang Gern is author of numerous publications revolving around Protestant Theology, Interculturality and Development Studies.

Bottom/Base of the Pyramid (BOP) and BOP markets are terms widely used for developing countries. However, there is a Bottom/Base of the income pyramid in affluent countries as well. What phenomena and individuals would you consider being part of the BOP in affluent countries?

Alexander Dietz: When we talk about developing countries, BOP means the population group living in absolute poverty. When we talk about countries like Germany, BOP can only mean the population group living in relative poverty. These are the people who are partially excluded from participation in society. This group is largely identical with those whose income is less than 60 or 50% of the median income. In Germany, this is about 16% of the population. The majority of these are people who have been unemployed for several years or work in the low-wage sector, and their families. Typical problems of this group are lack of affordable housing, rising energy costs, mobility restrictions, health problems, isolation, lack of prospects and suffering from social prejudice.

Steffen Boehm: First of all, I see the boundary between the Global South and the Global North continuously being eroded. I see general convergence of the political economies in broad terms between South and North, between what is sometimes called ‘developing countries’ and ‘affluent countries’. I know Latin America very well; and I also know parts of Asia like India and China quite very well. In these regions, you sometimes have more wealth concentrated than in many so-called ‘affluent’ parts of ‘the West’. If you look at the state of São Paolo in Brazil, for example – there are more millionaires than Berlin or Stockholm. And Beijing has more millionaires than

Toronto or Paris. And, at the same time, one can easily find poorer communities in say Northern England or the South Welsh valleys than in many parts of São Paolo state. Needless to say, you have very rich people in certain 'developing countries' and also a growing middle class as well, of course. And equally, if you look at many parts of the Anglo-Saxon world, UK and North America in particular, you have really entrenched areas of poverty which are comparable to way underdeveloped areas of the world. Essentially, I see a convergence. I don't necessarily see a huge difference between Global South and Global North anymore, but, of course, some of the differences remain existent. So, I don't just want to wish them away, they do exist, but there is a convergence. This is a long way of saying: of course, there are Base of the Pyramid dynamics, if you like, going on amongst individuals and communities not only in countries like the UK but also in Germany and many other European countries. You have large, for example, migrant communities. I have done quite a bit of work on migrant labour recently. I live in a very rural county in the UK. UK agriculture is more or less dependent on migrant labour. These workers often don't have proper contracts, often there is a black market for that kind of labour, they have less than minimum wage income, they have no voice, it is very difficult to even find them, never mind unionise them. Various unions have tried to reach out to them and get them organized and collectively bargain with their employers. I know these exist in Germany and in many other parts of Europe as well. In the food and hospitality sector in general you have huge swathes of work and labour, which is basically undervalued and underpaid, zero-hour contract work, below minimum wage, black market, modern slavery work, you name it. A whole lot. And all of this is basically happening in the so-called 'affluent countries' where you basically see a huge divide that has emerged over the last 30–40 years under successive governments which have basically tried to 'make labour markets more flexible', essentially make labour cheaper. The so-called 'affluent countries' are basically affluent because you have still a large privileged middle class, but then you have the bottom third – or bottom half, essentially – that lives very precarious lives. There is a term also called 'precariat' or 'precarious workers', sometimes in the new economy also called the 'Gig workers'; those who are delivery drivers, those who essentially are (self-employed) freelancers. They don't have any proper contracts and they are basically just used when needed, and in the current crisis [COVID-19], as we have seen, those are the workers who almost immediately lose their jobs, or they don't lose their jobs because there is no job left to lose. They just don't have any work. These are the people who are literally dependent on food banks. Food banks in the UK have seen huge rises in need for people who basically go hungry. You literally have 2 or 3 million people or more going hungry in the UK at the moment. Sorry, it's a very long answer, but basically, I have named a few examples, a few work groups, which would fall under the Base of the Pyramid type of category.

Wolfgang Gern, throughout his publications and the interview, continuously emphasised that it is crucial to talk about legislation, welfare systems, taxation and the historical development of these systems when it comes to BOP and thus poverty in affluent countries. Unfortunately, instances of minimum wage becoming the 'standard' salary instead of being the lower boundary are more common nowadays, as is prevalent for the growing low-income sector of society. Furthermore, evaluating the situation long-term, children of poor parents often also become poor eventually. Hence, in his words, 'if one does not like to talk about growing wealth in the hands of a few people, one should not talk about growing poverty among the many'. Classifying groups relevant for this 'sector', he names people below the relative-poverty threshold, homeless people, the working Poor, single parents with children, the growingly large number of individuals reliant on food banks, elderly people with low income and many more. Church-related and non-governmental organizations aiming to support these individuals further have the role to be the lobby for people at the BOP, but it is a public (i.e. governmental) duty to design a system preventing growing numbers of citizens to become poor. Concludingly, he insistently emphasised what London (2008) defined as the 'Principle of Focussing What Is "Right" at the BOP': BOPMs must be looked at closely, since there is reasonable suspicion that often-times the ones benefitting from such markets are not the ones that are affected the most.

What are the main characteristics of BOP markets or more generally BOP initiatives in affluent countries, in particular concerning innovation, business model, network, challenges, etc.? Furthermore, who do you consider to be the main players of BOP initiatives in affluent countries?

Alexander Dietz: I will illustrate this with the example of the 'Tafel' [German food bank]. This is the largest social initiative in Germany in recent decades. About 1000 of these initiatives provide about 1.5 million needy people with surplus food. Tafel work is based on voluntary commitment and donations.

> The degree of professionalisation is nevertheless high and continues to grow. Without full-time staff, it is difficult to ensure quality standards, to compete for donations and to perform the increasingly difficult volunteer management. The participation of those affected at eye level often does not yet function satisfactorily. Community-oriented networking is one of the key words for making initiatives sustainable and giving them a lasting impact. However, this approach is often hampered by specific state funding conditions and by a widespread inertia that does not want to think outside the box.

[Concerning the main players,] I am thinking here especially of non-profit organisations that are oriented towards the common good. In Germany, this area is dominated by welfare organisations. This tried and tested system is based on special legislation from the 1960s (neo-corporatist principle of subsidiarity). According to this principle, welfare state services should neither be provided directly by the state nor left to the free market. In this way, state failure and market failure should be excluded. Furthermore, tendencies towards a total state or a total market were to be avoided. Since the 1990s, this approach has been increasingly undermined, and the social sector has been economised. This favours an economic professionalisation of NPOs and the development of an ambivalent BOP market (compassionate economy).

Steffen Boehm: Well, I guess you know I come more from a sort of a critical political economy perspective, more from a sort of a critical social science approach to these kinds of questions. So, of course there are business models, of course there are innovations, there are things like frugal innovation and there are ways of coping. But I think these have to be understood on the basis of a good critical kind of understanding of what is actually going on. So, rather than going straight into the market aspects of it or how the markets solve these social, economic and environmental problems associated with the Base of the Pyramid, I do think we need a deep analysis of what is actually going on rather than a sort of a celebration of various business models that are trying to solve these kind of problems, which I am happy to elaborate on. Having said that, I am just writing a paper on precarious work and how precarious workers are coping with these situations and how they make a living under such kind of situations of zero-hour contracts; not just coping but how they are living their day-to-day live, how is their day-to-day experience. We have interviewed more than

70 people of these kind of – what you would call 'Base of the Pyramid' kind of workers – and it is difficult to say in a nutshell what these findings are but it's really interesting to see, what in England you would call 'how they are muddling through', you know, how they are muddling through their everyday life, how they are developing coping mechanisms as well as tactics, how they are developing ways to make something out of nothing, how they are mobilising their networks, how they are mobilising their friendships, how they are developing specific opportunistic kind of relationships in order to make it through, essentially. To feed their families, to feed themselves, to provide for their daily livelihoods. I haven't done a huge amount of work into sort of Base of the Pyramid business models as such, although I am quite interested in the frugal innovation approach. What I do think is happening in a widespread way, particularly in neoliberal countries, is basically that a lot of state capacity was being eroded over the last few decades, like in the UK. In the UK, there are a lot of areas where the state is not providing, you either organize yourself and come up with solutions yourself or you have nothing. That kind of bottom-up organising, these bottom-up innovation processes are quite widespread in countries where neoliberal policy has taken hold. The Base of the Pyramid kind of approach has to be seen hand-in-hand with, what I would call, the general neo-liberalisation of policy and market approaches. And a lot of that is innovative, I mean a lot of it is, I would say, good because you get grassroots bottom-up organising and you allude to the innovative creative capacity of people to do things rather than a centralised state from the top basically telling us what to do. In the UK, there are so many examples of that, and we can expand on that later if you like. But when you talk about business models in the UK, I mean we have community interest companies, we have charities, we have foundations, we have a whole range of legal formats and business models which are all geared towards basically giving communities, freelancers tools to essentially provide for themselves rather than waiting for the state to tell them what to do – there is a whole range of models available and a whole policy agenda has been implemented to empower the communities to do that, essentially. But of course, a critical approach would say, in terms of public service provisioning, a lot has been an overemphasis on that. Local councils, for example, in the UK through austerity measures etc. have been absolutely starved of any kind of resources since the financial crisis in 2008.

So, more than 10 years – and this will probably continue in the post-COVID-19-world – public services eroded. The reason why the UK has been so shambolic in its COVID-19 response is because the public services left, right and centre have been starved of resources for a long time and there is literally no capacity, no resources available to respond to such a huge pandemic and that can be translated in all sorts of other areas. So, there is the flipside; on the one hand you have this belief that communities basically should solve their own problems and people should solve their own problems … but on the other hand, suddenly, you have this pandemic and other crises coming and then you have no capacity of the state locally or centrally to respond to that and that's basically the conundrum we're dealing with. Again, a very long answer. I'm sorry I haven't used the concept of the Base of the Pyramid at all, but your approach inspired me to think about it in those terms and it's quite interesting to me.

Wolfgang Gern, taking his critical perspective towards market-based solutions, also illustrated this issue by using the working poor. In several industries, people tend to earn non-sufficient salaries, for example, the service industry or within manufacturing jobs. Rather than expecting (social) organisations to solve the issues of affected people by using market mechanisms, it is actually the unions that would play an important role in poverty-reduction by collectively bargaining and pressuring companies to fulfil, for example, safety standards. By disregarding their societal role and duty and basing poverty-reduction on BOP markets, one could even suspect an 'economic apartheid', where certain individuals are only allowed to participate through their social/economic stratum. This could even endanger democracy, something that is already somewhat happening when looking at decreasing voter turnout among the poorer part of society. He further illustrates his point of view by citing Helmut Simon, an influential German judge who, throughout his life, voiced his concerns for the weaker sector of society: '*he who has little in life must have much in justice. […] The strength of our society is measured by the welfare of the weak*'.

What are the main drivers and/or barriers of BOP markets or initiatives in affluent countries?

Alexander Dietz: Concerning the drivers, I am thinking of NPOs as well, in Germany especially welfare organizations. On the one hand out of self-interest, on the other hand in the sense of social advocacy for those affected. Far too seldom are the affected people themselves the driving forces. This has to do with the fact that the group of people affected

> by poverty has difficulty in mobilising itself as a lobby group because it is very heterogeneous, its composition is constantly changing, its lack of prospects paralyses it and it needs all its resources to cope with its life situations.

Concerning barriers, the more restrictive state financing conditions in Germany since the 1990s have led to a decline in the innovation potential of social work institutions. The reduction in benefit payments for the long-term unemployed and their families since 2005 and the sharp drop in subsidies for employment projects since 2012 have led to a larger group of people perceiving themselves as superfluous and without opportunities. One of the main problems is the prejudices against the BOP population group, which are increasingly promoted by the media and politicians. There is no other population group about which there are more widespread prejudices. They are considered lazy and anti-social. Anyone who works with them or for them, stays where they are, or shops where they shop, has to reckon with stigmatisation themselves.

Steffen Boehm: I think the main drivers are basically successive governments and a whole ideology of neoliberalism which needs to be mentioned here that you have had, essentially, public services being starved of resources out of a concrete political choice by successive governments left, right and centre – politically speaking. So there has been a whole ideological sort of movement around what is called 'neoliberal flexibilisation' of labour markets and, as a result of that, even in very affluent countries like Germany as well as the UK you essentially have the inequalities between people – the wealth and income inequalities between the different labour market segments – increasing massively over the last 40 to 50 years, as Thomas Piketty has shown in detail. Large parts of workers in the UK haven't seen a rise in income for the last 30 years or longer even while others have quadrupled (or more) their income or wealth. For me, this is one of the main drivers. I think the BOP markets, the political economic context around that is neoliberalism and flexibilisation of economies and the conscious choice by governments to not engage in certain activities and basically saying to individuals and to communities and to companies 'you sort the garbage yourself'. Which then, on the back of that, requires the emergence of what you would call BOP markets and initiatives to essentially cope with this brave new world; essentially coping mechanisms or mechanisms of responses to dealing with the arising certain social and economic

> problems. If the government says, 'okay, there is not enough money for social care', then essentially individuals and communities have to find other solutions. If the government is unable, or if the food system is unable, to feed its people in an adequate way, then you have the emergence of food banks. I mean, food banks are a particularly good example. The whole food bank system, which is now a very elaborate, huge system in the UK in all the main regions, for urban and rural populations they provide literally an essential lifeline and service to the millions of people in the UK. All basically done without governmental support. They are providing an essential service which … if that wasn't happening, then two things would happen: the supermarkets and the food system in general would have to deal with a lot of extra food waste and the government, at the same time, would have to deal with millions of people who potentially might be on the streets and might be protesting because they go hungry. So, you have these Base of the Pyramid markets which are actually providing certain resilience functions for the system to stay in place and maybe sediment certain inequalities and certain environmental externalities because essentially the food banks enable supermarkets to say 'our system is fine because our extra food we can't use just goes to food banks'. But that sediments the wastefulness of the supermarket-driven food system.

Wolfgang Gern referenced back the correlation between rich and poor. In his view, markets entice consumption, and the prevalence of wealth for some often-times works as a seductive mechanism that leads to indebtedness or even over-indebtedness for the poor at the BOP (e.g. Sivanathan and Pettit, 2010, illustrate this for the USA). These individuals often eventually use the services of debt counselling or similar programmes of charitable organisations. Exhorting about future developments, he warned that it will become increasingly difficult to establish solidarity among those affected by poverty, because the value patterns are geared to possession and consumption rather than to solidarity-based cohesion. An economy of enough would help above and below, indeed, would create solidarity – and the earth would be grateful to us as well as the generations to come. After all, '*growing inequalities will dissolve societies from within*'.

He furthermore emphasised the issue of long-term developments. Poor children tend to grow up to poor adults, and beyond the low purchasing power, there are increasingly informational deficits concerning economic behaviour in (permanently) financial distress situations. This especially has negative consequences for children. Providing an avenue for improvements, a basic provision for children would most likely be able to close supply gaps here. Public investment in the social and cultural infrastructure pursues a similar goal.

What negative consequences can BOP initiatives have and what could be possible ways to mitigate these?

Alexander Dietz: The initiatives are often – as already mentioned – ambivalent, since they can contribute as unintended side effects to the normalisation of poverty as a part of society, to the structural consolidation of poverty and to the legitimisation of misguided social policy, by relying on charity and voluntary commitment as a means of combating poverty, making users dependent on the existence of the society, renouncing political entitlement and calling into question the – in rich countries such as Germany – proven welfare state in the sense of state-guaranteed and financed benefits. To this extent, they must be linked with socio-political education work and lobbying.

Steffen Boehm: Well, the main problems for societies at large is to rely on BOP initiatives, essentially. They don't have the reach of state or municipality services. So, if you have a state-funded governmental or municipality public service, then you would expect – but, of course, that is not necessarily always happening – you would expect that the reach, the power and the capacity of the state would be able to basically provide an equal type of service throughout the population across or throughout the country. I mean, that's not necessarily always happening. There's a huge differentiation of the effectiveness and the availability of public services in the UK, the country that I know best. But, nevertheless, if you look at the NHS – the largest public service organization, one of the largest in the world with over 1 million employees and a kind of combination of centralised and decentralised decision-making and organizing and provisioning – essentially it is able to reach the whole of the population. In terms of the food banks, well, the food system is creating huge problems in the UK. You have lots of people who are basically obese, who eat too much and they eat bad, highly processed food, which is not nutritious, and then you have, on the other hand, lots of people who don't have enough food and they go hungry. And then, of course, you have affluent consumers who are basically buying the latest Jamie Oliver cookbook and buy the greatest food that is flown in from across the world. So, you have these huge inequalities in the food system creating all sorts of social, environmental and economic externalities. Food banks are just a BOP initiative to deal with these externalities but it's entirely self-organized, it's a lot of duplication of effort, it's a lot of struggle, and it's relying a lot on volunteering work. So, a lot of these BOP initiatives are relying on volunteers and very precarious finances and resources in these BOP organizations. I've seen a lot of volunteers and a lot of BOP organizations that are basically burning out because they are trying their best they can, but they are just completely overwhelmed. So, while, on the one hand, it's great to involve individuals and communities to essentially do charity work and to 'do good', you can never do it in such a way that you reach everyone in need, in an equal and widespread-reach way that governments could do. As a result, you always have 'patchy' services, you have a variety of organizational, financial and psychological struggles of those who are providing these BOP services. As a result, essentially you often don't get the widespread and consistent service that you would expect when it comes to a life and death thing such as food provision.

Wolfgang Gern discussed possibly unintended, negative consequences throughout this manuscript, reminding that business solutions are not the most viable way of mitigating poverty and consequences of being at the BOP. He thus gladly elaborated on possible mitigating approaches. Invest in education and work, expand poverty prevention, strengthen rather than weaken the welfare state. Only a strong tax state can be a strong welfare state. The following applies: strong shoulders can bear more than weak ones. At the same time, it helps to overcome exclusion, racism and violence – at all levels – and to practice a culture of non-violent conflict and fair democratic coexistence. Even before the pandemic, but even more so now: especially in times of crisis there is no other way than solidarity among people.

Is there an intersection between sustainability and BOP markets in affluent countries? How do BOP markets, or more generally BOP initiatives, contribute to sustainable development? Where are possible limitations?

Alexander Dietz: With regard to the ecological and economic aspects of sustainability, I consider the effects on society as a whole to be minimal (unlike in countries with a predominant subsistence economy). With regard to the social aspects of sustainability, I consider the effects on society as a whole to be very relevant, but with clear limits.

When we talk about poverty reduction, we must first distinguish between poverty alleviation, poverty prevention and poverty eradication. And secondly, between economic poverty, social poverty, health poverty, spiritual poverty and cultural poverty. With regard to economic poverty, BOP initiatives can only have poverty-reducing effects. Because offers of support do not usually change the framework conditions that cause material poverty. And job opportunities in this area are usually low-paid, so that poverty occurs despite work. With regard to social poverty (loneliness), spiritual poverty (lack of prospects) and cultural poverty (participation deficits), however, BOP initiatives can also have poverty-preventing or poverty-overcoming effects.

Steffen Boehm: If you look at the SDGs, the UN Sustainable Development Goals, as sort of the key framework for sustainable development, essentially that framework provides a very good guide, roadmap and summary of the challenges we are facing on this planet. You know, some of these are absolutely huge and I've mentioned some of them already: poverty, hunger, decent work provision. But essentially, these are societal norms and goals that I would argue can only be reached with organizations that have the capacity and reach to really affect widespread change in certain national jurisdictions. And these organizations need to have some sort of governmental support or need to be run by the governments themselves. Which is not to say that these should be top-down initiatives and the typical soviet model of 'the dictator decides everything'. That's not what I have in mind at all, but I think we need institutional innovations which combine private initiatives, community accountability and governmental capacity to essentially reach every community in a national jurisdiction. And basically, many Base of the Pyramid kind of initiatives, markets and organizations simply haven't got the capacity and the resource base nor the reach to essentially provide these very essential public services. I would say they can only patch certain holes, have a quick fix for certain problems but they are struggling to really scale up, they are struggling to reach everyone. I think that's the key problem, that's the key limit of the BOP initiatives. If we take the UN SDGs and sustainability in general seriously, then we need a combination of law making, of command and control from the top-down as well as bottom-up initiatives, accountability and involvement of widespread communities to make this happen. I'm quite interested in this sort of

> hybrid institutions concept. I think we essentially need innovative institutions and new institutional designs to make this happen, which involves both governmental institutions as well as community bottom-up kind of initiatives. At the moment we really haven't got the right institutional setup to deal with the grand social, economic and environmental challenges we face on this planet. We need new institutions, new approaches to effectively respond to these challenges.

Furthermore, I really don't want to lose that personal community initiative; I think that's vital. Otherwise we end up with top-down, autocratically organised economies and societies, which are never very effective in my mind. We do need the institutional entrepreneurs who do things differently. There is also another term: social movement organisations. These are basically bottom-up – as I would call them – bottom-up institutions, bottom-up organisations that are solving problems from the bottom-up through community participation, through mobilising resources locally to get stuff done. They are often looking after what is called the 'commons'. They are often finding ways to treat social, economic and environmental issues through a commons approach, which means that, rather than individualising and marketising everything, we need to collaborate and create buy-in from all to solve these problems together. But if that's the only thing that's happening, these will always struggle to scale up, they will always struggle to have the capacity to reach everyone. So, there also has to be a complementary process of where these bottom-up initiatives meet larger institutions, governmental institutions, that are able to support and create wider reach to tackle global commons issues.

Wolfgang Gern introduced the concept of 'prevention chains' for sustainable BOP initiatives. As he mentioned several times, children play a vital role in a longitudinal approach concerning the BOP. Especially during COVID-19, this need became prevalent: When schools in Germany closed, children were expected to participate in digitally organised classes. This is a viable approach for more affluent families, but especially poorer children tend to not have the resources to fully benefit from such approaches. Hence, in his mind, BOP initiatives that work throughout, that is '*from infant development to day-care, school, training and career entry, personality development, education and personal responsibility*', can be (socially) sustainable. Wherever local community and social responsibility are linked, initiatives and civil society actors can be supported. Where inclusion encourages decentralised action, community life is changed for the better, resulting in sustainable poverty reduction.

How would you predict future developments of BOP markets and initiatives as well as poverty in a more general sense in affluent countries?

Alexander Dietz: I assume that in rich countries relative poverty will continue to grow slowly but steadily. The BOP markets and initiatives will not change this. They will remain largely in the hands of NPOs, as profitability here is rather low.

Steffen Boehm: Well, I can approach this in two ways. One is a sort of a more normative way how I think they should develop and what I think should happen. So that's a normative response. But then there's also a sort of a more critical and realistic assessment of what I think will happen based on an analysis of current political economy and the current situation particularly in the post-COVID-19-world. The COVID-19-situation I think is such a fundamental event that has happened throughout the world and will have profound impact on the next 10–20 years. Not only because governments around the world have spent an absolute fortune to respond to this from a public health and economic-, security point of view. There will be huge state debts that will basically govern our lives for the next 10–20 years much more so than what we've seen in the last big crisis, the global financial crisis from 2008 onwards. I think there are sort of two responses to that: (1) either we will go back to a situation of deep austerity where essentially public services will continue to be starved because now the state has to pay off the debt and doesn't have any money. So, there will be austerity which means there will be ever more reliance on Base of the Pyramid kind of market initiatives to solve social, environmental and economic problems; so even more neo-liberalisation, even more starvation of public initiatives and funds. I think that might happen and probably will happen. (2) Having said that, in this COVID-19-crisis we have also seen the power of the state where consumers and citizens and the entire constituencies in countries have seen the capacity and the need for the state to organize and to respond to key social, economic and environmental problems. I have done a lot of work on climate change, for example. So, after COVID-19 we can't have any governments really claim anymore that they can't shut down certain economies or industries that they think are not basically contributing to the social, economic and environmental health of a country. They have the ability to shut down, they have the ability to direct, they have the ability and the capacity to enact profound social, economic and

> environmental change. I think that's quite a significant event as well, which will provide a path into the future. And I should also say that a lot of people and communities have realised that a different world is possible, a different way of life is possible. We don't necessarily need to fly around the world anymore, we can have these interviews, meetings and conferences online. A lot of people, to stay with the food system example, a lot of people have started to source their food locally. They have learned how to think about where their food comes from. They have maybe not gone into the big supermarkets but sourced their food through alternative provisioning schemes locally. There's been a lot of learning going on of how to deal with certain crises situations. Base of the Pyramid kind of initiatives are a response to a crisis – you know, they are responding to certain social, economic and environmental crises and the COVID-19 is a big crisis that is still ongoing and will probably not go away for some time to come. I see some positive signs of how a combination of local and community initiatives and governmental interventions can actually affect quite profound social, economic and environmental change. I think it's been a useful intervention in a way, but it's only been a test drill for much larger crises like the climate crisis that is still to come.

Wolfgang Gern, rather than predicting the unpredictable, preferred to focus on possible avenues how to reach improvements. Using words from Gustav Heinemann to summarise his point of view on poverty and wealth: '*the experiences of Weimar taught us that we need to connect both: rule of law and social care. Social foundation is a necessity for democracy. Social security belongs to the basic equipment of all citizens in industrialised countries as salient proof of practiced solidarity*'.

Concluding remarks

There is evidence that the lower tier of the income pyramid is growing in size throughout the developed world. While there are business solutions similar to the BOP approaches in developing countries, these tend to be less profit-driven than the vast majority of organisations in developing countries. However, the market approach of such initiatives is less about mutually beneficial business solutions, but rather about attenuating (effects of) poverty through support programmes. This is especially apparent through the plurality of ecclesiastical, non-profit and charitable organisations in this market segment.

There is further evidence that phenomena such as food banks, bottle collectors and modern slavery, and the underlying issues are far from being solved. In times of COVID-19, this segment of society is once again at the crossroad: past crises, such as the financial crisis of 2008, tended to erode the little financial resources for the population at the BOP. For instance, in Germany, the share of households without any relevant possession increased from 14% in 2003 to 19.5% in 2013 (Boockmann et al., 2015). While many affluent countries have implemented an additional safety net throughout the pandemic, only time will tell the long-term developments of this segment.

Our experts were persistent voices for more governmental control for the weakest of society, arguing that public institutions are able to reach more people, work more efficiently and have the clear goal of common good compared to private organisations. Given evidence from the literature (Dethier, 2007) that social security and welfare programmes reduced poverty in a significant way, this perspective seems plausible.

In this book, we have for the first time adapted the BOP concept to affluent countries. In this introductory chapter, we have developed a tripartite definition of BOPMs in affluent countries and discussed avenues for improvement at the BOP. The five chapters in the following will illustrate such approaches as well as issues for this segment. We call for future research especially within the management literature on such BOP initiatives, since research is mostly published in other scientific disciplines (e.g. sociology for street papers or bottle collectors). By looking at such initiatives from a business perspective, we are confident that members of the BOP in developed countries are supported throughout their financial struggle. They can find more effective ways to create value in resource-scarce situations.

References

Andrews, D, Jencks, C, & Leigh, A (2010). *Do rising top incomes lift all boats?* (IZA Discussion Papers No. 4920). Bonn: Institute for the Study of Labor (IZA).

Bergh, A, Dackehag, M, & Rode, M (2016). Are OECD policy recommendations for public sector reform biased against welfare states? Evidence from a new database. *European Journal of Political Economy*, *48*, 3–15.

Boockmann, B, Kleimann, R, Meythaler, N, Nasgowitz, A, Nielen, S, Späth, J, & Wegendt, S (2015). *Forschungsprojekt: Analyse der Verteilung von Einkommen und Vermögen in Deutschland. Projektbericht an das Bundesministerium für Arbeit und Soziales.* ZEW-Gutachten und Forschungsberichte.

Brady, D, Fullerton, AS, & Cross, JM (2010). More than just nickels and dimes: A cross-national analysis of working poverty in affluent democracies. *Social Problems*, *57*(4), 559–585.

Campbell, I, & Price, R (2016). Precarious work and precarious workers: Towards an improved conceptualisation. *The Economic and Labour Relations Review*, *27*(3), 314–332.

Dethier, JJ (2007). “Social Security: What can Developing Countries Learn from the Experience of Developed Countries?” in J von Braun, R Vargas and R Pandya-Lorch

(Eds.), *The Poorest and Hungry. Assessments, Analyses and Actions*, Washington, DC: International Food Policy Research Institute.

Erikson, RS (2015). Income inequality and policy responsiveness. *Annual Review of Political Science, 18*, 11–29.

Gaetz, S, Dej, E, Richter, T, & Redman, M (2016). *The State of Homelessness in Canada 2016*. Toronto: Canadian Observatory on Homelessness Press.

Gold, S, Muthuri, JN, & Reiner, G (2018). Collective action for tackling "wicked" social problems: A system dynamics model for corporate community involvement. *Journal of Cleaner Production, 179*, 662–673.

Hammond, AL, Kramer, WJ, Katz, RS, Tran, JT, & Walker, C (2008). The next 4 billion: Characterizing BoP markets. *Development Outreach, 10*(2), 7–26.

Hanks, S, & Swithinbank, T (1997). The big issue and other street papers: A response to homelessness. *Environment and Urbanization, 9*(1), 149–158.

Jacobs, L (2020, June 4). Corona Risikogruppe. Und wer rettet die Erntehelfer? *Zeit online*. Retrieved from https://www.zeit.de/arbeit/2020-06/erntehelfer-corona-risikogruppe-saisonarbeit-landwirtschaft-arbeitsbedingungen-hilfe (accessed on 22 June 2020).

Kalleberg, AL (2009). Precarious work, insecure workers: Employment relations in transition. *American Sociological Review, 74*(1), 1–22.

Kolk, A, Rivera-Santos, M, & Rufín, C (2014). Reviewing a decade of research on the "base/bottom of the pyramid" (BOP) concept. *Business & Society, 53*(3), 338–377.

Levanon, A (2018). Labor market insiders or outsiders? A cross-national examination of redistributive preferences of the working poor. *Societies, 8*(3), 72.

London, T (2008, August). "The Base-of-the-Pyramid Perspective: A New Approach to Poverty Alleviation", in *Academy of Management Proceedings* (Vol. 2008, No. 1, pp. 1–6). Briarcliff Manor, NY: Academy of Management.

London, Ted, & Hart, Stuart L (2004). Reinventing strategies for emerging markets: beyond the transnational model. Journal of International Business Studies, 35, 350–370. 10.1057/palgrave.jibs.8400099.

Maloney, WF (2004). Informality revisited. *World Development, 32*(7), 1159–1178.

Marina, P (2018). Buskers of New Orleans: Transgressive sociology in the urban underbelly. *Journal of Contemporary Ethnography, 47*(3), 306–335.

Martin, N (2012). "There is abuse everywhere" migrant nonprofit organizations and the problem of precarious work. *Urban Affairs Review, 48*(3), 389–416.

Mason, K, Chakrabarti, R, & Singh, R (2013). What are bottom of the pyramid markets and why do they matter?. *Marketing Theory, 13*(3), 401–404.

Möller, J (2016). Lohnungleichheit–Gibt es eine Trendwende?. *Wirtschaftsdienst, 96*(13), 38–44.

Muthuri, JN, & Farhoud, M (2021). "The Base of the Pyramid Markets in Africa: Opportunities and Challenges", in Judy N. Muthuri, Marlen Gabriele Arnold, Stefan Gold, Ximena Rueda (Eds.), *Base of the Pyramid Markets in Africa*. London: Routledge, pp. 3–22.

OECD (2009). Is work the best antidote to poverty? *OECD Employment Outlook 2009: Tackling the Jobs Crisis*. OECD.

OECD (2018). Secondary graduation rate. Retrieved from https://www.oecd-ilibrary.org/content/data/b858e05b-en (accessed on 14 July 2020).

OECD (2019a). Gross domestic product (GDP). Retrieved from https://www.oecd-ilibrary.org/content/data/dc2f7aec-en (accessed on 21 July 2020).

OECD (2019b). Society at a Glance 2019. Retrieved from https://www.oecd-ilibrary.org/content/publication/soc_glance-2019-en https://doi.org/10.1787/soc_glance-2019-en (accessed on 17 April 2020).

OECD (2020). Income distribution. Retrieved from https://www.oecd-ilibrary.org/content/data/data-00654-en (accessed on 14 July 2020).

Papaoikonomou, K, Kipouros, S, Kungolos, A, Somakos, L, Aravossis, K, Antonopoulos, I, & Karagiannidis, A (2009). Marginalised social groups in contemporary weee management within social enterprises investments: A study in Greece. *Waste Management*, *29*(5), 1754–1759.

Pollert, A, & Charlwood, A (2009). The vulnerable worker in Britain and problems at work. *Work, Employment and Society*, *23*(2), 343–362.

Prahalad, CK, & Lieberthal, K (1998). The end of corporate imperialism. *Harvard Business Review*, *76*(4), 68–80.

Renooy, PH (1990). *The Informal Economy: Meaning, Measurement and Social Significance*. Amsterdam: Koninklijk Nederlans Aardrijkskundig Genootschap.

Rogaly, B (2006). Intensification of work-place gegimes in British agriculture: The role of migrant workers. Sussex Migration Working Paper No 36. Sussex Centre for Migration Research, University of Sussex, Brighton

Sivanathan, N, & Pettit, NC (2010). Protecting the self through consumption: Status goods as affirmational commodities. *Journal of Experimental Social Psychology*, *46*(3), 564–570.

Statista (2008). Einkommensgrenzen zur Einstufung in Arm und Reich für Singles und Paare auf Basis des monatlichen Nettoeinkommens. Retrieved from https://de.statista.com/statistik/daten/studie/510/umfrage/einstufung-in-arm-und-reich-fuer-singles-und-paare/#professional (accessed on 4 July 2020).

Statista (2019). Studenten in Deutschland nach Nettoeinkommen im Vergleich mit der Bevölkerung im Jahr 2019. Retrieved from https://de.statista.com/statistik/daten/studie/860094/umfrage/umfrage-in-deutschland-zum-nettoeinkommen-der-studenten/ (accessed on 4 July 2020).

Tansel, A, & Ozdemir, ZA (2019). Transitions across labor market states including formal/informal division in Egypt. *Review of Development Economics*, *23*(4), 1674–1695.

Terry, P (2019). Shelter briefing: General debate on Housing. Retrieved from https://england.shelter.org.uk/professional_resources/policy_and_research/policy_library/polipo_library_folder/briefing_general_debate_on_housing (accessed on 27 March 2020).

The Big Issue Foundation (n.d.). What we do. Retrieved from https://www.bigissue.org.uk/about/what-we-do/ (accessed on 2 May 2020).

The Big Issue Foundation (2019a). The Big Foundation: Service Brokerage Model. Evaluation Report August 2018. Retrieved from https://www.bigissue.org.uk/wp-content/uploads/2019/09/Review-of-the-Big-Issue-Service-Brokerage-Model-Report-Final-Web-Version.pdf (accessed on 2 May 2020).

The Big Issue Foundation (2019b). Annual Report 2019. Retrieved from https://www.bigissue.org.uk/wp-content/uploads/2019/10/Annual-Report_Web-double.pdf (accessed on 2 May 2020).

United Nations (2015). Resolution adopted by the General Assembly on 25 September 2015. Washington: United Nations.

Yaouancq, F, Lebrère, A, Marpsat, M, Régnier, V, Legleye, S, & Quaglia, M (2013). L'hébergement des sans-domicile en 2012. Insee Première (1466).

Part II

Drivers and barriers of BOP markets

2 Feeding a rich nation

Modern slavery reporting in UK agriculture

Andrew Phillips and Alexander Trautrims

Feeding a rich nation: Modern slavery reporting in UK agriculture

It has been estimated that, in 2016, there were around 46 million people in slavery around the world, over three times the number that came out of Africa during the entire transatlantic slave trade (Bales et al., 2009b). Human trafficking and slavery is the third largest source of income for organised crime, after drugs and arms smuggling (Bales et al., 2009a). In the UK, many aspects of modern slavery policy sit with the Home Office, the government department responsible for law and order, immigration and security. Research conducted for the Home Office (Silverman, 2014) estimated there were between 10,000 and 13,000 slaves in the UK, mainly within the sex, construction and agricultural sectors.

We consider modern slavery to be at the nexus of sustainability, human rights, environmental, economic and business leadership issues. It is recognised as a sustainability issue in the UN Sustainable Development Goals: SDG 8 Decent Work and Economic Growth aims to 'Promote sustained, inclusive, and sustainable economic growth, full and productive employment, and decent work for all' It is a human rights issue: slavery is illegal in all countries. There are many national and supranational laws that address issues of slavery. It is an environmental issue: if today's slaves were a country, its carbon footprint would be the third largest in the world behind China and the US (Bales et al., 2016). It inflicts damage in the unregulated and marginalised areas where it takes place, through, for example, deforestation in the Amazon and in Africa, destruction of coastal ecosystems, illegal mining and quarrying and mercury poisoning of land. It is an economic issue: the removal of people from a community into slavery eliminates their economic power as consumers, and their introduction into other communities impacts on local wages and the availability of work for others (Bales et al., 2009a). Finally, and, certainly in the UK, it is a business leadership issue, given the reputational risk of being associated with modern slavery and the risk of prosecution.

Modern slavery is often associated with developing countries and global poverty; nevertheless, it also occurs in developed countries such as the UK.

Cases of modern slavery in the UK have been documented across a range of economic sectors, including agriculture where the UK's Gangmasters and Labour Abuse Authority (2018) repeatedly highlights a high modern slavery risk.

Crane (2013) portrays modern slavery as a business model in which financial gains are extracted from victims by the perpetrator and as such can occur in any country. Although the number of people in the UK who could be considered part of the bottom of the pyramid in absolute terms is low in comparison, relative poverty does of course exist in significant numbers and other factors besides poverty contribute to modern slavery vulnerability. Modern slavery tends to occur predominantly in low skill manual jobs where workers are easily replaceable and such jobs can be found in any economy.

It is important to highlight that although poverty is a factor that creates vulnerability towards modern slavery, poverty is not the same as modern slavery: modern slavery is defined as 'the exercise of the powers attaching to the right of ownership' and the loss of individual liberty (Allain, 2012). Although its occurrence is often related to poverty, as it creates vulnerability of victims, it is also linked to an absence of institutions, no access to justice, workers' rights and bargaining power and other development aspects such as corruption that enable the exploitation of workers and, in its most extreme form, of modern slavery. It therefore links directly to the bottom of the pyramid of formal and informal workers who are the most exposed to the risk of modern slavery through their heightened vulnerability. It must also be stressed that although migration – and the criminalisation of irregular migration – create a particularly vulnerable group of potential victims, the largest group of victims of modern slavery identified in the UK are British nationals (National Crime Agency, 2018).

The bottom of the pyramid has not only been researched as a source for innovation and as a significant consumer market (Hall et al., 2012; Kolk et al., 2014) but it has also been looked at as a part of global supply chains (Hahn and Gold, 2014; Khalid et al., 2015) and as a source of labour (Arya and Salk, 2006). Developing countries are often sourcing countries for commodities and low cost labour in global supply chains. The responsibility of buyers from developed countries for the conditions in developing countries – and the impact on bottom of the pyramid workers and communities – that form part of their supply chain is a relatively new aspect to this debate. More recently, such social sustainability considerations have been added to voluntary and compulsory disclosure frameworks in the developed world (Yekini et al., 2019).

This responsibility of buyers is reflected in the increased discussion on establishing legal responsibility for parts of the supply chain that are outside an organisation's own boundaries (Director of Labour Market Enforcement, 2018). In UK legislation, this debate has resulted in a reporting obligation on modern slavery aspects in supply chains.

The UK's Modern Slavery Act 2015 (MSA) not only codified the criminal offences of modern slavery which were previously dispersed in

UK legislation (Wen, 2016) but also section 54 (s54) introduced a requirement for all companies with a turnover of £36m or more to report in an annual statement what they are doing to address modern slavery in their organisation and in their supply chain. The agricultural sector, with its use of unskilled and seasonal labour, is a high-risk area for modern slavery, both globally and in the UK.

The starting question for our study was therefore how well the UK agricultural sector is engaging with the reporting requirements of s54. We use content analysis to assess the sector's engagement with the reporting requirements of the Act. Specifically, we (i) look at the existence, conformance, content and registration of statements; (ii) undertake a longitudinal analysis to assess whether engagement is improving and iii) set this in the context of a meta-study of other research into responses to s54.

The agricultural sector in developed countries has attracted relatively little research despite it being structurally exposed to high modern slavery risks (Chesney et al., 2019). Many existing studies analyse statements that have been produced and lodged with one of the voluntary registries, thus missing companies that are not producing statements or not registering their statements.

Research context of this chapter

In trying to understand the nature and extent of modern slavery across countries and sectors, four research initiatives are particularly useful. These estimate the risk of slavery and the number of slaves globally and by country and give an insight into the potential problem within the UK and within the agricultural sector. The International Labour Organisation (ILO) estimated in 2012 that 20.9 million people are the victims of forced labour globally (International Labour Organisation, 2012). Secondly, the Global Slavery Index (GSI) estimated that 45.8 million people are in slavery (Walk Free Foundation US Department of State, 2016), their definition encompassing both forced labour and forced marriage. They provides estimates by country. The GSI measure includes forced marriage in slavery, whereas the ILO forced labour statistics do not. Thirdly, Alliance 8.7 estimates 40.3 million victims of modern slavery (24.9 million in forced labour and 15.4 million in forced marriage). Finally, there is the Modern Slavery Index (MSI), an assessment of the risk of slavery based on how strong a country's laws are, the effectiveness of enforcement and the severity of violations (Verisk Maplecroft, 2017). There is not a universal acceptance of the definitions and methodologies used by these studies (Aronowitz, 2017).

Looking in more detail at the situation in the UK, the GSI estimates 11,700 living in slavery in the UK. One of the lead authors of the GSI, Kevin Bales, also worked on the Home Office estimate of UK slavery in 2015 which produced a figure of 10,000 to 13,000 (Bales et al., 2015; Silverman, 2014). Police recorded crime statistics show 880 modern slavery crimes in the year to March 2016, and 2,255 the following year. The National Referral

Mechanism (NRM) was introduced in 2009 to meet the UK's obligations under the Council of Europe Convention on Action against Trafficking in Human Beings, and identifies victims of human trafficking or modern slavery and works to support them. Labour exploitation (which includes slavery within UK agriculture) made up nearly half of cases referred in 2017. The 5,145 referrals (an increase of 35% on 2016 and up threefold from 1,745 in 2013) came from 116 different countries. For the first time, UK nationals topped the list of referrals by nationality, with 819 cases, followed by Albania (777 cases) and Vietnam (739 cases). These three countries accounted for 45% of the total. However, the NRM is not without its critics: in oral questions and evidence given at the Public Accounts Committee's (PAC) progress review (21 February 2018, HC 886, 2017–18), Beth Sizeland, Director for Tackling Modern Slavery and Exploitation at the Home Office, described the National Referral Mechanism as 'clunky' (response to question 15). The National Audit Office (NAO) concluded in 2014 that the NRM needed to be redesigned (ibid. question 75).

It is also believed that the risk of modern slavery is growing, both globally and in the UK. This risk is assessed to have increased in 20 EU countries (including the UK), where in 2017 the risk rose from low to medium: '… the presence of … vulnerable migrant populations in the primary countries of arrival [such as Romania, Greece, Italy, Cyprus, and Bulgaria] is a key contributor for increases in slavery across multiple sectors in the [EU], such as agriculture, construction, and services' (Verisk Maplecroft, 2017). Additionally, the National Crime Agency in the UK produces annual estimates of serious and organised crime, including the nature and scale of human trafficking: 'It is highly likely that the actual scale of modern slavery across victim and offender numbers, as well as incidence rates, has increased year-on-year. Analysis of drivers suggests this trend is likely to continue' (National Crime Agency, 2018, p. 15).

Having reviewed the extent of the problem, it is important to consider the differing nature of slavery compared to many other crimes: unlike a murder or a burglary, enslavement is not a discrete, time-bound event but has indeterminate duration. This contributes to the difficulty of defining and quantifying slavery, as highlighted in the work of Datta and Bales (2013, 2014) to assess the 'dark figure' of modern slavery – the gap between the actual and reported incidence of the crime. This method of estimating true crime rates, based on referrals and convictions, has proved less effective in this area.

Although no data has been found showing the statistical prevalence of slavery in different sectors within the UK, the literature often cites agriculture as being a key area (Anderson and Rogaly, 2005; Bryant, 2015; IASC, 2016; US Department of State, 2016). Bales et al. (2009b) sets out the concept of commoditised labour, where the tasks required of a worker are easily replicable and labourers are thus easily replaceable. Such tasks are a feature of agricultural work, making it by nature a higher risk sector. There is also constant pressure on food prices from UK supermarkets as they seek to gain competitive advantage: Wilkinson (2014) identifies this pressure on farmers to reduce costs as a key factor in the rise of seasonal and gang labour since the 1980s, another reason that the agricultural sector is high risk. Wilkinson also suggests that non-unionised sectors, of which agriculture is one, are more susceptible to worker exploitation.

An example of more detailed academic research into the extent of modern slavery in the UK is that commissioned by the Thames Valley Police Commissioner (Wager and Wager, 2017). This attempted to build on the statistical methods proposed by Datta and Bales (2013, 2014) and others in order to produce regional and national estimates of the prevalence of modern slavery in the UK, based on direct indicators of victimisation. The aim of these estimates is twofold: to provide a benchmark against which the performance of the criminal justice system can be judged; and to underpin work by organisations supporting victims of slavery. The research concludes that there could have been nearly 2,500 victims of modern slavery in the Thames Valley area in 2016. As official estimates from the Home Office are that there are between 10,000 and 13,000 victims across the entire UK, this more detailed approach suggests much higher levels nationally, and supports claims made by the National Crime Agency in August 2017 that the Home Office statistics were 'the tip of the iceberg', that the problem is 'far more prevalent than previously thought' and that modern slavery affects 'every large town and city in the country' (BBC, 2017).

This literature shows the difficulty of determining with accuracy the extent of slavery. But it does give a sense of the quantum and the nature of the problem, the most likely sectors where slavery will be found, and thus some of the challenges that will be faced when trying to address it. The identification and prevention of modern slavery in supply chains is a new challenge to supply chain management that requires the presence of institutions and the building of new capabilities across supply chains and within individual firms (Gold et al., 2015). Modern slavery further reveals the limitations of traditional approaches to corporate social responsibility (New, 2015) and the limitations to the expectation that corporations can police their supply chains through corporate mechanisms such as auditing and monitoring effectively and entirely (Pinheiro et al., 2019).

Coming at the problem from a different but very important angle, various authors have sought to capture the experiences and voices of those vulnerable to slavery, in slavery or freed from slavery, within the UK (Wilkinson, 2012, 2014). It is worth keeping in mind this human suffering, as exemplified in the following case of Brzezinski, when considering the wider picture being discussed in this chapter and what the MSA is trying to address. Most bottom of the pyramid research has been conducted in developing countries (Kolk et al., 2014). However, poverty and vulnerability occur in all countries. Victims of modern slavery can be in their home country or be trafficked to the UK for exploitation or indeed be UK nationals. Due to the presence of stronger institutions, lower levels of corruption, less cultural acceptance and other factors, modern slavery is often organised through adjusted and more hidden mechanisms of control and enslavement in developed countries than in developing countries.

One of the first prosecutions under the UK Modern Slavery Act took place in the agricultural sector (Brzezinski, 2017) and illustrates the challenges to the sector. In 2011, Sajmon Brzezinski brought a 38-year man from Poland to Nottingham. He withheld the victim's passport and told him he owed £2,000 for fees in getting him to this country and arranging work. He set up a bank account for the victim to receive his wages, but retained his bank card to prevent him accessing the money. Although the victim's official salary was £480 per week, he was given only £20 to £30 per week, the remainder was kept by Brzezinski. This happened without any involvement or knowledge by the farming business owners (Nottingham Post, 2017). The victim was employed, legitimately, by a £15m turnover business, on a farm near Arnold, Nottingham, from 2013. After a number of years, the victim confided to a colleague and the Gangmasters and Labour Abuse Authority (GLAA) became involved. Brzezinski was sentenced in June 2017 to an eight-year custodial sentence under the Modern Slavery Act 2015, the Coroners & Justice Act 2009 and the Fraud Act 2006.

Modern slavery is, therefore, a pressing sustainability issue and the UK agriculture sector a high risk area. The MSA is the UK government's latest legislative response to the issue. The remainder of this chapter will look at what others have said about the MSA, current approaches to evaluating modern slavery statements, how this study was designed and data collected, what was found, how these results fit with existing knowledge, and, finally, wider implications and ideas arising.

The legal context for modern slavery reporting for UK companies

Any organisation seeking to understand their responsibilities for reporting by reading the MSA itself should not be confused – it is relatively short and written in a straightforward way that is understandable for legal laymen. There are also Parliament's explanatory notes which accompany the Act (Parliament, 2015), guidance notes on the transparency in supply chains (TISC) section of the Act, produced by the Home Office (2015) in consultation with businesses and civil society organisations at the time of Act, and the statutory instruments which provided further parameters. In 2017, the Home Office guidance was revised to take a harder line: the six areas to be addressed in a TISC statement were previously suggestions for matters which organisations 'may' include: now they 'should aim to' include them (and will become obligatory if the 2017 Bill (see below) is enacted). The latest guidance is also clearer on timing – statements to be published within six months of the financial year-end – and suggests that previous year's statements should continue to be available online so that comparison and progress can be demonstrated.

The MSA established the role of the Independent Anti-Slavery Commissioner, who has produced guidance on what organisations need to do – for example, he produced an annual report after one year (IASC, 2016) and addressed the business community (Hyland, 2017). The Government commissioned a review of the Act, again after one year (Haughey, 2016). UK Police services have begun efforts to address modern slavery through, for example, an advice note to the agricultural sector (Derbyshire Police, 2014).

In July 2017, the Modern Slavery (Transparency in Supply Chains) HL Bill (2017–18) [57], had its first reading, in the House of Lords, introduced by Baroness Young of Hornsey, '[t]o make further provision for transparency in supply chains in respect of slavery and human trafficking'. Under this Bill (i) the reporting requirements of s54 are extended to include public authorities; (ii) organisations which should, but do not, produce a statement, would be excluded from participation in procurement under Public Contracts Regulations; (iii) the six areas which in the act an organisation 'may' include become obligatory ('must' now be included) and (iv) the Secretary of State must publish a list of all commercial organisations that are required to publish a statement. These provisions go a long way to address the early criticisms of s54, and, although not yet enacted, give an aspiring organisation clear pointers for improved engagement. Without engaging external advisers it is straightforward to determine what is required, not only to comply with the letter of the law but also the spirit.

How this study was designed and data collected

In assessing engagement, this study (i) looks at the existence, conformance, content and registration of statements; (ii) undertakes a longitudinal analysis of the same set of agricultural companies to assess whether engagement is improving and (iii) sets this in the context of a meta-study of other research into responses to s54. It uses content analysis as the central research method.

Research approach

In order to assess the most basic of questions around engagement – whether a statement has been produced or not – the starting point had to be the set of all companies that should be producing a statement, rather than the statements that had already been lodged with one of the registries.

The sampling frame was established as companies in specific UK Standard Industry Classification (SIC 2007) codes with a turnover of £36m or above. There is no sampling error – the sample is the entire population. The benefit of using UK SIC codes is that they have been generally accepted as a classification system for many years, are the prevalent approach used by researchers (Bryman and Bell, 2015) and (since the 2007 revision) are in line with the European Union's industrial classification system. Bryman and Bell (2015), in reviewing the development of the North American Industrial Classification Scheme

(NAICS), cite a criticism of SIC codes: that they focus on what is made rather than what is done. While this might have an impact for manufacturing or for new emerging sectors, the descriptions used in section A, 'Agriculture, Forestry and Fishing', are based on processes which cover the generally accepted concept of 'farming' activity and output. To provide context and comparison for the results of compliance testing, three further higher risk sectors – Food Processing and Packaging (FPP), Mining and Hotels – were selected, using the same approach. SIC codes and descriptions are set out in Table 2.1.

The Modern Slavery (Transparency in Supply Chains) HL Bill (2017–18) [57] (MSB) proposes adding a new section (10A) to the Act: 'The Secretary of State must publish a list of all commercial organisations that are required to publish a statement under this section'. This will remove any ambiguity about the completeness of the dataset to be analysed, but for now the dataset for these sectors has been defined based on these ranges of SIC codes.

For all four sectors, data was then extracted from the FAME database run by Bureau van Dijk, which covers information on over seven million companies and unincorporated business throughout the UK and Ireland. The search criteria were:

1. all active companies (not in receivership or dormant)
2. turnover, last available year: £36m minimum
3. UK SIC (2007): Primary codes (as above)
4. country: primary trading address, registered office address: England, Northern Ireland, Scotland, Wales (to give UK).

Table 2.1 Sector SIC codes

Sector	*SIC code*	*No.*	*SIC description*
Agriculture	011xx	25	Growing of non-perennial crops
	012xx	7	Growing of perennial crops
	013xx	0	Plant propagation
	014xx	23	Animal production
	015xx	16	Mixed farming
		71	
FPP	101xx	82	Processing and preserving of meat and production of meat products
	103xx	42	Processing and preserving of fruit and vegetables
		124	
Mining	05xxx	6	Mining of coal and lignite
	07xxx	15	Mining of metal ores
	08xxx	44	Other mining and quarrying
		65	
Hotels	551xxx	85	Hotels and similar accommodation
		85	
		345	

This search produced an initial population for the agricultural sector of 71 companies. It was then established that two companies were using inappropriate SIC codes – they are not, or are no longer, involved in farming activities. A further 21 companies were subsidiaries of others within the population and were removed to avoid double-counting, giving a final population of 48 companies.

Having established the population, compliance testing was undertaken. There are four mandatory elements to complying with s54:

Existence

1. a statement must be produced: s54 (4)(a) says companies must produce 'a statement of the steps the organisation has taken during the financial year to ensure that slavery and human trafficking is not taking place (i) in any of its supply chains and (ii) in any part of its own business, or (b) a statement that the organisation has taken no such steps'.

Conformance

2. visibility: the statement must be published on the organisation's website with a prominent link from the home page (s54 (7)), or, if no website exists, the company must respond to a written request to provide a copy of the statement within 30 days (s54 (8));
3. approval: the statement must be approved by the board of directors (s54 (6)(a)); and
4. sign-off: the statement must be signed by a director (s54 (6)(a)).

For each company in the population, company websites were reviewed to determine whether a statement existed. If a statement could not be found, the two registries were searched, and web searches using the term 'modern slavery statement' and the company name were undertaken.

For the agricultural sector round one analysis, data was taken in June 2017, and the follow-up data for round two in June 2018. For the comparative sectors, data was taken in December 2017.

Where a website existed it was reviewed to test visibility, to see if there was a prominent link to the statement on the homepage. Copies of the statements were downloaded and analysed to determine if the statement had approval and sign-off. For agricultural companies, that were also to be subjected to content analysis, if no company website was found, a written request was made for a statement to be provided.

Having undertaken compliance testing, we then used content analysis for assessing the quality of the s54 statements included in our study. The MSA explanatory notes say 'Section 54 does not mandate what a slavery and human trafficking statement must contain (beyond the actual steps taken or a statement that the organisation has taken no steps) nor require commercial organisations to take any particular action beyond preparation of the annual statement' (Parliament, 2015, p. 36). But there are *content suggestions,* and *improvement* is expected over time. Section 54(5) suggests six content areas that could be covered in statements: (1) organisational structure, business and supply chains; (2) policies relating to slavery and trafficking; (3) due diligence processes in the business and supply chains; (4) parts of the business where there is risk, and steps taken to address that risk; (5) effectiveness in ensuring slavery/trafficking is not taking place measured against appropriate performance indicators and (6) staff training. These provide the six themes which were searched for and graded using content analysis and mirrors the approach adopted by previous studies (e.g. by Ergon Associates, 2017; BHRRC 2017; Emberson, 2017) (Table 2.2).

The legislation and its guidance have been reviewed to determine required and recommended content and process elements, and from this flow the list of recording units, set out above. Each element is then scored on a subjective scale of coding categories from 0 to 5, 0 being no performance, 5 being exemplary. This covers steps 1 and 2 of the Weber protocol.

A sample statement was then coded and the ratings given were cross checked with an analysis undertaken on the same statement by an experienced third-party. The sample grading assessments were revised in the light of this feedback, although there had been a high degree of consistency. The entire population was then fully graded and scored.

In order to minimise as far as possible subjective error within the content analysis, statements were analysed in batches and the various categories compared within a batch, so as to ensure consistency of grading and correct ranking. When a new batch was analysed, examples from a previous batch were reanalysed, to achieve the same ends. At the end of the analysis, all statements were sorted in descending order of content rank, for each content category, and reviewed again, to ensure that the progression down the grading was justified.

Compliance: Existence and conformance

Of the 48 agricultural companies that should have prepared a statement, 24 had done so, a 50% existence rate. When mapping the existence of a statement against the size of company (measured by turnover), neither discernible pattern emerges nor is there a correlation between whether a statement was produced and legal form. None of the population prepared a statement saying they had taken 'no such steps'. Some of the weakest statements did not actually set out any steps 'taken … to ensure' – they simply expressed a commitment to ensure there is no modern slavery.

Eighteen of the 24 statements produced (75%) were signed by a director. Twelve (50%) were approved by the board. Of the subset of the population which had produced a statement and had a website (22 companies), 13 (59%)

Table 2.2 Content analysis grading criteria from Emberson (2017)

Content category	*0*	*1*	*2*	*3*	*4*	*5*
Organisation and supply chain	No information	Some description of business structure, services, products and customers	Detailed description of business structure, services, products and customers	As 2 plus some description about first tier suppliers	As 2 plus detailed description about first tier suppliers	As 2 plus description of second tier and beyond
Policies	No policy	Formal or informal policy under which business with unethical suppliers is not to be conducted	Relevant Modern Slavery policy	As 2 plus code of conduct	Relevant and specific MS policy and code of conduct	As 4 plus for the organisation and its' supply chain
Due diligence	No steps taken	Modern slavery is / to be included in the organisations risk assessment processes	New internal processes detailed for the organisation	As 2, but extended to its suppliers	As 3, including organisational-wide grievance mechanisms in place for targeted workers	As 4, including suppliers and their workers
Risk assessment	No assessment	Risk assessment conducted based on the nature of goods/services supplied to the business	As 1, plus supply chain	Risk assessment focussed on modern slavery and labour risks in its own business	As 3, plus supply chain	Assessment to include potentially effected rights holders and other stakeholders

(*Continued*)

Table 2.2 (Continued)

Content category	*0*	*1*	*2*	*3*	*4*	*5*
Effectiveness & KPIs	No measures	General statement re: numbers trained, complaints from whistle-blowing mechanisms	As 1, plus figures	General KPIs used	As 3, plus figures	Detailed KPIs and figures relevant to Modern Slavery
Training	No information	General training on ethical practice provided to employees	Training on Human Rights provided	Training on Modern Slavery provided	As 3 plus details of specific groups of employees targeted	As 4 plus annual update

had a link on their homepage, and a further 4 (18%) had a link from a drop-down menu or subsidiary page, typically called 'CSR' or 'Policies'. For four companies (18%) a statement was discovered either on the Internet using a browser search tool or via one of the statement registries, but there was no reference to it at all on their websites, not even through their own search functions where these existed. It is not clear why an organisation would produce a statement but then fail to provide any connection to it on their website.

Of the final population, 10% (5 of 48) had no website and were contacted by post. Of these, 60% failed to respond, and 40% responded, within the 30-day time period. For one of these it is suspected that the statement was produced as a result of them being contacted, an interesting example of the Hawthorne ('observer') effect, where behaviour is modified as a result of the observed becoming aware of their own observation.

Therefore, across all four measures (existence and three conformance), only 9 companies of 48 (19%) complied with all the requirements of s54. This can be compared with compliance rates amongst all UK companies for filings with Companies House: 97.6% comply with filing annual returns, and 98.1% with filing annual accounts (gov.uk, 2017).

Quality of content

This next section looks at the quality of the statements that were produced.

The grading scheme criteria are discussed above (Figures 2.1–2.6).

C1: Business and supply chain structure

The MSA says that an organisation's statement may include information about – 'the organisation's structure, its business, and its supply chains' s54(5)(a).

Average score 2.0.

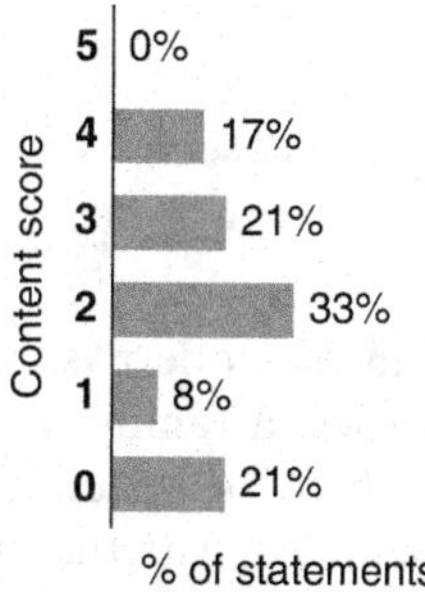

Figure 2.1 Content analysis scores re business and supply chain structure.

High scoring statements included data about the company – its products, processes, location and structure – and information about tier 1 suppliers so as to give a sense of the supply chain. No statements included information on tier 2 suppliers, but many of these companies have fairly flat supply chains: for example, one company grows organic produce on its own farms and delivers it direct to the end consumer.

Four companies' statements scored four points for their disclosure on structure, business and supply chains. For example, a large dairy farming and cheese production company from the West Country works through the relationship between the holding company and subsidiaries, setting out what each business does. It describes its sites, production processes and supply chains (which are relatively short) both in the UK and within a US-based joint venture. Another statement which scored well in this area (family company, vegetable grower and packer, turnover £127m, based in Lincolnshire) set out in a straightforward way the nature of their business, where and how they operate, who they supply and who their suppliers are.

When reading the four statements that scored zero points for this section, the reader does not get any information about the company, its products, services or customers – not even that they are involved in agricultural activity.

C2: Policies

The 'policies in relation to slavery and human trafficking' s54(5)(b).

Average score 2.7.

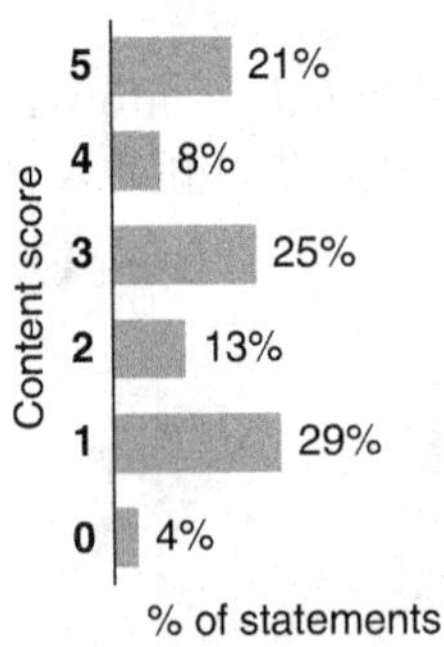

Figure 2.2 Content analysis scores re policies.

The highest scoring statements set out the company's modern slavery policy and how this links in with other company policies: a family-owned business with a turnover of £36.5m (just large enough to be required to produce a statement), that grows and packs root vegetables, lists the business policies it has in place, including policies on Ethical and Human Rights, Whistleblowing, Business Practice, Health & Safety, Prevention of Illegal working, and Anti-Bribery. A UK subsidiary of a major multinational has a supplier code of conduct which has been published in 30 languages as the company engages with its international supply chain. Some companies refer to their use of work done by trade bodies, for example the British Poultry Council Poultry Supply Chain Ethical Compliance Code of Practice.

Although they didn't have a specific modern slavery policy, a cheese making group (private limited company, turnover £84m, based in Somerset and Dorset), describe in their 2017 statement the policies they operate which contribute 'to the identification of modern slavery risks and steps to be taken to prevent slavery and human trafficking' in their operations. This includes details about their Whistleblowing policy, Employee code of conduct, Supplier code of conduct and Recruitment/Agency workers policy.

Poor statements included generic comments about zero tolerance to modern slavery, but gave no indication of how this was effected.

C3: Due diligence processes

'Due diligence processes in relation to slavery and human trafficking in its business and supply chains' s54(5)(c).

Average score 3.3.

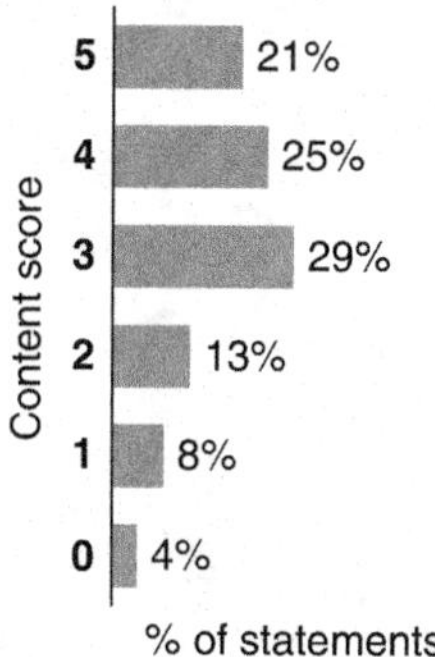

Figure 2.3 Content analysis scores re due diligence processes.

Overall this was the highest scoring area within the analysis. Proactive companies are members of SEDEX and/or the Ethical Trading Initiative (ETI). To assess their supply chain they use internal auditors or external auditors from ETI, SEDEX, Fairtrade, the GLAA Active Check service or the Association of Labour Providers. They have clear codes of conduct, and require use of the GLAA for all providers of contract labour. Poor statements gave no indication of any specific due diligence processes, using generic, aspirational comments.

One of the strongest statements in this area came from the parent of a public limited company group whose main business is growing, storing, processing and packing potatoes. They operate in the UK, Jersey, France and the Netherlands, with a turnover of £185m. Their statement remained unchanged from 2017 to 2018, and did not comply with all requirements, but it was particularly strong in setting out the due diligence work the group undertakes, including membership of SEDEX themselves and across their supply base, membership of the Association of Labour Providers, undertaking Gangmaster Licencing Act audits with temporary labour providers, using Ethical Trading Initiative (ETI) audits to SEDEX Members Ethical Trading Audit (SMETA) standards, and participation with the Stronger2gether campaign.

One major international agricultural company conducted over 21,500 audits of businesses in their supply chain in one financial year, in the process finding no incidences of forced labour. It might be thought that only larger companies would have the necessary resources to actively engage in this way, but the correlation between company turnover and score for due diligence was weakly negative at −0.28: smaller companies, if anything, more robust than larger.

C4: Risk and risk management

'The parts of its business and supply chains where there is a risk of slavery and human trafficking taking place, and the steps it has taken to assess and manage that risk's54(5)(d).

Average score 2.2.

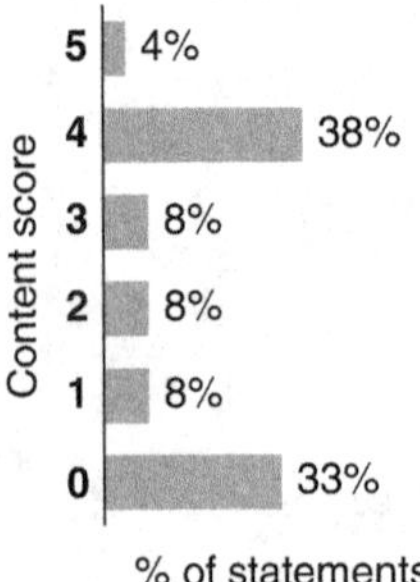

Figure 2.4 Content analysis scores re risk and risk management.

There is crossover between risk management and assessment and the previous content area, due diligence processes. Similar third parties can be used for both, and there was a moderately positive correlation between performance in these two areas (+0.41).

There is a real divide in this category, with around 40% (score 4 or 5) of companies who actively use risk analysis as a tool for identifying key areas for focus in their own businesses and supply chains and use tools such as ILO NORMLEX and NATLEX (information systems on international labour standards, national labour and social security laws, human rights issues). Additionally, there are 40% of companies who neither use risk appraisal as a tool nor identify areas of high risk (score 0 or 1).

Just one company gained maximum marks in this area (a private limited, UK-based international salad company with a turnover of £293m). They produced a high-scoring statement in 2017 and then revised and improved their statement in 2018. They had identified as higher risk their seasonal workers and external labour providers, and they set out the risk mitigations both within their own organisation and then within their supply chain to deal with these risks.

C5: Measured effectiveness & KPIs

'Its effectiveness in ensuring that slavery and human trafficking is not taking place in its business or supply chains, measured against such performance indicators as it considers appropriate' s54(5)(e).

Average score 0.4.

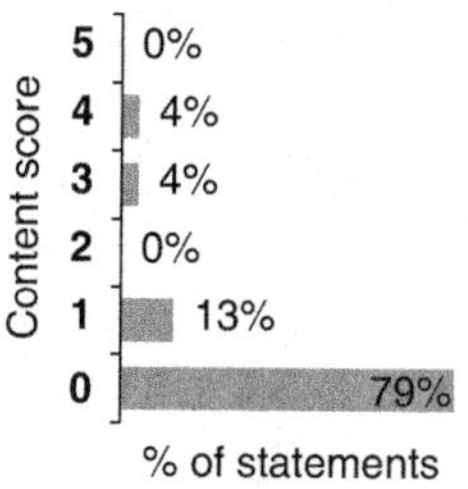

Figure 2.5 Content analysis scores re measured effectiveness and KPIs.

This is by far the weakest area in statements. Very few companies discussed any approach to assessing the effectiveness of what they were doing to address modern slavery. Only two companies included specific KPIs, and neither of these had any data to report or had set targets, as one would expect from the financial KPIs in annual financial statements.

While there are few good examples in the area of measured effectiveness, one comes from a small company, only just over the £36m turnover threshold (private limited company, based in Nottinghamshire, growing and marketing vegetable crops and cereals, selling mainly to the major UK supermarkets). This area was not covered in their 2017 statement, but the 2018 had been revised and improved, and included a reflection on their performance over the year on which they were reporting, and some targets for the subsequent year.

Nearly 80% included nothing on this area. Effectiveness measures could relate both to modern slavery itself (the number of incidences found, or notifications received through an internal reporting mechanism) or to the company's modern slavery policy and work, such as the proportion of its suppliers audited internally or externally, or the numbers of its staff who have received training on modern slavery.

It would be expected that KPIs would change over time as the focus of a company's work changes and it becomes more engaged with the issue. This very poor result may be a function of these reports being the first produced by the companies, but even statements of intent were rare. (Round two analysis, in 5.4, shows a slight increase in average score from 0.4 to 0.7, but it remains the worst area.)

C6: Staff training

'The training about slavery and human trafficking available to its staff' s54(5)(f).

Average score 2.3.

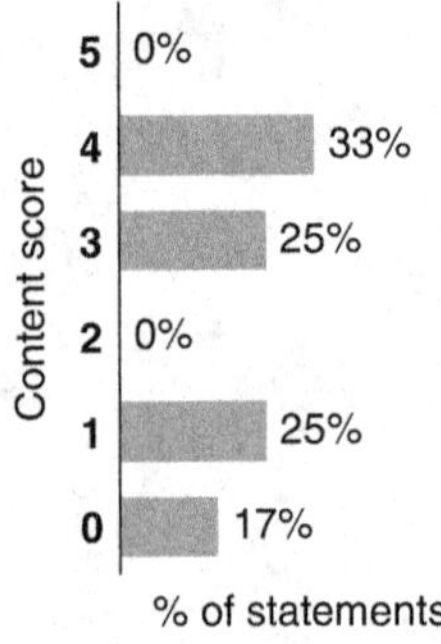

Figure 2.6 Content analysis scores re staff training.

Again, there was a clear divide in discussion of training. Companies with active training programmes in this area had differentiated training for different groups of staff (such as management, recruiters, operations teams), used company-wide awareness raising programmes and gave detailed disclosure about their training programmes.

Many had become involved in Stronger Together, a multi-stakeholder initiative aiming to reduce modern slavery, which offers support and guidance and multi-lingual resources. Engaged companies extend their training provision to their supply chain.

A chicken rearing company, part of one on the UK's largest food producing groups (public limited company, turnover £1.4bn) set out the differentiated training provided, from basic training for all staff to more specialist training for HR teams and supply chain operations teams. Another higher scoring company in this area had provided key members of staff with lead auditor training in SA8000, an international social accountability standard. But 42% of company statements gave little or no information about any training put in place.

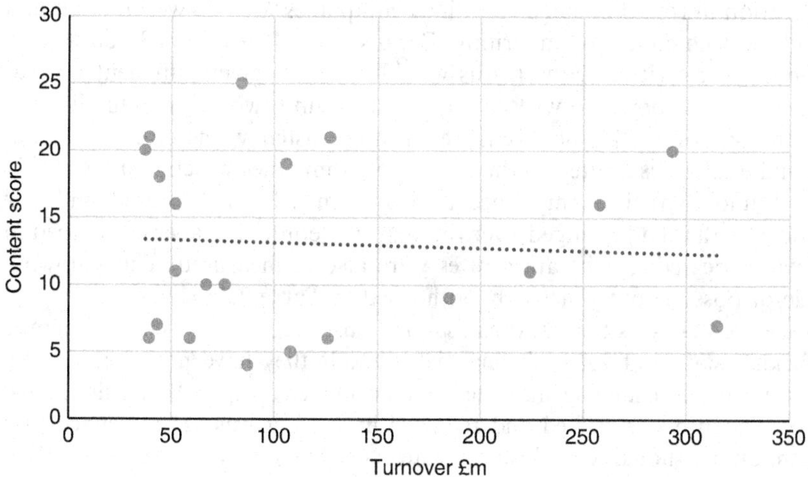

Figure 2.7 Content score mapped against size of company.

Just as with the testing for existence of a statement, these results do not allow any conclusion to be drawn about the nature of companies which are preparing higher scoring statements. There is no correlation between size of company and scoring: Figure 2.7 plots this, removing the two outlying largest companies, references 1 (turnover £976m) and 3 (turnover £576m). This gives a correlation coefficient (r) of −0.05, i.e. no correlation.

Nor is there any correlation between company profitability and scoring: profit margin percentages range from −2.8% to +9.3% (removing the one outlier at 59%), and the correlation coefficient between these and content score is 0.03. There is also no discernible correlation between legal form of company and higher scoring statements. The two public alternative investment market companies had an average score of 12.5, very close to the population average of 12.9.

Is there a correlation between quality and approval or sign-off, that is, does the active involvement of the board or a named individual produce better statements? The correlation coefficient of statement score and approval is 0.32, and between statement score and sign-off is 0.38. Both of these correlations are positive, but at less than 0.5 would generally be considered rather weak. The reasons behind better engagement with s54 must therefore be more nuanced, and suggest further areas for study, discussed in the chapter conclusion.

Comparison over two reporting periods

The final element of our study was a longitudinal analysis, looking at changes in engagement over a year of the same set of agricultural companies. By comparing the statements produced by companies in the agricultural sector at June 2017 with the statements of the same companies one year on, it is possible to see whether there has been any improvement. The final population in round one had contained companies with no website that had therefore been contacted in writing. Because the MSA allows 30 days for a response to a written request, this would not have given sufficient time to integrate the response to written requests in round two prior to finalisation and submission of this book chapter. For consistency, therefore, the longitudinal analysis is limited to the dataset of companies which had a website.

In round two, the compliance testing from 4.1 was repeated and, for statements that had changed over the year, the content analysis described in 4.2 was repeated. Registration rates were also re-measured. The following range of possible outcomes is hypothesised in Table 2.3:

Section 54 (1) says that an organisation 'must prepare a slavery and human trafficking statement for each financial year'. If they have not, even just by reviewing it and changing the date, they no longer comply. When the Home Office guidance was revised and re-issued in 2017, it was recommended that 'organisations should keep historic statements from previous years available online even when new statements are published' (Home Office, 2017, p. 14). These two aspects were introduced as additional compliance tests for round two.

The longitudinal work addresses one of the weaknesses identified in the existing literature (3.2) and explores a key aspect of the legislative guidance, that there should be development and improvement over time: Home Office guidance says that it is expected that organisations will 'build on their statements year on year and for the statements to evolve and improve over time' (Home Office, 2015, p. 6).

In his letter to CEOs one year after the MSA came into force, the Independent Anti-Slavery Commissioner noted: 'Despite some positive steps forward since the Modern Slavery Act and a number of good statements being published, I remain disappointed that analysis has shown the quality to be weak overall ... Even statements that do legally comply have a lot of room for improvement with many simply being reiterations of generic human rights policies ... I expect companies to be building on their statements year on year' (Hyland, 2017, p. 1).

Table 2.3 Range of possible outcomes is hypothesised

Engagement June 2017 (round one)	*Engagement June 2018 (round two)*	*Category*
Statement exists	Revised, better quality	Reviser, improving
	Revised, same quality	Reviser, static
	Revised, worse quality	Reviser, declining
	Not revised	Non-reviser
	Statement no longer exists	Dropout
Statement doesn't exist	Statement now exists	New engager
	Still doesn't exist	Non-engager

Existence over time

Of the 43 companies with a website, 51% (22) had produced a statement in round one (Table 2.3). One year later this existence rate had risen to 67%: two companies no longer produced a statement, and there were nine new engagers.

Of the original 22 statements from round one, 20 companies still have a statement, of which,

- ten statements have changed ('revisers' per 4.4)
  - six statements have been materially revised and needed to be subjected to content analysis, with four increasing in quality ('reviser, improver'), three by 2 points, one by 3 points and two staying the same ('reviser, static')
  - four statements have simply had the date changed for a new year but are otherwise identical ('reviser, static').
- ten statements have not been changed at all ('non-revisers'), and are therefore out of date
- two companies no longer have statements available ('dropouts')

Of the 21 companies that had not produced a statement in round one

- nice have now engaged ('new engagers')
- 12 still haven't ('non-engagers').

This takes the total existence rate from 51% in round one to 67% in round two, or 44% if the out-of-date statements are excluded, as they no longer comply. This is illustrated in Figure 2.8 which tracks engagement from round one to round two:

Compliance over time

Of the 20 companies producing a statement in both rounds, none had changed their conformance scoring with regards to visibility, sign-off or approval: of the ten revisers, none had addressed gaps around sign-off or approval from round one. For the nine new-engagers, conformance rates are shown in Table 2.4 and compared with round one revisers and non-revisers: poor performance from the new engagers has reduced the overall average:

As discussed in Table 2.4, round two compliance testing included an additional tests to check whether a statement had been produced for the new financial year. Ten of the round one 22 companies, the 'non-revisers', fall in to this category. Although the first statement still exists, the company no longer technically complies. Thus at round two the existence rate falls to 44%: despite nine new companies engaging, ten have not revised their statement and two have dropped out.

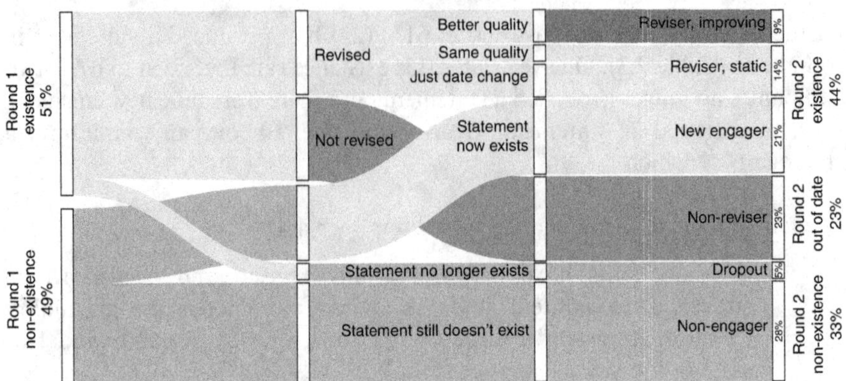

Figure 2.8 Engagement over time Acknowledgement to Bruce McPherson, desktop liberation, mcpher.com and bost.ocks.org for d3.js and Sankey diagram tool.

Table 2.4 Round two conformance of agricultural sector statements

	Existence		*Conformance*			
	Existence	*Revision*	*Visibility*	*Sign-off*	*Approval*	*All 3*
Round one revisers and non-revisers	51%	–	75%	75%	50%	35%
New engagers	–	–	67%	89%	11%	11%
All at round two	67%	44%	72%	79%	38%	28%

Quality over time

There are four clear findings from the longitudinal quality analysis:

i. those companies that were most engaged in round one were most likely to have revised their statements a year later. It will be recalled that scores can range from 0 to 30: the average round one score of those who went on to be revisers was 19.8, well above the average of 12.9. The six statements revised had round one scores of 16, 18, 20, 20, 20 and 25. In round two the revisers average increased to 21.3.
ii. new engagers have neither learned from the earlier engagers in their sector nor from the additional time they have had to engage: statements from new engagers were almost all weak, with scores ranging from 5 to 16, an average of 8.8, with only one statement above the round one average of 12.9.
iii. with the new engagers producing relatively poor statements, and with only 6 of the 22 round one statements being materially revised, the average quality score for the sector has fallen marginally, from 13.2 for all round one companies with websites, to 12.7 for round two.

iv. the content areas of relative strength and weakness remain the same: content area C3, due diligence, was the best addressed area amongst new engagers (albeit with an average score of 2.2, compared to 3.3 for round one) and C5, effectiveness and KPIs, the least well addressed (with a score of 0.2).

Two further observations emerge:

v. as noted in 4.4, official guidance suggests that websites should include all modern slavery statements, not just the current year, so that the public can compare statements and monitor progress within an organisation over time. No company website in the agricultural sector does this.

vi. some of the organisations which still do not have a statement on their website, do have homepage links to gender pay gap information and General Data Protection Regulation (GDPR) privacy notices, so it is clear they are aware of at least some aspects of their reporting responsibilities and do maintain their websites. Both GPG and GDPR come with very large – and very well promoted – financial penalties for non-compliance. This theme is revisited in the conclusions

Longitudinal summary

While existence rates have increased within the agricultural sector, up from 51% to 67% (for companies with websites), nearly half of those producing a statement in the first year have not revisited their statements and so no longer comply. The poorer performance of the new-engagers means that overall conformance rates have actually fallen year-on-year (from 35% of statements meeting all three requirements, to 28%) and the average content quality has also marginally fallen.

Contextualising and comparing the results

At face value, a 51% existence rate (round one, companies with websites), and a 19% overall compliance rate, seem poor. Average scores for content quality also seem low. These results have therefore been contextualised in two ways, first by extending the research of this study for compliance to other higher risk sectors, and secondly by drawing together both compliance rates and content quality information from the six existing UK work streams into a meta-study of results. How do the results and the analysis compare, and what common themes are there? Is the low level of engagement of the UK agricultural sector unusual?

Compliance within other UK sectors

We analysed three further high-risk sectors under the same approach to testing compliance, except that where no company website was found companies were not contacted in writing. Comparative statistics are therefore just for companies with websites as presented in Table 2.5.

Table 2.5 Compliance rates across different sectors

	Ag	*Comparative sectors*				*Total*
		FP	*Mining*	*Hotels*	*Total*	
Initial population	71	124	65	85		
Removals (wrong SIC code being used)	−2	0	0	−1		
Subsidiaries	−21	−30	−9	−26		
Final population	**48**	94	56	58		
No website	−5	−14	−8	−5		
Final population with websites	**43**	80	48	53	**181**	**224**
Statements found online	22	47	24	19	90	112
Existence:	**51%**	59%	50%	36%	**50%**	**50%**
Visibility	17	37	22	15	74	91
Sign-off	16	39	20	15	74	90
Approval	11	18	12	8	38	49
All compliance elements	8	13	10	8	31	39
Compliance rates (as % of final population of companies):						
Visibility	40%	46%	46%	28%	41%	41%
Sign-off	37%	49%	42%	28%	41%	40%
Approval	26%	23%	25%	15%	21%	22%
All compliance elements	**19%**	16%	21%	15%	**17%**	**17%**

Compliance rates across different sectors show similar results to those found within the agricultural sector: 90 of the 181 companies with websites in the three other sectors had produced statements, a 50% existence rate. Food processing and packing leads, at 59%, mining 50%, and then the hotels sector 36%. Across all four sectors, 50% of companies had produced a statement. The existence rate for the agricultural sector is therefore average. Overall compliance rates for the three other sectors were similarly close: mining at 21%, food processing and packing 16% and hotels 15%, giving an average of 17%, slightly behind the agricultural sector at 19%. The prima facie poor results for the agricultural sector appear to be par for the course.

Conclusions

By June 2017, only 50% of agricultural companies had produced a modern slavery statement, and only 38% of these statements conformed to all requirements, an overall compliance rate for the sector of 19%. One year on, 67% of agricultural companies have a statement, but as a number of these statements are now out-of-date, technically only 44% of companies have an in-date statement.

The quality of the content of the statements was low, with an average score of 12.9 out of 30. There are some areas of s54 that companies seem to find easier to comply with than others. An area of particular weakness is that of measured effectiveness and key performance indicators: if a company has no way to assess the effectiveness of the steps it is taking to ensure slavery is not taking place, the chances of driving change must be reduced.

There has been little development over time: the quality of statements has not improved. Those companies that were reporting in June 2017 have not made significant progress in the year since, and new engagers have not learned from the response of the earlier adopters, producing below-average quality statements. Only a quarter of companies have revisited their statements one year on, and only 9% of companies increased the quality of their statements. A small group is strategically engaged with the issue, and may well be frustrated by the increased scrutiny their transparency brings while the poor performance of the majority goes unaddressed. The inference is that the majority of companies have either failed to engage, or have put out a statement, considered the job done, and moved on from the issue, even though there is every indication the issue is a growing one.

Results from this study echo those found in other sectors and in the existing literature. This study contributes to the exploratory foundations on which more theoretical work can be built as to why engagement is poor: the conclusion for now must be to doubt the effectiveness of this example of regulated corporate reporting to bring about change for more sustainable business. The weakness of the provisions of s54 of the MSA manifests itself in this poor engagement: legislation requiring similar outcomes which is more robust achieves a greater impact, sooner. The efforts of civil society and Government to drive up engagement and improve standards show no signs of having had an impact in this sector.

The study supports the need for including the bottom of the pyramid parts of the supply chain in corporate responsibility as suggested by Hahn and Gold (2014). Keeping such responsibility at a voluntary basis without meaningful enforcement mechanisms, however, can be concluded to be an insufficient and largely naïve approach. It also demonstrates the clear need for state institutions in bottom of the pyramid supply chains where commercial logic does not support, and even contradicts, treating workers well.

Our study can be used for measuring success of the UK's Modern Slavery Act supply chain provision and backs up the Commissioner's and the Public Accounts Committee's conclusions that s54 statements were a 'tick-box exercise' and that 'Having a series of regulations with which two-thirds ... are not compliant is not world leading' (IASC, 2018, question 63 & 64). In essence, the poor quality of many statements indicates a *tactical* response to the MSA and the issue of modern slavery – box ticking and minimal compliance – from the UK agricultural sector, and more widely. If sustainability issues such as modern slavery are going to be successfully addressed through mandated corporate reporting, this must fully engage these companies and elicit a more meaningful *strategic* response.

References

Allain, J (2012). *The Legal Understanding of Slavery: From the Historical to the Contemporary*. Appendices. Oxford: Oxford University Press, pp. 375–380.

Anderson, B, & Rogaly, B (2005). Forced labour and migration to the UK. *Prevention*, 1–68.

Aronowitz, AA (2017). *Human Trafficking: A Reference Handbook*. Santa Barbara: ABC-CLIO.

Arya, B, & Salk, JE (2006). Cross-sector alliance learning and effectiveness of voluntary codes of corporate social responsibility. *Business Ethics Quarterly, 16*, 211–234. https://doi.org/10.5840/beq200616223

Bales, K (2016). *Blood and Earth: Modern Slavery, Ecocide, and the Secret to Saving the World*. New York: Random House.

Bales, K (1999). *Disposable People: New Slavery in the Global Economy*. Berkeley: University of California Press.

Bales,K, Hesketh, O, & Silverman, B (2015). Modern slavery in the UK: How many victims? *Significance, 12* (3), 16–21.

Bales, K, Trodd, Z, & Williamson, AK (2009a). *Modern Slavery: A Beginner's Guide*. Oxford: Oneworld.

Bales, K, Trodd, Z, & Williamson, AK (2009b). *Modern Slavery: The Secret World of 27 Million People*. Oxford: Oneworld.

BBC (2017). Modern slavery and trafficking "in every UK town and city." Retrieved from http://www.bbc.co.uk/news/uk-40885353

BHRRC (2017). *First Year of FTSE 100 Reports Under the UK Modern Slavery Act: Towards Elimination?* Retrieved from https://business-humanrights.org/sites/default/files/FTSE100Report Public.pdf

Bryant, K (2015). Identifying what works: a meta-evaluation of modern slavery evaluations. In *Proceedings from the Freedom from Slavery Conference*, 9th October 2015 (pp. 1–16).

Bryman, A, & Bell, E (2015). *Business Research Methods* (4th ed.). Oxford: Oxford University Press.

Brzezinski (2017). R v Brzezinski [2017] Nottingham Crown Court.

Chesney, T, Evans, K, Gold, S, & Trautrims, A (2019). Understanding labour exploitation in the Spanish agricultural sector using an agent based approach. *Journal of Cleaner Production, 214*, 696–704.

Crane, A (2013). Modern slavery as a management practice: Exploring the conditions and capabilities for human exploitation. *Academy of Management Review, 38* (1), 49–69.

Datta, MN, & Bales, K (2013). Slavery in Europe: Part I, estimating the dark figure. *Human Rights Quarterly, 35* (4), 817–829.

Datta, MN, & Bales, K (2014). Slavery in Europe: Part 2, testing a predictive model. *Human Rights Quarterly, 36* (2), 277–295.

Derbyshire Police (2014). *Modern Slavery: A Briefing for the Agricultural Sector*. Retrieved from http://www.derbyshire.police.uk/Documents/Safety-Advice/HumanTrafficking/Agricultural.pdf

Director of Labour Market Enforcement (2018). *United Kingdom Labour Market Enforcement Strategy 2018/19*. Retrieved from https://assets.publishing.service.gov.uk/government/uploads/system/uploads/attachment_data/file/705503/labour-market-enforcement-strategy-2018-2019-full-report.pdf.

Emberson, C (2017). *Modern Slavery Act Statements in the University Sector – The Start of the Journey.* Retrieved from https://www.hepa.ac.uk/Resources/News/View?g=a2c633b3-9d77-454c-8bc5-d2f96c5256f9&m=4&y=2017

Ergon Associates (2017). *Modern Slavery Statements: One Year on.* Retrieved from http://ergonassociates.net/wp-content/uploads/2016/03/MSA_One_year_on_April_2017.pdf

Gangmasters and Labour Abuse Authority (2018). *The Nature and Scale of Labour Exploitation across all Sectors Within the United Kingdom.* Retrieved from http://www.gla.gov.uk/media/3537/external-nature-and-scale-of-labour-exploitation-report-final-version-may-2018.pdf.

Gold, S, Trautrims, A, & Trodd, Z (2015). Modern slavery challenges to supply chain management. *Supply Chain Management: An International Journal, 20* (5), 485–494.

gov.uk (2017). *Companies House Management Information 2016/17.* Retrieved from https://assets.publishing.service.gov.uk/government/uploads/system/uploads/attachment_data/file/638401/Companies_House_Management_Information_2016-17.xlsx

Hahn, R, & Gold, S (2014). Resources and governance in 'base of the pyramid'-partnerships: Assessing collaborations between businesses and non-business actors. *Journal of Business Research, 67* (7), 1321–1333.

Hall, J, Matos, S, Sheehan, L, & Silvestre, B (2012). Entrepreneurship and innovation at the base of the pyramid: A recipe for inclusive growth or social exclusion? *Journal of Management Studies, 49* (4), 785–812.

Haughey, C (2016). *The Modern Slavery Act review.* Retrieved from https://assets.publishing.service.gov.uk/government/uploads/system/uploads/attachment_data/file/542047/2016_07_31_Haughey_Review_of_Modern_Slavery_Act_-_final_1.0.pdf

Home Office (2015). *Transparency in Supply Chains etc. A Practical Guide* (Vol. 54). London. Retrieved from https://www.gov.uk/government/uploads/system/uploads/attachment_data/file/471996/Transparency_in_Supply_Chains_etc__A_practical_guide__final_.pdf

Home Office (2017). *Transparency in supply chains etc. A practical guide – 2017* (Vol. 54). London. Retrieved from https://assets.publishing.service.gov.uk/government/uploads/system/uploads/attachment_data/file/649906/Transparency_in_Supply_Chains_A_Practical_Guide_2017.pdf

Hyland, K (2017). *Letter to CEOs.* Retrieved from http://www.antislaverycommissioner.co.uk/news-insights/letter-to-ceos-one-year-on-from-section-54-of-modern-slavery-act/

IASC (2016). *Independent Anti-Slavery Commissioner Annual Report 2015-16.* Retrieved from http://www.antislaverycommissioner.co.uk/media/1164/iasc_annual-report-16-17-web.pdf

IASC (2018). *Calling on FTSE 100 Companies to Combat Modern Slavery.* Retrieved from http://www.antislaverycommissioner.co.uk/news-insights/calling-on-ftse-100-companies-to-combat-modern-slavery/

Khalid, RU, Seuring, S, Beske, P, Land, A, Yawar, SA, & Wagner, R (2015). Putting sustainable supply chain management into base of the pyramid research. *Supply Chain Management: An International Journal, 20* (6), 681–696. https://doi.org/10.1108/SCM-06-2015-0214

Kolk, A, Rivera-Santos, M, & Rufín, C (2014). Reviewing a decade of research on the "base/bottom of the pyramid" (BOP) concept. *Business & Society, 53* (3), 338–377. https://doi.org/10.1177%2F0007650312474928

National Crime Agency (2018). *Modern Slavery and Human Trafficking: National Referral Mechanism Statistics.* Retrieved from http://www.nationalcrimeagency.gov.uk/publications/national-referral-mechanism-statistics/2018-nrm-statistics.

New, SJ (2015). Modern slavery and the supply chain: The limits of corporate social responsibility? *Supply Chain Management: An International Journal, 20* (6), 697–707.

Nottingham Post (2017). *Farmer lifts lid on how he uncovered slave master.* Retrieved January 29, 2018, from https://www.nottinghampost.com/news/local-news/farmer-lifts-lid-how-uncovered-647470

Parliament (2015). Explanatory notes - Modern Slavery Act 2015. *TSO (The Stationery Office), The Houses of Parliament.* Retrieved from http://www.legislation.gov.uk/ukpga/2015/30/pdfs/ukpga_20150030_en.pdf

Pinheiro, S, Emberson, C, & Trautrims, A (2019). 'For the English to see' or effective change? – How supply chains are shaped by laws and regulations and what that means for modern slavery exposure. *Journal of the British Academy, 7* (s1), 167–190. doi: 10.5871/jba/007s1.167

Silverman, B (2014). *Modern Slavery: An Application of Multiple Systems Estimation* (Vol. 2014). Retrieved from https://www.gov.uk/government/uploads/system/uploads/attachment_data/file/386841/Modern_Slavery_an_application_of_MSE_revised.pdf

U.S. Department of State (2016). Trafficking in Persons Report 2016 – Introductory Material.

Verisk Maplecroft (2017). Modern Slavery Index 2017. Retrieved from https://maplecroft.com/portfolio/new-analysis/2017/08/10/20-eu-countries-see-rise-modern-slavery-risks-study/

Wager, N, & Wager, A (2017). Estimating the extent of modern slavery: Proposed model and formula for Thames Valley Police and Crime Commissioner, available at: https://www.thamesvalley-pcc.gov.uk/victims-first/modern-slavery/

Wen, S (2016). The cogs and wheels of reflexive law - Business disclosure under the modern slavery act. *Journal of Law and Society, 43* (3), 327–359. https://doi.org/10.1111/j.1467-6478.2016.00758.x

Wilkinson, M (2012). Out of sight, out of mind: the exploitation of migrant workers in 21st-century Britain. *Journal of Poverty and Social Justice, 20* (1), 13–21(9).

Wilkinson, M (2014). Demonising "the other": British government complicity in the exploitation, social exclusion and vilification of new migrant workers. *Citizenship Studies, 18* (5)499–515.

Yekini, K, Li, H, Ohalehi, P, & Chijoke-Mgbame, AM (2019). CSR disclosure and corporate sustainability: Evidence from the Shenzhen Stock Exchange. *International Journal of Business Governance and Ethics, 13* (3), 300–322.

Part III

Roles, cooperation and structure in BOP markets

3 Bottle collectors between societal exclusion and inclusion in affluent countries

Wolfgang Bichler-Riedl, Annika Mies, and Stefan Gold

Introduction

For some time, recycling is named one of the most important concepts to decreasing raw material footprints on the one hand and waste on the other (Hayes, 1978). Its importance is reflected in United Nations Sustainable Development Goal (SDG) 12.2, which postulates: 'by 2030, substantially reduce waste generation through prevention, reduction, recycling, and reuse' (General Assembly of the United Nations, 2015). Amongst the drivers of ever increasing raw material consumption, research has highlighted 'affluence' (Myers and Kent, 2003; Weinzettel et al., 2013; Wiedmann et al., 2015).

For European countries, raw material consumption is particularly a problem due to a scarcity of natural resources (European Commission, 2010). Hence, recycling and therefore the usage of secondary materials in the sense of urban mining assists in decreasing dependence from raw material import while preserving the environment through reduced waste. The ongoing efforts of the European Union and its member states like Germany result in numerous publications calling Europe a 'recycling society' (Fischer and Davidsen, 2010; Lazarevic et al., 2010) as well as the World Economic Forum stating: 'Germany recycles more than any other country' (Gray, 2017). One major factor for this assessment is the introduction of a bottle-deposit system in Germany in 2003 with different incentive-mechanisms for the usage of multipath systems.

First of all, several publications from private organisations (e.g. Albrecht et al., 2011) as well as governmental agencies (Cantner et al., 2010) have since evaluated the German system regarding its ecological, social and economic dimensions. However, surprisingly, one phenomenon crucial to the increasing return-rate of bottles is not mentioned in the literature while being more and more obvious, in particular in Germany's inner cities: so-called bottle collectors, who search for containers, thrown away by other citizens, and return them to gain the associated deposits. Generally speaking, bottle collectors can be classified as the affluent-countries' version of so-called waste-pickers or scavengers. In the following, these terms will be used for German collectors as synonyms.

Nevertheless, evaluating scavengers is crucial for drawing a complete picture on this form of recycling. In many countries, the waste management systems could not function without people collecting for refunds (Wilson et al., 2006). For instance, Dhokhikah and Trihadiningrum (2012) found that at least 10% of total waste in Indonesia is solely collected by scavengers. Unlike most developing countries, Germany has an overall functioning public waste management system, even though there are ongoing exports to developing countries for sorting and disposing. Furthermore, in Germany most of the collected bottles are found in garbage cans, so we argue that the issue is mostly about consumers returning the raw material like PET to the raw material cycle. This can also be illustrated by the amount of deposits: especially for smaller breweries, that do not manufacture their own bottles, the deposit is actually lower than the costs for a new bottle (Moritz, 2013). Hence, while scavengers in developing countries have a strong ecological and economic impact due to the lacking waste management systems, bottle collectors in affluent countries serve the market primarily in an economic way.

Both waste pickers in developing and affluent countries have in common that they mostly belong to the low end of the income pyramid, compared to their socio-economic environment. Furthermore, in both cases, they operate in an informal market sector, an essential aspect of the so-called bottom of the pyramid (BOP) concept (London, 2008). Comparing developing countries with the case of Germany can provide some valuable insights. For instance in Nicaragua, Vazquez reports collectors are living in extreme poverty and social exclusion (Vázquez, 2016); Germany's scavengers are most likely not endangered of starvation and returns for bottles are much higher than returns for recycled materials in developing countries. Hence, for the heterogeneous group of scavengers in affluent countries, the question arises why they strive for the extra income and what they use it for (Moser, 2014).

Affluent countries are often labelled as consumption societies, where people like to show their wealth. This leads to people living at the bare minimum searching for alternative income options to participate (i.e. include themselves) in society. This process of collecting bottles for money hence could constitute an inclusion mechanism for people at the BOP in affluent countries, similar to what reports from Greece suggest (Papaoikonomou et al., 2009). If so, it could not only contribute to SDG 12.2 but also to SDG 10.2, which calls for inclusion for all (General Assembly of the United Nations, 2015). Bottle collecting is not restricted to individuals at the BOP. Moser (2014) also describes instances of middle-class individuals collecting easily accessible bottles (e.g. bottles standing next to garbage bins) as 'easy money'. As societal inclusion is particularly relevant for people at the bottom of the pyramid, we focus on the activity of collecting, rather than bottle collectors. This scope allows us to evaluate the inclusion mechanisms of bottle collecting for individuals living in poverty (i.e. at the BOP) compared to a heterogeneous field of scavengers with different reasoning and socio-economic backgrounds. These considerations thus lead to the following research question:

> In how far is collecting bottles an inclusion mechanism for people at the bottom of the pyramid in an affluent country like Germany?

Since the motivation of scavengers, their situation, and other relevant criteria in affluent countries is mostly unknown, an exploratory approach is appropriate. We conducted semi-structured interviews and applied the Gioia method as a qualitative, interpretivist evaluation approach. Interpretivist research focusses on subjective insights and reasoning of individuals, in this case bottle collectors. Understanding their lives can only be achieved by voicing their values, reasoning and other possible factors. This further allows us to ensure that all included individuals belong to our BOP scope.

The paper is structured as follows: the next section provides the theoretical background from existing literature. Subsequently, research design and the methods applied are described. Next, the findings are presented and conceptualised into a model of bottle collectors between exclusion and inclusion. The chapter concludes with a discussion and suggestions for future research.

Literature review

Base of the pyramid, poverty and the deposit system in Germany

The base or bottom of the pyramid (BOP) was described by Hahn (2009) as 'the bottom-tier of the world income pyramid […] characteris[ing] a particular cross-national class of population' (pp. 313–314). While the definitions of poverty and BOP are not fully congruent, they are still closely tied to their basis of economic income. London (2008) defines BOP members to mostly exist within the informal market economy due to a lack of resources that somewhat go beyond monetary funds. To understand situations of people at the BOP, it is thus essential to take a closer look at their economic status and the market system they primarily act in. The former will be evaluated for Germany in the following, the latter will be discussed in the subsection 'Understanding bottle collectors' after a brief introduction into the German deposit system.

Although economies in industrialised countries tended to grow for the last decades, increasing income inequality leaves many citizens decoupled from these improvements (Möller, 2016). The German Federal Statistical Office reported for 2015 that one in five people in Germany is endangered of poverty (Destatis, 2016). Accordingly, the BOP from a poverty perspective does not only concern people in developing countries but also applies to affluent countries (Hahn, 2009).

Moser (2014) reported that many scavengers within Germany have income issues due to, for example, illnesses, unemployment or small retirement funds and thus fall into the resource-scarce perception of people at the BOP. Since the introduction of the bottle deposit system in Germany, many started collecting bottles to gain extra income; however, not all containers have the same deposit and weight, so different strategies are prevalent. Therefore, the German deposit system will be briefly explained in the following.

There are three major recycling systems in Germany targeting private households (Albrecht et al., 2011): a multipath and a single-use system for bottles with monetary deposits, and a dualistic system for single-use material without deposits. Multi-use systems with short distances are the most efficient from the ecological point of view while single-use is preferred economically mostly due to smaller transportation costs (Albrecht et al., 2011). The amount of monetary deposits varies, depending on the material and size of the container. Single-use PET as well as cans have the highest deposit and are therefore the most profitable to collect (Figure 3.1); PET bottles furthermore constitute 481.000 tons of Germany's plastic production (roughly 11%) for 2019 (Statista, 2020).

The deposit system was established in 2003 and entailed several amendments since then. The probably most important amendment took place in 2006 ruling that all retailers selling a certain type of bottle must return deposits, no matter where the container was initially bought (BMUB, 2014, p. 6). This means, if a store sells single-use PET containers, it must refund all kind of single-use PET bottles with deposits. This rule may be considered the starting point for bottle collecting as a socio-economic phenomenon in Germany. Collectors interviewed by Moser (2014) often times reported that 2006 was the year they started.

Layout adapted from Einweg-mit-Pfand (2018), content from Verbraucherzentrale (2019), Einweg-mit-Pfand (2018), German Bundestag (2019).

Understanding bottle collectors

Existing literature provides a general understanding of bottle collectors in Germany, their reasoning, place in society and 'work ethic'. Moser (2014) defines the activity of collecting bottles as 'an informal-economic act with the goal of collecting containers with deposits and returning said containers for increasing the own socioeconomic possibilities' (p. 248). Scavengers are further using the collection of containers to structure their day, uphold social contacts as well as proving themselves capable of working (Pitz, 2009; Moser, 2014; Catterfeld and Knecht, 2015). Since they rarely collect in groups, Moser (2014) compared them to tiny, mostly one-person businesses. He even describes some sort of addiction towards finding the next container similar to, for example, stamp collection. Crucially, bottle collectors *do not*

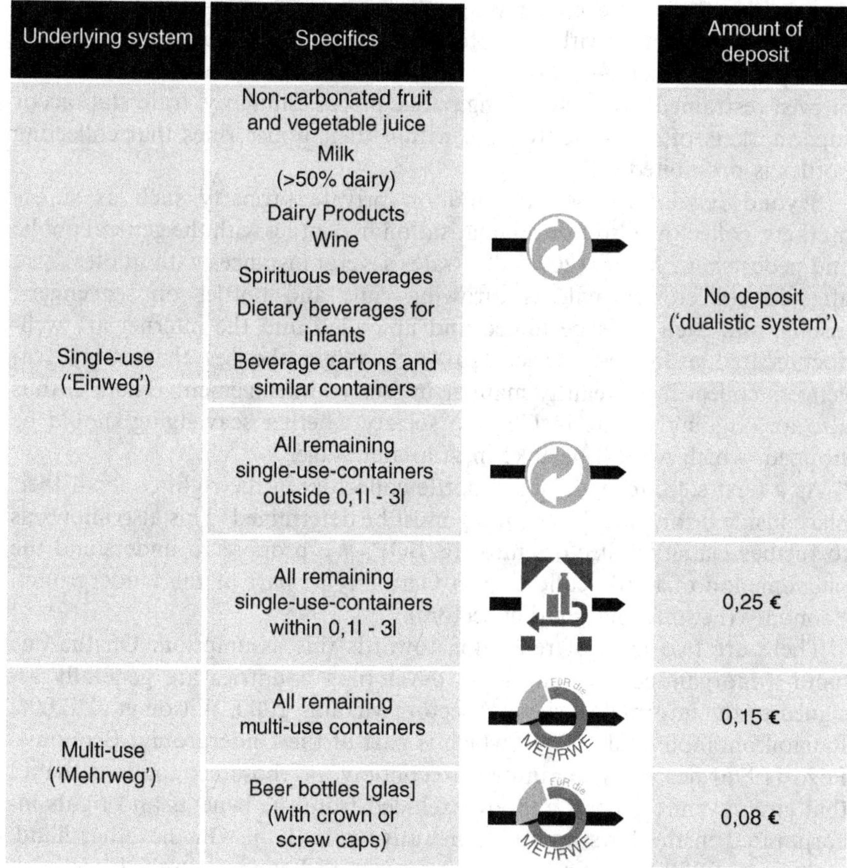

Figure 3.1 Overview on monetary deposits of beverage containers in Germany.

have to be at the bottom of the pyramid, since there are instances of middle-class individuals collecting for money (Moser, 2014).

Furthermore, scavengers' working days vary according to the individual's idiosyncrasies. Some collectors go out regardless of weather conditions while others combine the collection process with running errands. Some use tools such as a flashlight or gloves and collect anonymously while others ask people sitting in parks for their empty bottles. Thus, there is much diversity within the field depending on personal attitude (Pitz, 2009; Moser, 2014; Catterfeld and Knecht, 2015).

Moser (2014) also hypothesises that professions tied to any form of 'garbage' (Pitz, 2009; Moser, 2014; Catterfeld and Knecht, 2015) faces stigmatisation and are ostracised from public life. This is even manifested by urban planning nowadays, as illustrated by below-ground garbage bins in several German cities. These containers are only accessible by specialised personnel and thus prevent scavengers from collecting. Similarly, collectors often face dissensions with regulatory agencies and the police. Due to their weak position of socio-economic and societal exclusion, they are often fined or even restrained from re-entering public places. Similarly, train stations or supermarkets often explicitly state within their house rules that collecting bottles is prohibited.

Beyond regulatory agencies and on private property such as supermarkets, collectors also face stigmatisation in contact with the general public and pedestrians. Moser (2014) illustrates several instances with quotes from affected collectors. Civilians throwing cans and bottles on scavengers, insults, and even violence filmed and uploaded into the internet are well-documented examples. Moser (2014) thus hypothesises that many scavengers collect in a stealthy manner in fear of infringement. There is thus also an ongoing debate in German society whether scavenging should be stopped, which we will partake in at a later stage.

As a next step, to understand bottle collectors in the right context, their place inside or outside the economy must be determined. This also allows us to further classify collectors into the BOP. We propose to understand the phenomenon of bottle collecting in Germany as part of the Underground Economy (i.e. informal market sectors).

There are two lines of reasoning towards this assumption. On the one hand, (unorganised) scavengers in developing countries are generally assigned to the informal (recycling) sector (Medina, 2000; Wilson et al., 2006; Papaoikonomou et al., 2009), which is part of the Underground Economy. Pozo (1996) describes the informal economy as 'those economic activities that circumvent the costs and are excluded from the benefits and rights incorporated in the laws and administrative rules […]'. On the other hand, scavengers fulfill the definition of Underground Economy itself. In defining this concept, Frey and Schneider (2000) and Tanzi (1980) focus on an activity's role within the national accounting. They state that whenever an activity adds value and is not considered in the nation's GDP, it falls within the Underground Economy. Although scavengers should report their earnings according to German tax legislation, this is often not the case (e.g. Moser, 2014). Therefore, collectors fit the informal market sector definition of London (2008) as well as definitions of resource-scarce individuals. We thus evaluate scavengers from a BOP-market perspective.

Inclusion and exclusion

For evaluating in how far bottle collecting can be regarded an inclusion mechanism, societal boundaries as well as inclusion and exclusion must be defined first. According to Braeckman (2006), there is an ongoing debate about what inclusion and exclusion does specifically mean. Following his argument, the definitions of Niklas Luhmann will be adopted: '[…] there can only be inclusion, when exclusion is possible. Only the existence of persons or groups that cannot be integrated reveals social cohesion and makes it possible to specify its conditions' (Luhmann, 1997 cited from Braeckman, 2006, p. 67). Thus, one is not included in all of society, or as Braeckman (2006, p. 68) puts it: 'persons do no longer belong to only one subsystem [...] but participate simultaneously in different subsystems'. Hence, one is rather included in a specific area by outlining (excluding) other individuals.

Furthermore, in modern society, people are not excluded a priori by relevant subsystems, since, in theory, everybody can have a role in any societal area like politics, art, economics etc. Hence, accessibility for any wished-for subsystem exists and individuals can make efforts to be included in such. We apply Braeckman's argumentation that inclusion within subsystems is less random and more open nowadays. The fact that individuals are often part of many subsystems leads to issues of identity that, according to Luhmann, cannot be solved by society, hence, 'the individual's identity automatically becomes the work of the individual itself' (Braeckman, 2006, p. 71). This is contrary to pre-modern society, where identity was mostly derived from social stance (e.g. born a peasant/duke/king).

Modern society is based on the concepts of *freedom and equality* (Luhmann, 1995 cited from Braeckman, 2006, p. 70), where everybody has, in theory, access to every subsystem. These possibilities raise the question of why people choose the particular areas of interest such as cultural activities. Luhmann (1997, cited from Braeckman, 2006, p. 71) argues, 'the modern individual is only what it is by virtue of its (partial) inclusion in the various function systems'. Hence, interdependences between personality and the chosen subsystems further influence the personal identity and individual decision-making.

Accessibility, however, does not mean that every individual is included. Financial resources are often a necessity for joining subsystems with few exceptions like religion (Braeckman, 2006). Bauman (1997, 2009) also argues that consumption is one of the major factors within the identity-formation-process. In affluent countries, people have shifted from (subsistence) 'producers' to 'consumers', making consumption a major factor for identity formation. Hence, we propose that individuals in an affluent country like Germany often need financial resources to include themselves in subsystems of their choosing; these depend on an individual's identity and personality.

In this context, poverty and loss of (regular) employment can be seen as a threat to an individual's personality (e.g. Petzall et al., 2000; Sivanathan and Pettit, 2010). According to the self-affirmation theory, such a threat is addressed by ego-protection mechanisms like avoidance or denial. As an applied example, Sivanathan and Pettit (2010) furthermore identify consumption of status goods as an ego-protection mechanism. Steele (1988) states that self-affirmation mechanisms, such as strengthening other facets of the individual's personality, can counteract and compensate the initial aim to solve the (identity-) threat with an ego-protection-mechanism (e.g. consumption of status goods). Self-affirmation mechanisms thus can lead to better decision making among affected individuals and shift the focus away from (debt-funded) consumption, towards alternative prioritisations (Sivanathan and Pettit, 2010).

Methodology

We chose a qualitative, inductive approach based on semi-structured interviews that aims at developing a model of bottle collectors between social exclusion and inclusion in an affluent country like Germany. The Gioia-methodology (Gioia and Chittipeddi, 1991) is part of Grounded Theory approaches (Glaser and Strauss, 1967), which aim to analyse data systematically in an inductive way. Since collectors' motivations, situations and biographies are reportedly heterogeneous and are thus expected to provide a wide variety of responses, a systematic approach helps preventing to get 'lost in data' during the analysis process.

As 'first-order concepts', we coded values and interpretations of bottle collectors regarding their activity, thus building the basis of analysis. As a next step, we derived 'second-order concepts'. Within these categories, the researchers summarised and grouped the participants' input of the first-order concepts. This resulted in gaining a better overview as well as reaching a more theoretical level by iterative comparison of source data with possible theoretical interpretations. Importantly, during this abstraction process, we used existing theory from our literature review and beyond, to understand collectors' way of reasoning. By constantly discussing and reevaluating our findings, we gained confidence in our second-order concepts, and condensed them further towards aggregate dimensions. These provided the general structure of our data and gave important guidance for inductively conceptualising bottle collectors between societal exclusion and inclusion.

Data collection process

We conducted two phases of semi-structured interviews within two months of spring (starting in March) in one medium-to-large German city: in the first phase, questions were based on a literature review, drawing mostly from the publication of Moser (2014), and guided by our research question. The second-phase questionnaire was revised based on additional literature and the experience during interview phase one. Hence, a snowball technique comparable to Corley and Gioia (2004) emerged. Taking notions from phase one (that we felt to be of high importance) and including them in the questions of the second-phase questionnaire helped validating our results as well as provided a deeper focus on certain issues raised in the first four interviews. Both questionnaires consisted of a trinomial structure. The introductory part (e.g. 'Are you from here?') aimed at gaining trust and starting the interview. In the subsequent part, we asked questions about the individual (e.g. 'What was your profession before?' or 'Do you also have other income?') to ensure that participants fall into our research scope. This also allowed us to control for middle-class collectors in some viable manner. We expect people having, for example, regular, mostly sufficient income from other professions to not fall into the bottom of the pyramid *per definition.* Furthermore, this section allows us to derive implications on their personal reasoning for collecting. Based on our research question, we further asked participants about individual specifications of collecting bottles (e.g. 'Are you collecting every day?', 'Do you collect all kinds of bottles?' or 'Why are you collecting?'), allowing us to evaluate the activity. We controlled for leading-the-witness questions by only asking questions *indirectly* concerning in- and exclusion. On the one hand, participants let us know what their general perspective on society is (e.g. 'We are ruled by authorities of darkness', #1); on the other hand, questions about the reasons for collecting or usage of money gave valuable clues concerning the subsystems, in which the bottle collectors wished to include themselves. Naturally, individuals were explicitly told they could decide whether they wanted to respond to a question, but a refusal to respond did not occur for any question.

For the identification of potential interviewees, the first author started approaching random bottle collectors within a major German city. He started to search in areas where we expected a high frequency of people and thus, many collectable containers. He always brought a 0.25€ or 0.15€ bottle as a possible ice-breaker for a conversation. After monitoring people looking into garbage bins for a longer period, he approached them carefully asking whether the person was collecting bottles for deposit refund. After affirmation, the brought-along bottle was offered, and the collector was asked to participate in a short interview. Further, all participants were offered a small sum (approx. 5€) to thank for their time and a hot beverage whenever a café or restaurant was nearby. All except for one refused the compensation at first because they believed the researcher was close to their socio-economic group. After explaining that their willingness to participate was appreciated and their time should be compensated for, all accepted the compensation. This payment of their time might contribute to bias, however, creating the impression of eye level was expected to be more important than the possible bias. Since reports of officials like police discriminating against collectors are prevalent, we wanted them to feel comfortable enough sharing even sensitive information.

Since many scavengers were expected to be skeptical and careful not to overshare, we implemented compensation as well as encouragement within our interviews. Encouragement consisted of positive reinforcement such as 'I understand completely' or 'That's an interesting point' in an extensive way. Having also interviewed BOP individuals, O'Flaherty (1996) came across similar issues, arguing that there is no obvious, formal way of interviewing. If we did not encourage participants, much information such as their health

Table 3.1 Overview on characteristics of conducted interviews

#	*Name*[a]	*Duration*[b]	*Age*[c]	Place	Phase
1	Frederik	20 min	50–60	Pedestrian zone	1
2	Johann	12 min	50–60	Side road	1
3	Paul	7 min	<20	Pedestrian zone	1
4	Richard	31 min	30–40	University	1
5	Andreas	38 min	20–30	Park	2
6	Anna	7 min	>60	Pedestrian zone	2
7	Maria	15 min	>60	Tram station	2
8	Stefan	14 min	40–50	Pedestrian zone	2

[a] Anonymised.
[b] Rounded.
[c] Stratified.

issues or personal relationships would most likely not have been reported. These issues, however, were crucial for our assessment. Compensation and encouragement could implement bias, however, due to constant discussion and keeping other research like Moser (2014), Catterfeld (2015), or Pitz (2009) in mind, we are still confident in our approach.

A special focus was put upon finding diverse scavengers regarding age, gender and ethnicity. This was difficult in the first phase; however, within the second phase two women agreed to the interview. Only native German speakers participated (Table 3.1).

All but one interview was tape recorded. The interviewee who refused the recording had consented that the researcher was allowed to take notes during the interview. The original audio recordings were distorted immediately after the interview to comply with existing data-protection legislation in Germany. A lot of information was provided nonverbally during the interviews. Further, none of the conversations was finished after the interview itself ended. All participants continued talking and provided additional information after formal conclusion of the interview. A short time period (usually 1–2 days) was taken before a new participant was searched for, to reflect and transcribe the interview. This helped to include valuable details and avoid confusing the provided insights with these of other participants.

Altogether, from 15 people asked, 8 agreed to the interview, that is 4 participants for each of the two phases of data collection (Figure 3.2 and Table 3.1).

Research quality and limitations

In line with Gioia-methodology (Gioia and Pitre, 1990; Gioia et al., 2013), we took several steps to gain as much confidence in our results as possible as well as providing the necessary rigor and ensuring a high research quality. To ensure

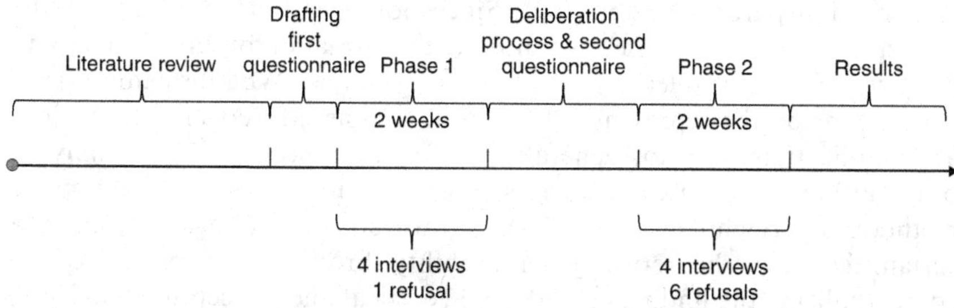

Figure 3.2 Detailed representation of data collection process.

Table 3.2 Overview on characteristics of conducted interviews

#	*Age-stratum*[a]	*Characteristics*[a]	*Reason for refusal*	*Place*
1	60+	Native German, male	*'I'm not willing to participate'* – *'I'd even give you a couple Euros for your time'* – *'I don't want your money!'*	Pedestrian zone
2	60+	Native German, male	*'I'm not ready for that!'*	Pedestrian zone
3	50+	Latvia, male	*'No German'*	Pedestrian zone
4	60+	Native German, male	*'Sorry, I don't want to talk about it'*	Park
5	60+	Non-native German, male	*'No German'*	Side road
6	60+	Native German, female	*'I'm writing a paper about bottle collection and …'* – *'I don't do it for these reasons!'*	End of Pedestrian zone
7	50+	Non-native German, male	*'No German'*	Park

[a] Anonymised.

appropriateness of our research design, as well as internal validity of our analysis of the interview data and the model derived there-of, we had regular discussions among the team of authors as well as with independent researchers. Corley and Gioia (2004, p. 184) referred to this as 'peer-debriefing'.

The interviews were conducted with presumably only a fraction of the bottle collectors within a medium-sized city in Germany during daytime. While we intended to interview as diverse a group of collectors as possible, this turned out to be more difficult than expected, due to unavailability or refusals to participate. We included the information on the refusals for the sake of transparency (Table 3.2). Since bottle collection is part of the underground economy, there are no exact information on the number and diversity of people collecting bottles in public areas. We thus cannot draw conclusions on the representability of our sample. Moreover, our findings and implications are not generalisable for all collectors in Germany or other affluent countries, which is a general limitation of the applied methodology (Gehman et al., 2018). However, our findings may claim a certain degree of theoretical generalisability through our approach of de-contextualising the findings based on theoretical and conceptual reasoning (Avenier, 2010).

During the process of analysing data through Gioia-methodology, a special focus was put upon using the participant's own language rather than the author's interpretations in order to minimise interpretational bias. As we also included nonverbal information and observations into our analysis, a certain level of subjectivity could not be excluded. The interviews were all conducted and coded (in particular regarding first-order concepts) by the first author, which contributes to the consistency of the data collection and data analysis, but again entails a certain potential for subjectivity bias. Since the interviews were conducted in German, they were translated as closely as possible, with a firm focus on maintaining the spirit of the given answers.

Findings

Figure 3.3 shows our emerging data structure. According to the Gioia methodology, the first-order concepts consist mostly of phrases of the participants, which is shown by the quotation marks in every instance. The second-order concepts are phrases given by the author team. Lastly, the second-order concepts were further condensed into three aggregate dimensions, which are crucial for our derived model of societal exclusion and inclusion of bottle collectors in Germany. These three aggregate dimensions thus ultimately arose from the questionnaire and given answers. However, we appropriate a certain interconnectedness between the dimensions and predefined concepts such as exclusion/inclusion or BOP as follows: (1) Personal attitude gives insights into collectors' identity and willingness to include themselves in general. (2) Social status aims to control for middle-class individuals to keep the BOP scope. (3) Financial reasoning somewhat reassesses aspects (1) and (2): answers of participants concerning *what* they use the income for is relevant for the willingness to include [1] as well as controlling for other income, e.g. regular jobs, which has implications for belonging to the BOP as discussed before [2]. In the following, the most crucial relationships between first-order, second-order, and the aggregate dimension will be explained as shown in Figure 3.3, namely personal attitude, social status and financial reasoning.

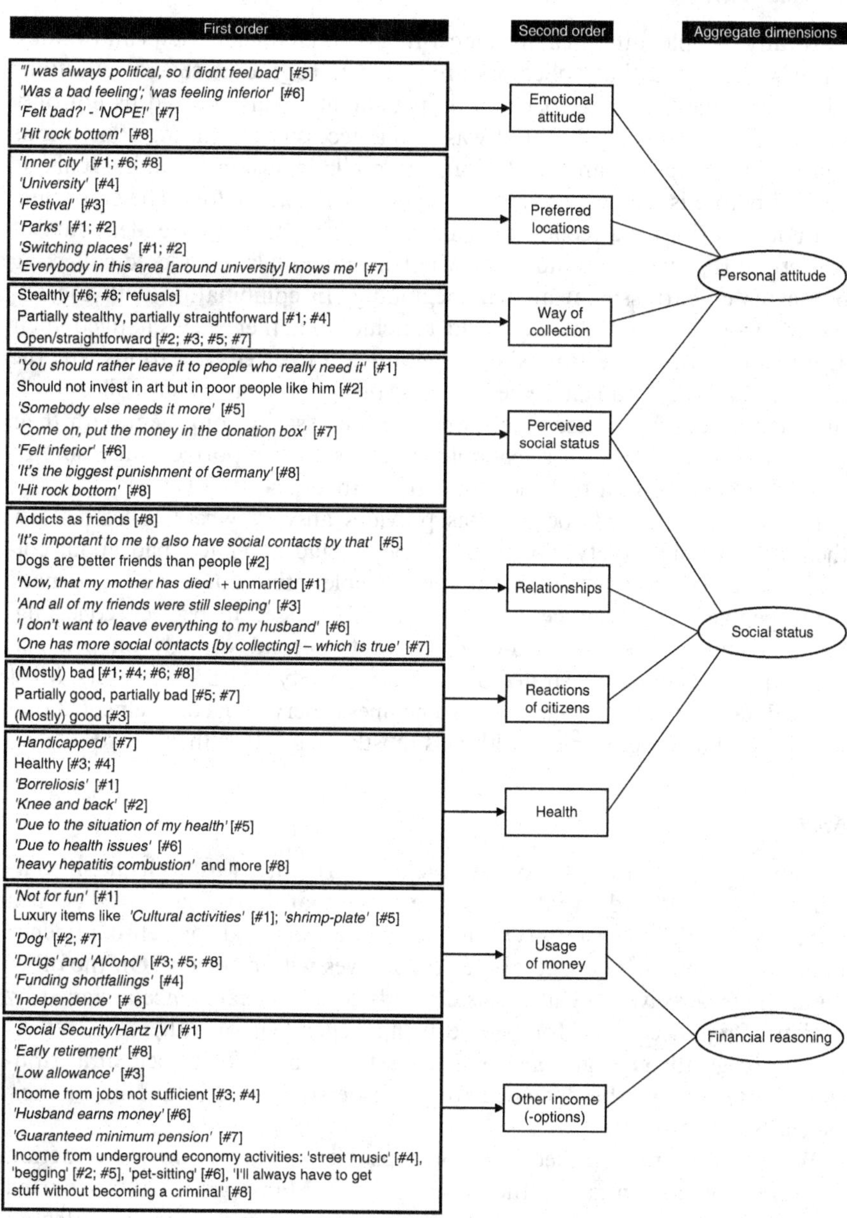

Figure 3.3 Data structure.

Personal attitude

Naturally, people differ heavily concerning their character, views and values. Since we assumed that collectors are very heterogenous, several questions within our questionnaire focussed on personality. This allowed us not only to maintain a focus on BOP but was also a necessity for stating conclusions concerning inclusion and exclusion; after all, inclusion of individuals as defined before is based on a *willingness to include themselves*. The emotional attitude describes the feeling of collectors during their first endeavours of collecting. It serves as an indicator whether individuals considered collecting bottles as embarrassment at their beginning. In combination with the observed way of collection, we could conclude whether they changed their attitude towards collection since beginning. Preferred Locations are the stated areas within the city where each scavenger assumed that collection is the most successful. These places were not necessarily congruent with their actual collecting areas, for example Andreas (#5) reported some sort of rivalry preventing him to collect in certain areas.

Lastly, the perceived social status provides answers where collectors saw themselves within society. Some stated they would never feel bad about collecting since it serves the community as a whole; other times, we experienced many people being 'ashamed' or at least embarrassed to be seen collecting. Summarising, all these second-order concepts depend strongly on personal values and attitudes as illustrated by the heterogeneity within the answers. Most of the data was from interviews, but sometimes observation complemented oral interview data, for example stealth was mostly seen rather than heard.

Social status

Perceived social status, as shown in the data structure, was both classified as personal attitude and social status. We argue that due to 'perceived', it is a mixture of both dimensions. On the one hand, it depends on self-confidence and self-worth, where collectors see themselves within society. On the other hand, their perceived social status depends on the social stance assigned by society. Prejudices exist for people being dependent on others as well as having to go through garbage bins for extra income. This societal attribution, however, may be detached from the personal understanding of their 'Social status'.

We furthermore identified Relationships, Health status quo and Reaction of citizens as influential for their Social status. Many participants reported personal health issues which are widely linked to having a negative effect at least towards their subjective social status (e.g. Sapolsky, 2004; Demakakos et al., 2008). We also found different enumerabilities of existing relationships ranging from an individual's pet being their best friend to being married and having children. Both Health and Relationships were mostly reported without explicit questioning.

Financial reasoning

Lastly, collectors would most likely not collect without financial incentives. Hence, we asked them about their other income (-options). All interviewees reported that funds such as social security are simply not sufficient for the life they want to live. Nevertheless, nearly everybody reported regular income, many from other types of underground economy activities such as begging, street music or pet sitting.

Furthermore, to evaluate whether people try to include themselves in subsystems with their extra income, their usage of money was asked for. Luckily, many explained their reasoning unsolicitedly. Again, there was a big heterogeneity in answers; however, most reported that the extra income was not a necessity for survival. This marks an important difference to most waste pickers in developing countries, who use their recycling income for their daily survival.

Conceptualising bottle collectors between exclusion and inclusion

From our data structure, the following model was derived that conceptualises bottle collectors between societal exclusion and inclusion in an affluent country like Germany (Figure 3.4). The model was devised by means of 'disciplined imagination' (Weick, 1989), linking data to theory in iterative cycles, while findings and implications were continuously discussed within the research team. For reasons of clarity, we provide a step-by-step explanation appropriating the example of Frederik (#1) and Maria (#7) as a straightforward/open collector and Anna (#6) as a stealthy collector.

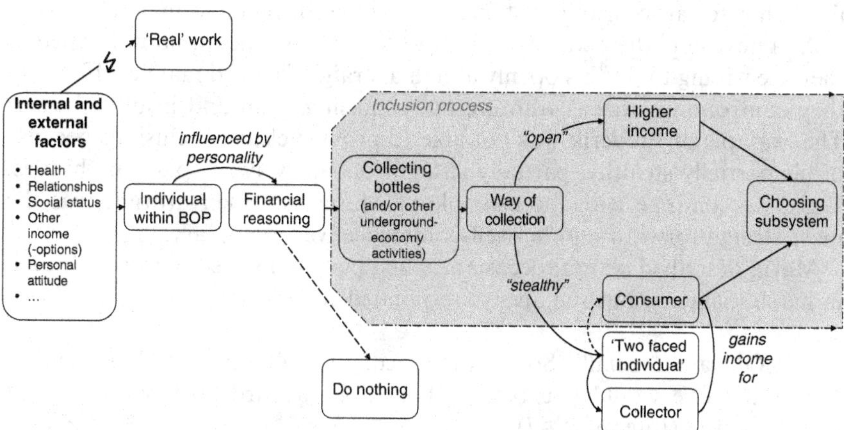

Figure 3.4 Conceptualising bottle collectors between exclusion and inclusion.

Step-by-step explanation of our conceptualisation

There are several internal and external factors of why people are or become members of the BOP in an affluent country. For instance, we found that often-times the individuals inadvertently moved to the BOP due to health issues or past relationships. Since our research focussed on the inclusion process, these factors only represent examples and cannot claim to be a comprehensive compilation. For example, Frederik (#1) was not able to work due to internal and external factors. In the past, he was infected with Borreliosis [health]. Since his mother's terminal illness, he decided to nurse her for her remaining life [relationships]. These two factors combined resulted in Frederik not having enough income for his preferred life and becoming an individual within [the] BOP based on his limited income and him mostly operating within the informal economy.

Due to his Financial reasoning, which was illustrated by his admiration for a 'cultural activity'(Interview #1) in his city, he did not decide to just collect his welfare check/social security, use this money to survive and do nothing, but rather search for a way to generate more income, resulting in an activity within the Underground Economy. This marks the starting point for the inclusion process, since scavenger's personalities and financial reasoning make them willing to participate in additional societal sub-systems rather than just Do[ing] nothing. Ashenmiller (2010) reports a decreasing of petty crime rates for any US-American state having introduced bottle deposit legislation. She argues that collecting for refunds provides an alternative to crime for BOP individuals looking to increase their income. Hence, based on our impressions and the findings of Ashenmiller, we assumed that Frederik (#1) chose collecting bottles to improve his income, instead of possible alternatives like criminality or begging. His decision is made due to his personality as shown between the individual within the BOP and his financial reasoning (i.e. realising that social security is not enough income for him and his preferences).

As a next step, their way of collection is relevant. The question is whether they are willing to do this openly and in a straightforward manner. If so, are they confronting citizens who are marginalising them and insulting them? The example of Frederik was not able to provide clear conclusions because of his partially stealthy, partially straightforward way of collecting bottles. Thus, we continue with the example of Maria, since her attitude was the most straightforward and her self-confidence was exemplary.

Maria described several occasions when people insulted her at first, even in harsh manners, but she always responded superiorly:

> "YOU are asocial!" So, I responded: "I ain't no asocial person!" – "What else would you be!?" – I have a standard response: "A great woman."[1] (Interview #7)
>
> Her self-confident attitude then gave her somewhat of a 'competitive advantage' towards other collectors. She mentioned young people who

> insulted her heavily, but after her interactions with them, "[…] they also donated [a bottle] to me". In another instance, people were stopping her, saying "My friend called, you should go over there, he has his car's trunk full of cans!" (Interview #7)

Since we never heard something like that from the 'stealthy' collectors, we expected 'openly collecting' individuals to have more income than their counterparts do, which we explained by their attitude towards collecting as well as their general personal attitude (self-confident vs. shy/embarrassed). We explain this with the possibilities for collaborations with citizens and a change in reactions of the general public due to confrontations: Maria illustrated this once more in a perfect manner:

> "Two months ago, a teacher came to me and said: "My colleague and me, we are now collecting all the bottles that are left on the premises for you"; every Thursday I shall come and collect." (Interview #7) How would a stealthy collector get such collaborations?

Interestingly, stealthy collectors develop what we call a '*two-faced individual*': we classified them as '*Consumer*' on the one hand and '*Collector*' on the other. Due to their collecting-activity, they obviously increase their income. They use this money to consume, but both of those 'personalities' are separated from one another: Anna (#6) was invited to having the interview in a café or restaurant, which she declined heavily, explaining she would not feel comfortable talking about her collecting in public. At the same time, she reportedly uses the additional income for keeping her independence within her marriage, so that her husband does not have to pay bill. Since she also told us that both did not get social security due to enough existing income, we assumed that she did not collect for subsistence but for (luxury) goods or services. Hence, she is splitting these two parts of her personality, the *consumer* and the *collector*, resulting in only the consumer part trying to include herself as shown in our model. This interestingly constitutes an intra-person exclusion/inclusion process in the sense of Luhmann: as cited before, Luhmann expects inclusion only to be possible if in-group members exclude out-group members (Luhmann, 1997 cited from Braeckman, 2006). Since collectors are obviously well aware of stigmatisation and discrimination from other members of society towards scavengers, they choose to exclude the 'collecting' part of their personality to being able to include the 'consuming' part. Interestingly, the two-faced individual thus represents a similar exclusion-determines-inclusion mechanism *on an individual level* that operates similar to Luhmann's theory of inclusion, where you need excluded individuals to maintain a feeling of inclusion. We will discuss the two-faced individual during the subsection 'Consumption, Inclusion and Exclusion' within the discussion.

These personalities, 'consumer' on the one hand and 'collector' on the other, would not exist without its counterpart: if she did not collect, she would not have money to consume; if she did not consume, she would not need the money from collection due to her husband's earnings. We would furthermore argue that this situation is prevalent for many collectors collecting stealthily. Also, this is most likely the reason why – according to our study – collectors do not gain social contacts, as previously mentioned by Moser (2014). Hence, this stealthy not only limits their additional income compared to open collectors as illustrated in higher income but also affects their social status by preventing scavengers to increase social contacts and possibly results in solitude.

Due to our research question, we explained their choice of subsystems (i.e. where to include) by their Personal attitude as shown in the following examples.

- Frederik explained to us, when asked for his main reason, that he used this money for the before-mentioned 'cultural activity'. He further illustrated: 'when going there, 50 Euros are gone, you cannot do that as a normal social-security-recipient, it's not possible' (Interview #1). Hence, he used his collection money for additional cultural activities and the related subsystem.
- Rudi (#2) used his earnings mostly for his dog which he described as his best friend. This reduced his loneliness, possibly increased income when begging, simplified social contacts with other animal lovers, and therefore included him in the according subsystem. Instances of collectors using a significant amount of their financial resources for a pet occurred more than once during our research.
- Andreas (#5) told us that his income was enough for surviving. However, he stated: 'that's not the issue that you simply want to survive, but to a certain degree, you want to have more in your life [than the bare minimum]' (Interview #5). He provided the example of going to festivals or occasionally being able to afford a 'Shrimp-plate', thus improving his standard of living.

Discussion

In this section, we discuss main findings against the current state of knowledge. Furthermore, we point to limitations of our scope of research and to avenues for future research.

The issue of ending scavenging

Before we started conducting our interviews, we were wondering what would be necessary that people, many times elderly or sick individuals, stopped collecting. Hence, we also asked participants what they each perceived as necessary to end their scavenging career.

After starting the data-gathering-process, it quickly became apparent that the issue of ending scavenging entailed certain sustainability tensions (Hahn et al., 2010, 2015). On the one hand, there are environmental issues that are reduced by scavengers collecting containers such as raw material getting back into the recycling process. These materials otherwise would have been burnt with the remaining garbage. However, on the other hand, there are ethical issues with our recycling quota being upheld by BOP citizens that need the extra income to participate in social life. Hence, from the ecological point of view, bottle collection is desirable while it is ethically questionable from a social perspective.

To solve this tension, we can draw on the Greek example by Papaoikonomou et al. (2009). The authors reported several issues affecting Roma people and citizens with disabilities scavenging for raw materials due to nescience of rights or recycling programme details. Furthermore, on societal level, citizens mostly do not know about scavengers' reasoning and benefits from recycling for money resulting in, for example, stigmatisation (Papaoikonomou et al. 2009). By organising affected people into social enterprises, their societal stance as well as income is increased while maintaining, or sometimes even increasing the environmental services they provide. This seems plausible for Germany as well, knowing there are socio-economic differences between both countries.

Nevertheless, we argued that better organising and collaborations within scavengers lead to higher income as well as social acceptance like the open/straightforward collectors compared to stealthy collectors. Approaches for better organising could be taken from the example of Greece; however, to adapt this to the Germany context, future research is necessary.

Concludingly, we are not certain there is a decent way to end scavenging anyways. There are two reasons for this argument. First, we asked every participant how to end scavenging. While many reported 'higher social security' for a possible reason to end, others voiced their concern that some people would still collect just to buy some luxury goods even if their income was subsistent. Since we argued identity nowadays is closely tied to consumption and financial resource, there is no reason to believe fulfilled basic needs would prevent people searching for more income. Secondly, people will have to be willing to include themselves in social subsystems, which might not always be the case as implied by Moser (2014). Since Luhmann argues that inclusion lies within the responsibility of an individual, avenues for future research on impacting factors for this willingness arises. Hence, in our view, it is crucial searching for ways to improve BOP people's lives for whatever activity they chose rather than trying to end possibly undesired outcomes altogether (i.e. scavenging). However, the phenomenon of collecting cannot be classified as a homogenous group of people. We thus name the small number of participants as a limitation for the validity of this discussion.

The possible professionalisation process of collectors

Moser (2014) names several characteristics of collectors such as collecting individually, facing stigmatisation and discrimination, mostly collecting in a stealthy manner to avoid infringement, maintain social contacts through collecting, and constant issues with regulatory agencies. These findings are mostly congruent to ours, whereas we identify one important enhancement. As argued within the two-faced individual section, a straightforward manner of collecting bottles helps generating higher revenue and changes the attitude of (confronted) civilians. While it is intuitive to link different collecting styles to the heterogeneity of individuals, we add time consideration and related learning processes as another plausible explanation. Moser's study was conducted during the early stages of bottle collecting in Germany from 2008 to 2014. Imagining a collector scavenging for a decade, professionalisation and learning processes might have led certain individuals to find income and 'working conditions' optimisations, for example by asking people for their containers or confronting stigmatisation. Spillover effects between scavengers of different skill and experience levels might further contribute to professionalisation of regularly collecting individuals, transforming the field of scavenging altogether. Since we did not conduct a longitudinal study, the explanatory power of our deliberations is limited in this regard. Further research might thus corroborate and further explore either one of these possible explanations.

Our model's delimitation from non-BOP collectors

It is important to note that the scope of our model focusses on the inclusion mechanism used by BOP individuals in form of collection. However, there was one instance during our interviewing process that cannot be explained by our model. Richard (#4) was a university student that has legal work as a student assistant. Due to the nature of his work, he sometimes had funding shortcomings whenever his contract was not renewed in time. His collecting thus did not serve the purpose of inclusion but aimed at compensating missing income. Hence, he only fell into the BOP-stratum during these periods. In our view, this illustrates the income inequality and insufficiency of income spreading into normally unaffected social stratums like middle-class. Furthermore, it serves as a good example why we focussed on the activity rather than the individual. Most of the time, Richard is beyond our scope due to his regular job and hence might differ profoundly compared to other participants (e.g. when asked if he collected during times of regular income, he not only affirmed but also stated that he only collects easily accessible containers, hence further confirming Moser's (2014) finding of middle-class individuals collecting). By evaluating his temporary solution of collecting bottles for mitigating financial bottlenecks, we were able to gain insights into the blurred territory at the margins of the concept of BOP. However, middle-class individuals collecting regularly should be distinctly targeted by future research.

Consumption, inclusion and exclusion

Regarding inclusion and exclusion, we drew on the work of Luhmann, Braeckman and Bauman, arguing that subsystems are chosen based on individual preferences, situation and engagement, ultimately depending on their personality. It leads to a very limited understanding of inclusion, since it is based mostly on Luhmann and thus sociology. Due to our argumentative background of individuals including themselves in a subgroup of their choosing based on their personality, psychological insights concerning identity or personality might further illuminate the phenomenon. For instance, Sivanathan and Pettit (2010) used self-affirmation theory to understand consumption of status goods. Following their argument, poverty imposes a threat to an individuals' positive self-image. Affected individuals often use consumption of so-called status goods as an (unhealthy) ego-protection mechanism. Therewith, they aim to be part of a subsystem they de facto are not. Meanwhile, (externally, e.g. researcher) imposed self-affirmation mechanisms, such as reaffirming other personality aspects (e.g. 'doing it for the family') can be used to better compensate personality threats (e.g. poverty). This can ultimately lead to better decision-making among threatened individuals and hence less consumption (of status goods). Applied to our concept of subsystems, self-affirmation mechanisms may somewhat shift away the focus from consumption-driven inclusion (e.g. 'big-car-owners') towards alternatives (e.g. family).

Thus, the question arises, whether the consumption of scavengers consists also heavily of status goods. Looking at our participants, luxury goods such as a 'shrimp plate' (#5, Andreas) or the visit of a "cultural activity" (#1, Frederik) were paid for by scavenging-earnings. However, in our view, these purchases represent occasional treats rather than a 'façade' consisting of status goods. In our impression, scavengers within the BOP prove their 'work spirit' and 'capability' by *the activity* of bottle collecting, as previously reported for Germany (Moser, 2014) and the USA (Ashenmiller, 2010, 2011). Within our first-order concepts, there is also vague evidence of this phenomenon: Richard (#4), when asked about scavengers in general, stated:

> [a scavenger] is trying to make the best of a bad situation. He has survival strategies!

For poverty, Richard is drawing the line between people accepting poor living conditions and people (i.e. bottle collectors) trying to improve their situation. We understand this procedure as an ego-protection mechanism. Poverty constitutes a threat to the individuals' identity that must be compensated. While some BOP members buy status goods to *externally* signal a 'higher' subsystem-membership, we argue that scavengers *internally* prove their capability in the sense of an ego-protection mechanism. This could also serve as an explanation for the fact that bottle collectors accept their relatively hard work for low salaries as reported by previous publications (e.g. Ashenmiller, 2009; Moser, 2014).

Besides the consumption of status goods, self-affirmation theory describes avoidance or denial of a threat as examples of ego-protection mechanisms (Steele, 1988). Correspondingly, stealthiness and straightforwardness of scavengers can be understood as different ego-protection mechanisms depending on personal preferences. On the one hand, by collecting stealthily, collectors aim at avoiding the threat of others stigmatising them. As hypothesised by Moser (2014), professions tied to garbage face profound discrimination by the general public, similar to people facing poverty (Hall et al., 2014). Through splitting their profession (i.e. Collector) and their social selves (i.e. Consumer) within our concept of the two-faced individual, we argue that stealthy collectors include one part of their personality by explicitly hiding (i.e. excluding in the sense of Luhmann, 1997) the section of personality that might face stigmatisation. This is especially apparent by statements of some of our participants whose friends and family are not necessarily aware of their activity of collecting but are aware of their activity of shopping and consuming. This represents a manifestation of our proposed theoretical splitting of the activity of collecting from the individual: scavengers might not include themselves altogether but use the activity and resulting income to include a part of themselves. In our view, this inclusion-by-excluding mechanism works similar on an individual level to Luhmann's argumentation concerning societal exclusion and inclusion: since collectors know about and have been subject to stigmatisation from the general public, they need to find a way to deal with resulting feelings or anxieties. By collecting stealthily, and not telling (all of their) friends or family, they are actively giving up a part of their selves for being able to include the desirable parts – just like subsystems in the sense of Luhmann actively give up parts of society to maintain social cohesion. On the other hand, we found some evidence that societal acceptance can be increased long-term if scavengers collect bottles in a straightforward manner and if needed, confront bystanders. Self-affirmation theory could possibly provide the tools for better understanding scavengers and developing political, social and individual measures for improving affected lives. However, other psychological theories may also provide further directions. Especially, research on identity in general (Ramarajan, 2014) can improve the conceptual understanding, since identity research contributes explanations for, for example behaviours, well-being or commitment.

Due to language barriers, we could not interview non-native collectors. We expect different nationalities and cultural backgrounds to affect motivation and rationale for engaging in this activity, which illustrates a further limitation of our research and requires future research.

Conclusion

Due to the enumerability of bottle collectors in Germany's inner cities and the various services they adopt, it can be considered important to evaluate the deposit system and scavengers more closely in order to increase recycling quotas as well as decreasing social stigmata towards people collecting bottles.

We find within our scope that many waste pickers start collecting because they face financial issues in order to overcome or mitigate them. They use this extra income to include themselves in social subsystems of their choosing. Social stigmata and sometimes even insults prevent many to be straightforward about their activities, although they serve the community, the economy, for example small(er) breweries as well as the environment.

Combining our understanding of inclusion and exclusion with self-affirmation theory, we argue for an activity-based understanding of collecting with an individual sensemaking of threats and inclusion. Collecting bottles serves as an inclusion-mechanism for BOP individuals as well as an (internal) ego-protection-mechanism. Furthermore, the different ways of collection (stealthy vs. straightforward) represent the external ego-protection-mechanisms based on the individual's personality.

There are first implications from Greece how to increase their social stance and secure their income by formalising informal fields of work, that is grouping them into social enterprises. Nonetheless, due to different socio-economic conditions between Germany and Greece, implications for business practice and policy-making can only be transferred with due caution. We thus call for future country-contingent research about the BOP in affluent countries.

Note

1 Due to trying to remain her spirit, an English slang was used: 'I ain't no […]' = 'I am not an […]'.

References

Albrecht, P, Brodersen, J, Horst, DW, & Scherf, M (2011). *Mehrweg- und Recyclingsysteme für ausgewählte Getränkeverpackungen aus Nachhaltigkeitssicht.* Available at: http://www.duh.de/uploads/tx_duhdownloads/DUH_Getraenkeverpackungssysteme.pdf.

Ashenmiller, B (2009). Cash recycling, waste disposal costs, and the incomes of the working poor: Evidence from California. *Land Economics, 85*(3), 539–551.

Ashenmiller, B (2010). Externalities from recycling laws: Evidence from crime rates. *American Law and Economics Review, 12*(1), 245–261.

Ashenmiller, B (2011). The effect of bottle laws on income: New empirical results. *The American Economic Review, 101*(3), 60–64.

Avenier, M-J (2010). Shaping a constructivist view of organizational design science. *Organization Studies, 31*(9–10), 1229–1255.

Bauman, Z (1997). *Postmodernity and its Discontents.* Cambridge: Polity Press.

Bauman, Z (2009). *Leben als Konsum* (1st ed.). Hamburg: HIS Verlagsgesellschaft.

Braeckman, A (2006). Niklas Luhmann's systems theoretical redescription of the inclusion/exclusion debate. *Philosophy & Social Criticism, 32*(1), 65–88.

BMUB (Ed.) (2014). *Fragen und Antworten zur Pfandpflicht.*

Cantner, J, Gerstmayr, B, Pitschke, T, Tronecker, D, Hartleitner, B, & Kreibe, S (2010). *Bewertung der Verpackungsverordnung: Evaluierung der Pfandpflicht.* Dessau-Roßlau. Available at: www.umweltbundesamt.de/uba-info-medien/mysql_medien.php?anfrage=Kennummer&Suchwort=3931.

Catterfeld, P, & Knecht, A (Eds.) (2015). *Flaschensammeln: Überleben in der Stadt.* Konstanz, München: UVK Verlagsgesellschaft Konstanz.

Corley, KG, & Gioia, DA (2004). Identity ambiguity and change in the wake of a corporate spin-off. *Administrative Science Quarterly, 49*(2), 173–208.

Demakakos, P, Nazroo, J, Breeze, E, & Marmot, M (2008). Socioeconomic status and health: The role of subjective social status. *Social Science & Medicine (1982), 67*(2), 330–340.

Destatis (2016). *Anteil der von Armut oder sozialer Ausgrenzung bedrohten Bevölkerung in Deutschland nahezu unverändert.* Wiesbaden. Available at: https://www.destatis.de/DE/PresseService/Presse/Pressemitteilungen/2016/11/PD16_391_634.html (accessed on 17 February 2019).

Dhokhikah, Y, & Trihadiningrum, Y (2012). Solid waste management in Asian developing countries: Challenges and opportunities. *Journal of Applied Environmental and Biological Science, 2*(7), 329–335.

Einweg-mit-Pfand (2018 n.d.). "*Das neue Verpackungsgesetz. Förderung des Recyclings für mehr Ressourcen- und Umweltschutz.*" Available at: https://einweg-mit-pfand.de/verpackungsgesetz.html (accessed 18 February 2019).

European Commission (Ed.) (2010). *Being Wise With Waste: The EU's Approach to Waste Management.* Luxembourg: Publ. Off. of the European Union.

Fischer, C, & Davidsen, C (2010). *Europe as a Recycling Society: The European Recycling Map.* ETC/SCP Working Paper 5/2010, Copenhagen.

Frey, BS, & Schneider, F (2000). *Informal and Underground Economy.* Available at: https://www.econstor.eu/bitstream/10419/73197/1/wp0004.pdf (accessed on 19 February 2019).

Gehman, J, Glaser, VL, Eisenhardt, KM, Gioia, D, Langley, A, & Corley, KG (2018). Finding theory–method fit: A comparison of three qualitative approaches to theory building. *Journal of Management Inquiry, 27*(3), 284–300.

General Assembly of the United Nations (2015). *Transforming our world: The 2030 agenda for sustainable development. A/Res/70/1*, in *Resolution adopted by the General Assembly on 25 September 2015.*

German Bundestag (2019 2017). *Gesetz zur Fortentwicklung der haushaltsnahen Getrennterfassung von wertstoffhaltigen Abfällen: VerpackG, 2017 Teil I.*

Gioia, DA, & Chittipeddi, K (1991). Sensemaking and sensegiving in strategic change initiation. *Strategic Management Journal, 12*(6), 433–448.

Gioia, DA, Corley, KG, & Hamilton, AL (2013). Seeking qualitative rigor in inductive research. *Organizational Research Methods, 16*(1), 15–31.

Gioia, DA, & Pitre, E (1990). Multiparadigm perspectives on theory building. *The Academy of Management Review, 15*(4), 584–602.

Glaser, B, & Strauss, A (1967). *The Discovery of Grounded Theory: Strategies of Qualitative Research.* Chicago: Aldine.

Gray, A (2017). *Germany Recycles More Than Any Other Country.* Available at: https://www.weforum.org/agenda/2017/12/germany-recycles-more-than-any-other-country/.

Hahn, R (2009). The ethical rational of business for the poor – integrating the concepts bottom of the pyramid, sustainable development, and corporate citizenship. *Journal of Business Ethics, 84*(3), 313–324.

Hahn, T, Figge, F, Pinkse, J, & Preuss, L (2010). Trade-offs in corporate sustainability: You can't have your cake and eat it. *Business Strategy and the Environment, 19*(4), 217–229.

Hahn, T, Pinkse, J, Preuss, L, & Figge, F (2015). Tensions in corporate sustainability: Towards an integrative framework. *Journal of Business Ethics, 127*(2), 297–316.

Hall, CC, Zhao, J, & Shafir, E (2014). Self-affirmation among the poor: Cognitive and behavioral implications. *Psychological Science, 25*(2), 619–625.

Hayes, D (1978). *Repairs, reuse, recycling – first steps toward a sustainable society.* Worldwatch Paper 23, Library of Congress Catalog Card Number 78-644.

Lazarevic, D, Aoustin, E, Buclet, N, & Brandt, N (2010). Plastic waste management in the context of a European recycling society: Comparing results and uncertainties in a life cycle perspective. *Resources, Conservation and Recycling, 55*(2), 246–259.

Luhmann, N (1995). *Die Soziologie und der Mensch, Soziologische Aufklärung/Niklas Luhmann*, 6. Opladen: Westdt. Verl.

Luhmann, N (1997). *Die Gesellschaft der Gesellschaft, Suhrkamp-Taschenbuch Wissenschaft.* Frankfurt am Main: Suhrkamp.

Medina, M (2000). Scavenger cooperatives in Asia and Latin America. *Resources, Conservation and Recycling, 31*(1), 51–69.

Möller, J (2016). Lohnungleichheit – Gibt es eine Trendwende? *Wirtschaftsdienst, 96*(13), 38–44.

Moritz, R (2013). *Probleme am Flaschenhals. Im harten Wettbewerb der Brauer geht der Trend zur individualisierten Flasche: Premiumbrauereien prägen ihre Markennamen ins Glas - mit schlimmen Folgen für regionale Brauereien und die Umwelt. Handelsblatt.com.* 20 September.

Moser, SJ (2014). *Pfandsammler: Erkundungen einer urbanen Sozialfigur.* Dissertation (1st ed.), Hamburg: Hamburger Ed.

Myers, N, & Kent, J (2003). New consumers: The influence of affluence on the environment. *Proceedings of the National Academy of Sciences of the United States of America, 100*(8), 4963–4968.

O'Flaherty, B (1996). *Making Room: The Economics of Homelessness* (1st ed.). Cambridge: Harvard University Press.

Papaoikonomou, K, Kipouros, S, Kungolos, A, Somakos, L, Aravossis, K, Antonopoulos, I, & Karagiannidis, A (2009). Marginalised social groups in contemporary WEEE management within social enterprises investments: A study in Greece. *Waste Management, 29*(5), 1754–1759.

Petzall, BJ, Parker, GE, & Stoeberl, PA (2000). Another side to downsizing: Survivors' behavior and self-affirmation. *Journal of Business and Psychology, 14*(4), 593–603.

Pitz, A (Ed.) (2009). *Arme habt ihr allezeit: Vom Leben obdachloser Menschen in einem wohlhabenden Land, Edition Chrismon.* Frankfurt: Überarb. und erw. 2. Aufl., Hansisches Dr.- und Verl.-Haus.

Pozo, S (1996). "Introduction", in Pozo, S (Ed.), *Exploring the Underground Economy: Studies of Illegal and Unreported Activity*, Kalamazoo: W.E. Upjohn Institute, pp. 1–4.

Ramarajan, L (2014). Past, present and future research on multiple identities: Toward an intrapersonal network approach. *The Academy of Management Annals*, *8*(1), 589–659.

Sapolsky, RM (2004). Social status and health in humans and other animals. *Annual Review of Anthropology*, *33*(1), 393–418.

Sivanathan, N, & Pettit, NC (2010). Protecting the self through consumption: Status goods as affirmational commodities. *Journal of Experimental Social Psychology*, *46*(3), 564–570.

Steele, CM (1988). The psychology of self-affirmation: Sustaining the integrity of the self. *Advances in Experimental Social Psychology*, *21*, 261–302.

Tanzi, V (1980). The underground economy in the United States: Estimates and implications. *PSL Quarterly Review*, *33*(135), 427–453.

Vázquez, JJ (2016). The stigma of making a living from garbage: Meta-stereotypes of trash-pickers in León (Nicaragua). *Scandinavian Journal of Psychology*, *57*(2), 122–128.

Verbraucherzentrale (2019). Mehrweg oder Einweg: Verwirrung total beim Pfand. Available at: https://www.verbraucherzentrale.de/wissen/umwelt-haushalt/abfall/mehrweg-oder-einweg-verwirrung-total-beim-pfand-11504 (accessed on 18 February 2019).

Weick, KE (1989). Theory construction as disciplined imagination. *Academy of Management Review*, *14*(4), 516–531.

Weinzettel, J, Hertwich, EG, Peters, GP, Steen-Olsen, K, & Galli, A (2013). Affluence drives the global displacement of land use. *Global Environmental Change*, *23*(2), 433–438.

Wiedmann, TO, Schandl, H, Lenzen, M, Moran, D, Suh, S, West, J, & Kanemoto, K (2015). The material footprint of nations. *Proceedings of the National Academy of Sciences of the United States of America*, *112*(20), 6271–6276.

Wilson, DC, Velis, C, & Cheeseman, C (2006). Role of informal sector recycling in waste management in developing countries. *Habitat International*, *30*(4), 797–808.

Part IV

Design, integration, innovation and change of BOP markets

4 Varieties of capitalism and the base of pyramid population segment in affluent economies: Discussion on entrepreneurship financing and skills development

Ahmad Arslan, Asif Ruman, Pia Hurmelinna-Laukkanen, and Tahir Ali

Introduction

The *base of pyramid* also referred by some as the bottom of pyramid (BOP) population segment represents the single largest portion of residents on the planet (Prahalad, 2006; Leposky et al., 2020). BOP focussed research in different fields of social sciences has rapidly expanded since the introduction of this specific term by Prahalad (e.g. 2002, 2006). At the same time, BOP-focussed research has primarily focussed this population segment in the developing economies of in Africa, Asia and Latin America. These studies have addressed a range of topics like frugal innovation, social enterprises, social value creation, technology use by entrepreneurs, role of microfinance, and product, and services marketing strategies of both local and foreign firms (e.g. Cieslik, 2016; Ghauri and Wang, 2017; Armstrong et al., 2018; Bhatti et al., 2018; Leposky et al., 2020). Despite interesting insights by these studies, the focus on only developing economies' context has perhaps biased some of the knowledge accumulated in this area. We suggest that it is important to acknowledge that BOP population segment is not only limited to emerging and developing economies but also exists in affluent (developed), mostly western economies. This issue or its relevance are not explicitly (or significantly) present and acknowledged in the extant economics, entrepreneurship, management, policy and sustainability studies. Hence, our chapter tries to conceptually address this gap in the literature.

Economics literature has generated ample evidence on the existence of poverty and significant inequality in affluent economies (e.g. Jäntti and Danziger, 2000; Smeeding, 2006; Dorling, 2018). This poverty and inequality are manifested in a particular section of population that becomes marginalised with limited participation in economic activities (e.g. Morris et al., 2018; Sutter et al., 2019). This marginalised section of population can be caught in conditions similar to BOP conditions in many developing economies. Even though conditions of BOP residents in affluent economies are not necessarily life threatening and may not represent extreme poverty as in most developing countries (e.g. Sutter et al., 2019), the phenomenon is observable. Therefore, BOP population segment (residents) in affluent economies (like developed economies of western Europe and Northern America), needs a closer analysis, for better understanding of this under-researched context.

Significant differences exist in affluent primarily western economies due to differences in their institutional structures and systems of economic governance. These differences have been specifically addressed by the typology of the varieties of capitalism (VOC) developed by Hall and Soskice (2001). VOC perspective focusses on the differences in liberal market economies (LMEs) compared to coordinated market economies (CMEs). We argue that BOP population segment in affluent western economies needs to be analysed using VOC lens. This is because all the associated aspects with easing the BOP condition, such as regulations, access to welfare benefits, entrepreneurial possibilities including access to financing and entrepreneurial skills development, tend to differ in CMEs compared to LMEs (e.g. Hall and Soskice, 2001; Huber et al., 2018; Walker et al., 2018). We suggest that having a clearer understanding of how VOC connect to the features of the BOP population segment, and especially the means to ease the situation through entrepreneurial opportunities, allows introducing more efficient means to address the related challenges.

The discussion presented above forms the basis for our chapter's focus. We aim to offer a conceptual overview on BOP population segment in selected western affluent economies. As no specific BOP definition exists in the context of affluent economies, we aim to address this issue by incorporating views from multiple relevant academic disciplines. We discuss the differences of LMEs and CMEs focussing especially on the entrepreneurial possibilities in relation to access to financing and relevant skills development. These delimitations are grounded in existing knowledge: access to financing (including credit) has been identified as a driver for entrepreneurial activities (e.g. Kuzilwa, 2005) like training and skills development (e.g. Hermelin and Rusten, 2018; Nguyen, 2018). Furthermore, there is a linkage between training and funding considering that training on the financial opportunities and its terms and conditions links to the ability and willingness of potential entrepreneurs to rely on specific funding instruments (see, e.g. Amesheva et al., 2019; Damian and Manea, 2019). At the same time, both economics and management literatures have established that entrepreneurship is a key in improving living conditions of people (Sutter et al., 2019); thereby, making it an important tool for easing BOP conditions for that population segment.

We incorporate conceptual insights from extant literature regarding the role of financing (e.g. Bruton et al., 2015; Chiu et al., 2018), and link it with entrepreneurial possibilities for BOP residents in affluent economies. We argue in this context, that if people in BOP population segment are unable to access appropriate financing especially from formal channels, they may not (be able to) embrace entrepreneurship (e.g. Herkenhoff et al., 2016) as a possibility to ease the BOP conditions. We further suggest that for BOP residents, alternative financing modes supported by institutions of affluent countries can be useful in this concern. The discussion offered is substantiated by presenting some relevant statistics as well as highlighting different financing possibilities for entrepreneurs in selected affluent economies. Furthermore – besides access to financing – training and entrepreneurial skill development have been mentioned as important factors for the success of the ventures especially in developed economies (Karlan and Valdivia, 2011; Hermelin and Rusten, 2018; Nguyen, 2018). Prior studies mention that significant variance exists in training and skill development policies and practices across developed affluent economies (e.g. Busemeyer and Trampusch, 2012). However, training and skills development are not straightforward issues. For example, at the same time, CMEs like Nordic countries tend to offer better social benefits than LMEs, which can potentially reduce motivation to engage in entrepreneurship (e.g. Saunders, 2017; Raitakari et al., 2019). Moreover, entrepreneurship specific training and skills development for BOP population segments in affluent economies, has been rather lacking. We also address this specific aspect later in the chapter.

In order to make the discussion focussed substantiated with some relevant statistics and examples, our chapter focusses on the Nordic countries (Denmark, Finland, Norway and Sweden) as representative of CMEs. LMEs in our chapter are represented by Ireland and UK. This delimitation helps to offer structured insights in the discussion. This choice of representative countries for CMEs and LMEs, in line with the country categorisations presented by established VOC scholars like Hall and Soskice (2001), and Hall and Gingerich (2009). These studies indicate that CMEs and LMEs differ in terms of regulation, welfare benefits, financing support for entrepreneurship, and entrepreneurial possibilities (see, e.g. Becker-Ritterspach et al., 2017; Saunders, 2017; Walker et al., 2018). Hence, this categorisation helps in making the discussion offered in our chapter more specific.

The rest of the chapter is organised as follows. The next sections will address BOP population segment in affluent economies and explicate why VOC perspective is needed to better understand this specific context. This is followed by the section on dynamics of entrepreneurship financing for BOP population segment being addressed using VOC lens. The section after that specifically addresses skills development in relation to entrepreneurship in this context. The chapter concludes with presentation of implications, limitations and future research directions.

BOP in affluent economies and VOC perspective

Defining the BOP in affluent (primarily western European and North American) economies can be rather difficult due to no established definition of this population segment being available so far. Furthermore, it has been argued earlier that majority of BOP research has focussed on developing and emerging markets, which means that a fitting definition may be even more difficult to find. For example, Angot and Plé (2015) have conducted one of the few studies focussing on serving BOP market in rich economies, offering several examples of products and services developed by firms as well as discuss business models in this context. However, they do not specifically define what is meant by BOP in the affluent (rich) countries' context.

Keeping in view, this dearth of specific research on BOP population segment in affluent economies and lack of its clear definition, we resort to nearest research domain. Poverty has been studied to a notable extent in both developed and developing economies' context. In order to better understand BOP population segment, we argue that relative, rather than absolute poverty (Sen, 1983, 1992) is a relevant concept. Within affluent economies, poverty perceptions and dynamics differ significantly between Northern, central and Southern European countries, and North America or Asia Pacific. We further acknowledge the argument by Sen (1992, p. 115) that poverty is a state characterised by the levels of capabilities that are, in the view of society, unacceptably low, and we advocate that a multi-dimensional perspective is needed when BOP segment is considered (see Misturelli and Heffernan, 2012). Approached in this manner, poverty may involve a variety of challenges beyond economic ones, including capability deprivation, marginalisation, discrimination and poor health (Amorós et al., 2011). These aspects are important because individual's capabilities and their development (or lack thereof) is not only a function of their personal choices, working and learning but are also contingent upon the institutional and welfare regime of the country they live in (Esping-Andersen et al., 2002). Therefore, we believe that inclusion of VOC perspective in this discussion is relevant.

VOC has been considered as a very useful theoretical perspective to understand not only the differences in types of capitalistic models in countries but also the influence of differences in socioeconomic aspects such as welfare, unemployment and business development (Hall and Soskice, 2001; Schröder, 2013). VOC categorises economies in LMEs comprising primarily English-speaking countries like the USA, UK, Ireland, Australia, Canada, and to the CMEs of Continental Europe and Scandinavia (Hall and Soskice, 2001). We focus on CMEs from Nordic region (Denmark, Finland, Norway and Sweden), and LMEs from British Isles (Ireland and UK) for discussion and analysis purposes. In order to further build a case for the use of VOC perspective to understand BOP population segment in affluent economies, we start by referring to relative poverty statistics. According to World Bank, dataset developed by Demirguc-Kunt et al. (2018), relative poverty in UK and Ireland has been between 15% and 20% during last decade while Nordic countries have shown statistics of around 10% during this time. Another widely used measure of inequality in society is GINI coefficient. World bank statistics reveal that latest available GINI coefficient of Denmark is 28.7, Finland is 27.4, Ireland is 32.8, Norway is 27.0, Sweden is 28.8 and UK is 34.8 (World Bank, 2020). These statistics clearly show that in affluent economies of western Europe, inequality and poverty are significantly more visible in the examined LMEs of Ireland and UK compared to Nordic CMEs. Therefore, it is reasonable to argue that BOP population segment in UK and Ireland is relatively higher compared to Nordic CMEs. This is understandable and in line with arguments in prior studies that have referred to relatively high percentage of people suffering from economic deprivation in LMEs compared to CMEs with stronger social safety net (welfare) (e.g. Schröder, 2019; Alper et al., 2019).

Even though VOC perspective can offer useful insights to BOP research, it has not been specifically applied to analyse this topic so far. At the same time, some researchers have used VOC to explain differences in governmental approaches to addressing poverty in rich economies. However, the focus of most of these studies has been on redistribution and taxation strategies (e.g. Chauvel and Bar-Haim, 2016; Behringer and van Treeck, 2017). An important role that entrepreneurship can potentially play in uplifting BOP population segment has been rather under-researched, and its analysis from the perspective of VOC has been very limited. Only recently, scholars have shown that VOC is strongly linked to entrepreneurship in the developed economies (e.g. Dilli et al., 2018). However, the question of how VOC plays a role in relation to key aspects of entrepreneurship in affluent economies like financing and skills development, still awaits analysis by academic researchers. Considering the relevance of VOC perspective in relation to entrepreneurship by BOP population segment, the next two sections offer specific discussion on entrepreneurship financing and skills development in affluent economies by highlighting the differences in selected CMEs and LMEs.

Entrepreneurship financing and BOP in affluent economies

In recent years, scholars from multiple fields including development, economics and management studies have suggested that entrepreneurship provides a viable solution to the extreme poverty (e.g. Jones Christensen et al., 2015; Sutter et al., 2019). However, most of the prior research on this topic has focussed on the developing and emerging economies with people mostly living at or below subsistence level. As a result, such prior studies offer useful insights to BOP research in developing and emerging markets context. However, what this means for BOP population segment, or what the role of entrepreneurship is in advanced affluent economies, is not as clear.

Entrepreneurship is widely defined as 'situations in which new goods, services, raw materials, markets, and organising methods can be introduced through the formation of new means, ends, or means-ends relationships' (Eckhardt and Shane, 2003, p. 336). More recently, entrepreneurship has been viewed as encompassing transformational change that may extend to social or institutional spheres (e.g. Battilana et al., 2009). We argue that the second definition captures the influence of entrepreneurship on the lives of BOP population segment in affluent economies; changing the conditions of BOP population segment in terms of entrepreneurship (e.g. with transformation in training and funding schemes) has far-reaching influence.

For entrepreneurship to reach its potential as a remedy for easing BOP conditions, access to financing for entrepreneurship among BOP population segment is highly relevant. Entrepreneurial finance is developing rapidly, and many new forms of financing along with traditional banking and support channels have emerged in recent years (Bruton et al., 2015). Even though majority of scholarly work on financing for entrepreneurship has focussed on developing or emerging economies, it has been gradually acknowledged also that financial inclusion – defined as access to formal financial services at an affordable cost in a fair and transparent manner – is decreasing in traditionally developed and affluent economies (e.g. Swamy, 2014). Lack of financial inclusion (i.e. financial exclusion) in affluent economies is visible from the fact that in EU out of total population, 11.6% are without bank account, 35.4% have no credit card or other forms of borrowing possibilities and 23% are at risk of poverty (Pedrini et al., 2016).

At the same time, dependence of BOP population segment on welfare is relatively high in affluent CMEs, compared to the situation in LMEs like UK, where many employed people tend to fall in working poor category where their income need to be supplemented by welfare payments by the states to reach viable levels (Moller et al., 2003; Copeland and Daly, 2012). Before proceeding further, it is important to refer to recent statistics concerning entrepreneurship or self-employment in our focus countries. According to recent statistics from 2019, 15.26% of labour force is self-employed in UK (Trading Economics, 2020a), while in Ireland the number is 15.2% (Trading Economics, 2020b). In Nordic CME countries, percentage of self-employed entrepreneurs in Denmark is 8.2 (Trading Economics, 2020c), the number in Finland is 13.12% (Trading Economics, 2020c), the number in Norway is 6.5 (Trading Economics, 2020d) and the number in Sweden is 9.81% (Trading Economics, 2020d). These findings indicate that entrepreneurship is a relevant source of income, and when supported, can provide a source of transforming the conditions for the BOP population segment.

However, together, financial exclusion and dependence on welfare as a relevant supplement to income indicate that there is relatively little manoeuvring for those who would like to improve their situation. Statistics on the financial inclusion data by the world bank (Demirguc-Kunt et al., 2018) show that the people not part of labour force, presumably representing BOP population segment have limited access to traditional banking and credit services in LMEs of Ireland and UK compared to Nordic SMEs. This aspect also resonates with the differences in CMEs and LMEs already indicated in existing literature (see, e.g. Hall and Soskice, 2001; Huber et al., 2018; Walker et al., 2018). Hence, if BOP population segment members are to be motivated for entrepreneurship, financing aspects need to be considered thoughtfully by policy makers.

Keeping in view, limitations associated with traditional banking and financing, it is no wonder that in developed (affluent) European economies, entrepreneurs are increasingly combining traditional debt and equity start-up finance (e.g. friends, family, capitalists and occasionally banks) with microfinance (e.g. Pedrini et al., 2016), crowdfunding (e.g. Belleflamme et al., 2013, 2014), and a range of other financial innovations (e.g. Bruton et al., 2015). Prior literature has mentioned certain unique features of these financial innovations. An important feature relates to the fact that these innovations may have arisen in one part of the world, but they quickly diffused across the globe. For example, microfinance emerged as a solution to a lack of capital for those living in poverty in developing economies, yet it has spread to developed economies (Eriksson et al., 2011; Pedrini et al., 2016). In fact, microfinance is the only medium which BOP population segment can utilise for starting a business – crowdfunding and other financial innovations having mostly been technology and innovation focussed (Pedrini et al., 2016; Chmelíková et al., 2018). Moreover, some prior studies have shown that biggest beneficiaries of microfinance are ethnic minorities, immigrants, women and young people especially in developed western economies (e.g. Kraemer-Eis and Conforti, 2009; Jayo et al., 2010; Hudon et al., 2019). Some of these have also been found to be more visible in BOP population segment due to a variety of reasons. Therefore, microfinance and other relevant financing initiatives should be linked to specific policy interventions in order to foster entrepreneurship in BOP population segment in both types of affluent economies.

Entrepreneurial skills development and BOP in affluent economies

Skills development and training have been identified as important pre-requisites for the success of entrepreneurial ventures in both developed and developing economies (Beaver, 2002; Eze and Nwali, 2012; Ogundele et al., 2012; O'Reilly et al., 2015; Thurman, 2016). However, in case of developed affluent economies of western Europe, such skill development and training can be even more important, as these markets are highly competitive and to an extent saturated, which makes survival of entrepreneurial ventures even harder (e.g. Kollmann et al., 2016). In fact, earlier research has revealed the existence of differences in LMEs vs. CMEs regarding specific aspects of skills development of population. It has been argued that vocal training is rather weak in LMEs due to lack of industry apprenticeships and as a result of formal education being focussed more on generic academic topics rather than specific skills (Thelen 2004; Busemeyer and Trampusch, 2012). At the same time in CMEs, industry specific skills development has been rather strong, but it is dependent on training system (mostly by firms) providing these opportunities (Thelen, 2004). Historically, many low-skilled employees in CMEs have had the possibility to gain long-term employment in industrial organisations, which developed their skills over time (Harcourt and Wood, 2007). However, due to the changing nature of CME economies, outsourcing of low-tech industries to developing economies, and turbulence in work life caused by shortening work periods in same organisations and frequent career transitions; such opportunities are increasingly becoming limited. As a result, such employees who end up losing industrial jobs can potentially end up being part of BOP population segment as their re-employment opportunities are limited due to a relative lack of skills (Crettaz, 2011). Challenges in LMEs and CMEs vary in nature, but they can be equally tough.

As this specific phenomenon represents a huge policy challenge, we can observe that irrespective of CME vs. LME categorisation, governments (public bodies) are increasingly being forced to play a visible role in skills development for BOP population segment as well as generally. For example, the Entrepreneurship Competence Framework (EntreComp) developed by the Joint Research Centre (JRC) of the European Commission on behalf of the Directorate General for Employment, Social Affairs, and Inclusion (DG EMPL), has been designed to improve the entrepreneurial capacity by providing holistic overview of needed competences and learning outcomes (see Bacigalupo et al., 2016). Examples can be found also in the national level, such as in the introduction of apprenticeship degrees in UK that are receiving significant public funding at the same time when other academic degrees have rather high fees (Bradley et al., 2019). In CMEs including Nordic economies, national and regional governments are progressively attempting to develop vocational degree programmes targeted at entrepreneurship (Chiu, 2012), and in countries like Finland entrepreneurship is already a natural part of primary school education (Lepistö and Ronkko, 2013; Hietanen, 2015; Deveci and Seikkula-Leino, 2018). In fact, an important advantage of CMEs in this concern relates to availability of training infrastructure for vocational training, which earlier was mostly oriented towards industrial skills development (Nyland and Rossvall, 2019). An interesting strategy in this concern has been to make entrepreneurship a visible part of schooling starting already from early years in order to develop those skills in future generations as industrial jobs are increasingly going to be limited in the future (e.g. Rasmussen and Fritzner, 2016).

Eurostat statistics on continuing vocational training (Eurostat, 2020) show that in Nordic CMEs, adult participation in continuous learning programmes is relatively higher compared to LMEs of Ireland and UK. However, at the same time, percentage of firms employing vocational training participants is relatively low in both CMEs and LMEs being analysed in the current chapter (Eurostart, 2020). This gives further credence to our argument that along with training BOP population segment for getting jobs, entrepreneurship specific training and skills development is highly needed in both CMEs and LMEs (see also Hermelin and Rusten, 2018; Nguyen, 2018); self-employment is very important and there are observations that entrepreneurship in this segment is actually increasing.

A good example in case of CMEs is of Finland, where, self-employing entrepreneurs, represent around 50% of all entrepreneurs (Statistics Finland, 2017). Also, it has been found in a recent survey that entrepreneurial vocational skills are in demand even in CMEs like Finland as many entrepreneurs are increasingly looking forward to sub-contract their activities (Statistics Finland, 2018). It should further be noted that reasonable work has been done for entrepreneurial education and skills development in all Nordic CMEs, as depicted by Chiu's (2012) report on state of entrepreneurial education in Nordic countries. However, most of this work is undertaken at a general level and specificities of skills development for BOP population segment have not been fully addressed. Similar observation can be made for LMEs like Ireland and UK. We argue that it is important for the researchers as well as policy makers to work on developing entrepreneurial skills set which offer realistic possibilities to BOP population segments in these economies.

Implications, limitations and future research directions

The purpose of the current chapter was to address BOP population segment in less researched context of affluent economies using VOC perspective as a lens. We present entrepreneurship financing and entrepreneurial skills development as possible strategies for providing support for BOP residents to improve their conditions. To make our discussion specific, we use some public statistics from Nordic countries to provide insight into the situation in CMEs, while data from Ireland and UK did the same for LMEs. Our review supports the notion that there are significant differences in CMEs and LMEs with regards to entrepreneurship financing possibilities and skills development for BOP population segments. Based on these findings, our chapter offers several theoretical and policy implications.

A key theoretical insight relates to highlighting the specificity of affluent economies in relation to BOP research. As significant BOP research has been undertaken in emerging or developing economies, relevant constructs and their definitions tend to be more linked to that context. We argue that BOP theorists should try to develop and agree on definition of this population segment that would also accommodate underlying features of affluent economies' context. Moreover, since based on our overview of CMEs and

LMEs, there is a variation across almost all discussed aspects from the nature of BOP population segment to the potential remedies and their antecedents; a key theoretical implication relates to applicability of VOC to better understand BOP population segment in affluent economies. We believe that such theoretical framing might significantly enhance the potential applicability of VOC perspective in BOP research especially in affluent economies and provide the needed theoretical tools for generating appropriate measures and indicators.

A key policy implication emanating from the discussion in this chapter relates to highlighting specificities of entrepreneurship financing and skills development for BOP population segment. Our illustrations show that the participation in vocational and entrepreneurial skills training is relatively high in Nordic CMEs compared to LMEs. Looking at how and why this works might provide the needed tools to transfer and translate best practices and approaches more widely to varying affluent economies. For example, it seems that taking entrepreneurial skills development as a part of specific continuous learning programmes in these countries, rather than generic ones, would be a viable approach.

The above argument receives support from another finding in our analysis: we found that percentage of firms employing vocational training participants is relatively low both in CMEs and LMEs. This aspect needs specific attention from the policy makers. It seems that if generic vocational training programmes do not inculcate required employability skills in BOP residents, then potential influence of such trainings on entrepreneurial success will also be limited. Therefore, entrepreneurship-specific vocational training programmes need to be developed in line with dynamics of the local context. We also found that even though significant emphasis is being placed on entrepreneurial education especially in Nordic CMEs, most of the work done so far is rather generic and tries to incorporate entrepreneurship to be part of educational curriculum from early on. It is important for policy makers to work in close coordination with interdisciplinary researchers, so that a specific tool set of entrepreneurial skills can be developed for BOP population segment in relevant CMEs and LMEs. In the same vein, it has been referred in some prior research on entrepreneurship education, that trainers should also be trained properly (Chiu, 2012, p. 68). We believe that this argument is especially valid in context of entrepreneurial skills development for BOP population segment. Policy makers should ensure that trainers in such programmes understand the sociological and psychological roots of BOP phenomenon properly in overall context of CME vs. LME dynamics. In this way, the trainers can help BOP residents to attain needed skills for success of entrepreneurial initiatives. Otherwise, without incorporating BOP context in these training and vocational programmes, chances of success are relatively low in our view.

Finally, the discussion presented in our chapter revealed relatively higher financial exclusion of BOP population segment especially in LMEs. This calls for policy makers in those countries to look for non-conventional financial instruments like microfinancing, which has proven to be useful in developed economies as well despite its origin in developing economies (e.g. Eriksson et al., 2011; Pedrini et al., 2016). In the context of microfinance, it is important to mention that profitability of microfinance initiatives is low in western European countries (Germany, Italy, Spain and UK), and in many cases, they need government subsidies to survive (e.g. Kraemer-Eis and Conforti, 2009). At the same time, research on microfinance in Nordic CMEs is very limited, but the same argument can be valid in these as well. Hence, a suggestion for policy makers is to link subsidies of microfinance for entrepreneurship with overall welfare spending, as it would support operations of such financial players and simultaneously reduce financial exclusion. Moreover, our analysis indicated that savings propensity for entrepreneurship is lesser among BOP residents in the Nordic CMEs compared to LMEs of Ireland and UK. Although this is understandable due to better welfare benefits and safety net in CMEs, policy makers need to think about policies and financial instruments which incentivise savings for this specific purpose.

Our chapter does have several limitations like any other academic work. Firstly, the discussion offered in the chapter is mostly conceptual, which is augmented in some cases by secondary, and descriptive data based on different publicly available data sources. Hence, lack of primary data and its analysis is a major limitation, which also influences potential generalisability of arguments presented in it. Likewise, more sophisticated data analysis could provide more nuanced evidence on the relationships between the different constructs. We believe that if interviews can be conducted with policy makers, relevant public bodies (including vocational education providers) and BOP population sample in selected CMEs and LMEs; more specific insights to the role of entrepreneurship financing and skills development can be achieved. In particular, the reasons behind the patterns that our analysis revealed are important factors that need to be considered in further theory development. Therefore, this is one aspect which future studies can focus on and enrich BOP literature by undertaking country specific as well as comparative studies. Our initial analysis despite its limitations – can provide the needed starting points.

References

Alper, K, Huber, E, & Stephens, JD (2019). *Work and Poverty in Post-Industrial Democracies* (No. 763). LIS Cross-National Data Center in Luxembourg. Available online at (last time accessed on 29 May 2020) http://www.lisdatacenter.org/wps/liswps/763.pdf

Amesheva, I, Clark, A, & Payne, J (2019). "Financing for Youth Entrepreneurship in Sustainable Development. Sustainable Development Goals", in J Walker et al. (Eds.), *Harnessing Business to Achieve the SDGs through Finance, Technology, and Law Reform*. Chichester: John Wiley & Sons. pp. 253–273.

Amorós, JE, Cristi, O, & Minniti, M (2011). Entrepreneurial volatility: A cross country study. *Annual Proceedings of the Wealth and Well-Being of Nations, Ill,* 159–176.

Angot, J, & Plé, L (2015). Serving poor people in rich countries: The bottom-of-the-pyramid business model solution. *Journal of Business Strategy, 36*(2), 3–15.

Armstrong, K, Ahsan, M, & Sundaramurthy, C (2018). Microfinance ecosystem: How connectors, interactors, and institutionalizers co-create value. *Business Horizons, 61*(1), 147–155.

Bacigalupo, M, Punie, PKY, & Van den Brande, G (2016) EntreComp: The Entrepreneurship Competence Framework. Science for Policy report by the Joint Research Centre, European Union. Available online at (last time accessed on 29 May 2020) http://publications.jrc.ec.europa.eu/repository/bitstream/JRC101581/lfna27939enn.pdf

Battilana, J, Leca, B, & Boxenbaum, E (2009). How actors change institutions: Towards a theory of institutional entrepreneurship. *Academy of Management Annals, 3*(1), 65–107.

Beaver, G (2002). *Small Business, Entrepreneurship and Enterprise Development.* Harlow: Pearson Education.

Becker-Ritterspach, F, Lange, K, & Becker-Ritterspach, J (2017), Divergent patterns in institutional entrepreneurship of MNCs in emerging economies. *Critical Perspectives on International Business, 13*(3), 186–203.

Behringer, J, & van Treeck, T (2017). *Varieties of Capitalism and Growth Regimes: The Role of Income Distribution* (No. 194). IMK Working Paper. Available online at (last time accessed on 29 May 2020) https://www.boeckler.de/pdf/v_2017_11_11_behringer.pdf

Bhatti, Y, Basu, RR, Barron, D, & Ventresca, MJ (2018). *Frugal Innovation: Models, Means, Methods.* Cambridge: Cambridge University Press.

Belleflamme, P, Lambert, T, & Schwienbacher, A (2013). Individual crowdfunding practices. *Venture Capital, 15*(4), 313–333.

Belleflamme, P, Lambert, T, & Schwienbacher, A (2014). Crowdfunding: Tapping the right crowd. *Journal of Business Venturing, 29*(5), 585–609.

Bradley, J, Newhouse, C, & Mirza, N (2019). Driving social mobility? Competitive collaboration in degree apprenticeship development. *Higher Education, Skills and Work-based Learning, 9*(2), 164–174.

Bruton, G, Khavul, S, Siegel, D, & Wright, M (2015). New financial alternatives in seeding entrepreneurship: Microfinance, crowdfunding, and peer-to-peer innovations. *Entrepreneurship Theory and Practice, 39*(1), 9–26.

Busemeyer, MR, & Trampusch, C (Eds). (2012). *The Political Economy of Collective Skill Formation.* Oxford: Oxford University Press.

Chauvel, L, & Bar-Haim, E (2016). *Varieties of Capitalism (VoC) and Varieties of Distributions (VoD): How Welfare Regimes Affect the Pre-and Post-Transfer Shapes of Inequalities?* (No. 677). LIS Working Paper Series. Available online at (last time accessed on 29 May 2020) https://www.econstor.eu/bitstream/10419/169237/1/677.pdf

Chiu, R (2012). *Entrepreneurship Education in the Nordic Countries–Strategy Implementation and Good Practices.* Nordic Council of Ministers. Available online at (last time accessed on 29 May 2020) https://norden.diva-portal.org/smash/get/diva2:707249/FULLTEXT01.pdf

Chiu, J, Dong, M, & Shao, E (2018). On the welfare effects of credit arrangements. *International Economic Review*, *59*(3), 1621–1651.

Chmelíková, G, Krauss, A, & Dvouletý, O (2018). Performance of microfinance institutions in Europe — Does social capital matter?. *Socio-Economic Planning Sciences*, *68*, 100670.

Cieslik, K (2016). Moral economy meets social enterprise community-based green energy project in rural Burundi. *World Development*, *83*(*1*), 12–26.

Copeland, P, & Daly, M (2012). Varieties of poverty reduction: Inserting the poverty and social exclusion target into Europe 2020. *Journal of European Social Policy*, *22*(3), 273–287.

Crettaz, E (2011). *Fighting Working Poverty in Post-Industrial Economies: Causes, Trade-offs and Policy Solutions*. Cheltenham: Edward Elgar Publishing.

Damian, D, & Manea, C (2019). Causal recipes for turning fin-tech freelancers into smart entrepreneurs. *Journal of Innovation & Knowledge*, *4*(3), 196–201.

Demirguc-Kunt, A, Klapper, L, Singer, D, Ansar, S, & Hess, J (2018). *The Global Findex Database 2017: Measuring financial inclusion and the fintech revolution*. The World Bank. Available online at (last time accessed on 29 May 2020) https://openknowledge.worldbank.org/handle/10986/29510

Deveci, I, & Seikkula-Leino, J (2018). A review of entrepreneurship education in teacher education. *Malaysian Journal of Learning and Instruction*, *15*(1), 105–148.

Dilli, S, Elert, N, & Herrmann, AM (2018). Varieties of entrepreneurship: Exploring the institutional foundations of different entrepreneurship types through 'Varieties-of-Capitalism'arguments. *Small Business Economics*, *51*(2), 293–320.

Dorling, D (2018). "Inequality in Advanced Economies", in Clark, L et al. (Eds.), *The New Oxford Handbook of Economic Geography*. Oxford: Oxford University Press. pp. 39–62.

Eckhardt, JT, & Shane, SA (2003). Opportunities and entrepreneurship. *Journal of Management*, *29*(3), 333–349.

Eriksson, PE, Kraemer-Eis, H, & Conforti, A (2011). "Microfinance in Europe", in M Delia (Ed.), *APS Bank Occasional Papers*. Malta: APS Bank Publications. pp. 49–86.

Esping-Andersen, G, Gallie, D, Hemerijck, A, & Myles, J (2002). *Why We Need a New Welfare State*. Oxford: Oxford University Press.

Eze, JF, & Nwali, AC (2012). Capacity building for entrepreneurship education: The challenge for the developing nations. *American Journal of Business Education*, *5*(4), 401–408.

Eurostat (2020). Continuing vocational training survey (CVTS). Available online at (last time accessed on 29 May 2020). https://ec.europa.eu/eurostat/statistics-explained/index.php?title=Glossary:Continuing_vocational_training_survey_(CVTS)

Ghauri, PN, & Wang, F (2017). "The Impact of Multinational Enterprises on Sustainable Development and Poverty Reduction: Research Framework", in Ghauri et al. (Eds.), *Multinational Enterprises and Sustainable Development*. Bingley: Emerald Publishing Limited, pp. 13–39.

Hall, PA, & Gingerich, DW (2009). Varieties of capitalism and institutional complementarities in the political economy: An empirical analysis. *British Journal of Political Science*, *39*(3), 449–482.

Hall, PA, & Soskice, D (2001). "Introduction to varieties of capitalism", in Hall, P, & Soskice, D (Eds.), *Varieties of Capitalism: The Institutional Foundations of Comparative Advantage*. Oxford: Oxford University Press, pp. 1–68.

Harcourt, M, & Wood, G (2007). The importance of employment protection for skill development in coordinated market economies. *European Journal of Industrial Relations*, *13*(2), 141–159.

Herkenhoff, K, Phillips, G, & Cohen-Cole, E (2016). *The Impact of Consumer Credit Access on Employment, Earnings and Entrepreneurship*. Available online at (last time accessed on 29 May 2020). https://www.tuck.dartmouth.edu/uploads/centers/files/entrepreneurship.pdf

Hermelin, B, & Rusten, G (2018). A place-based approach to social entrepreneurship for social integration–Cases from Norway and Sweden. *Local Economy*, *33*(4), 367–383.

Hietanen, L (2015). Entrepreneurial learning environments: Supporting or hindering diverse learners? *Education+ Training*, *57*(5), 512–531.

Huber, E, Petrova, B, & Stephens, JD (2018). *Financialization and Inequality in Coordinated and Liberal Market Economies* (No. 750). LIS Working Paper Series. Available online at (last time accessed on 29 May 2020) http://www.lisdatacenter.org/wps/liswps/750.pdf

Hudon, M, Labie, M, & Szafarz, A (2019). *A Research Agenda for Financial Inclusion and Microfinance*. Cheltenham: Edward Elgar Publishing.

Jäntti, M, & Danziger, S (2000). "Income poverty in advanced countries", in A Atkin et al. (Eds.), *Handbook of Income Distribution*. Amsterdam: Elsevier, pp. 309–378.

Jayo, B, González, A, & Conzett, C (2010). *Overview of the Microcredit Sector in the European Union 2008-2009*. Paris: EMN. Available online at (last time accessed on 29 May 2020) https://www.findevgateway.org/sites/default/files/mfg-en-paper-overview-of-the-microcredit-sector-in-the-european-union-jun-2010.pdf

Jones Christensen, L, Siemsen, E, & Balasubramanian, S (2015). Consumer behavior change at the base of the pyramid: Bridging the gap between for-profit and social responsibility strategies. *Strategic Management Journal*, *36*(2), 307–317.

Karlan, D, & Valdivia, M (2011). Teaching entrepreneurship: Impact of business training on microfinance clients and institutions. *Review of Economics and Statistics*, *93*(2), 510–527.

Köhler-Ulbrich, P, Hempell, HS, & Scopel, S (2016). *The Euro Area Bank Lending survey: Role, Development and Use in Monetary Policy Preparation* (No. 179). ECB Occasional Paper. Available online at https://www.econstor.eu/bitstream/10419/154632/1/ecbop179.pdf

Kollmann, T, Stöckmann, C, Hensellek, S, & Kensbock, J (2016). European startup monitor 2016 report available online at https://europeanstartupmonitor.com/fileadmin/esm_2016/report/ESM_2016.pdf

Kraemer-Eis, H, & Conforti, A (2009). *Microfinance in Europe–A Market Overview* (No. 2009/01). EIF Working Paper. Available online at (last time accessed on 29 May 2020) https://www.eif.org/news_centre/publications/EIF_WP_2009_001_Microfinance.pdf

Kuzilwa, JA (2005). The role of credit for small business success: A study of the national entrepreneurship development fund in Tanzania. *The Journal of Entrepreneurship*, *14*(2), 131–161.

Lepistö, J, & Ronkko, ML (2013). Teacher students as future entrepreneurship educators and learning facilitators. *Education+ Training*, *55*(7), 641–653.

Leposky, T, Arslan, A, & Dikova, D (2020). "Value co-creation in multinational enterprises' services marketing at the bottom-of-the-pyramid markets", in M Marinov et al. (Eds.), *International Business and Emerging Economy Firms, Volume I: Universal*

Issues and the Chinese Perspective. Cham: Palgrave MacMillan (Springer Nature). pp. 89–116.

Misturelli, F, & Heffernan, C (2012). The shape of change: A memetic analysis of the definitions of poverty from the 1970s to the 2000s. *Journal of International Development*, *24*, S3–S18.

Moller, S, Huber, E, Stephens, JD, Bradley, D, & Nielsen, F (2003). Determinants of relative poverty in advanced capitalist democracies. *American Sociological Review*, *68*(1), 22–51.

Morris, MH, Santos, SC, & Neumeyer, X (2018). "Understanding poverty", in *Poverty and Entrepreneurship in Developed Economies*. Cheltenham: Edward Elgar Publishing.

Nguyen, N (2018). The role of government in the development of ethnic entrepreneurs: The qualitative study on Vietnamese ethnic entrepreneur in Finland. Available online at (last time accessed on 29 May 2020) http://www.utupub.fi/handle/10024/145652

Nylund, M & Rosvall, PÅ (2019). Vocational education, transitions, marginalisation and social justice in the Nordic countries. *European Educational Research Journal*, *18*(3), 271–277.

Ogundele, OJK, Akingbade, WA, & Akinlabi, HB (2012). Entrepreneurship training and education as strategic tools for poverty alleviation in Nigeria. *American International Journal of Contemporary Research*, *2*(1), 148–156.

O'Reilly, J, Eichhorst, W, Gábos, A, Hadjivassiliou, K, Lain, D, Leschke, J, & Russell, H (2015). Five characteristics of youth unemployment in Europe: Flexibility, education, migration, family legacies, and EU policy. *Sage Open*, *5*(1), 2158244015574962.

Pedrini, M, Bramanti, V, Minciullo, M, & Ferri, LM (2016). Rethinking microfinance for developed countries. *Journal of International Development*, *28*(2), 281–302.

Prahalad, CK (2006). *The Fortune at the Bottom of the Pyramid*. Chennai: Pearson Education India.

Prahalad, CK, & Hammond, A (2002). Serving the world's poor, profitably. *Harvard Business Review*, *80*(9), 48–59.

Raitakari, S, Juhila, K, & Räsänen, JM (2019). Responsibilisation, social work and inclusive social security in Finland. *European Journal of Social Work*, *22*(2), 264–276.

Rasmussen, A, & Fritzmer, A (2016). From dream to reality: Learning outcomes and didactic principles for teaching entrepreneurship in Nordic schools. Nordic Council of Ministers. Available online at http://norden.diva-portal.org/smash/get/diva2:902861/FULLTEXT02.pdf

Saunders, P (2017). *Welfare to Work in Practice: Social Security and Participation in Economic and Social Life*. Oxon: Routledge.

Schröder, M (2013). *Integrating Varieties of Capitalism and Welfare State Research: A Unified Typology of Capitalisms*. Baskingstone: Palgrave MacMillan.

Schröder, M (2019). Varieties of capitalism and welfare regime theories: Assumptions, accomplishments, and the need for different methods. *KZfSS Kölner Zeitschrift für Soziologie und Sozialpsychologie*, *71*(1), 53–73.

Sen, A (1983). Poor, relatively speaking. *Oxford Economic Papers*, *35*(2), 153–169.

Sen, AK (1992). *Inequality Reexamined*. Oxford: Oxford University Press.

Smeeding, T (2006). Poor people in rich nations: The United States in comparative perspective. *Journal of Economic Perspectives*, *20*(1), 69–90.

Sobel, RS (2008). Testing Baumol: Institutional quality and the productivity of entrepreneurship. *Journal of Business Venturing*, *23*(6), 641–655.

Statistics Finland (2017). *YRITTÄJÄT SUOMESSA 2017*. Available online at (last time accessed on 29 May 2020). http://www.stat.fi/tup/julkaisut/tiedostot/julkaisuluettelo/ytym_201700_2018_21465_net.pdf

Statistics Finland (2018). *Self-Employed Persons in Finland Favour Subcontractors*. Available online at (last time accessed on 29 May 2020). https://www.stat.fi/uutinen/self-employed-persons-in-finland-favour-subcontractors

Sutter, C, Bruton, GD, & Chen, J (2019). Entrepreneurship as a solution to extreme poverty: A review and future research directions. *Journal of Business Venturing*, *34*(1), 197–214.

Swamy, V (2014). Financial inclusion, gender dimension, and economic impact on poor households. *World Development*, *56*, 1–15.

Thelen, K (2004). *How Institutions Evolve: The Political Economy of Skills in Germany, Britain, the United States, and Japan*. Cambridge: Cambridge University Press.

Thurman, PW (2016). *Entrepreneurship and Sustainability: Business Solutions for Poverty Alleviation from Around the World*. Oxon: Routledge.

Trading Economics (2020a). *United Kingdom - Self-Employed; Total (% of Total Employed)*. Available online at (last time accessed on 29 May 2020) https://tradingeconomics.com/united-kingdom/self-employed-total-percent-of-total-employed-wb-data.html

Trading Economics (2020b). *Ireland - Self-Employed; Total (% of Total Employed)*. Available online at (last time accessed on 25 May 2020) https://tradingeconomics.com/ireland/self-employed-total-percent-of-total-employed-wb-data.html

Trading Economics (2020c). *Denmark - Self-Employed; Total (% of Total Employed)*. Available online at (last time accessed on 29 May 2020). https://tradingeconomics.com/denmark/self-employed-total-percent-of-total-employed-wb-data.html

Trading Economics (2020d). *Finland - Self-Employed; Total (% of Total Employed)*. Available online at (last time accessed on 29 May 2020). https://tradingeconomics.com/finland/self-employed-total-percent-of-total-employed-wb-data.html

Trading Economics (2020e). *Norway - Self-Employed; Total (% of Total Employed)*. Available online at (last time accessed 29 May 2020). https://tradingeconomics.com/norway/self-employed-total-percent-of-total-employed-wb-data.html

Trading Economics (2020f). *Sweden - Self-Employed; Total (% of Total Employed)*. Available online at (last time accessed on 29 May 2020). https://tradingeconomics.com/sweden/self-employed-total-percent-of-total-employed-wb-data.html

Walker, J, Wood, G, Brewster, C, & Beleska-Spasova, E (2018). Context, market economies and MNEs: The example of financial incentivization. *International Business Review*, *27*(1), 21–33.

World Bank (2020). *GINI index (World Bank Estimate)*. Available online at (last time accessed on 29 May 2020). https://data.worldbank.org/indicator/si.pov.gini

5 Tiny Houses as innovations for the Base of Pyramid markets in Germany: A critical perspective under the lens of sustainability

Anne Fischer and Marlen Gabriele Arnold

Introduction

Around 8% of the global population lives in extreme poverty on less than $2 a day (World Data Lab, 2018). If the ability to generate global income and wealth distribution is measured in terms of an economic pyramid (Prahalad, 2005), this part of the population can be assigned to the Base of the Pyramid (BOP). The designations mainly refer to less developed countries. Accordingly, there is a wide range of literature that examines BOP in the context of these countries (e.g. Dembek et al., 2018; Kuo et al., 2018; Palomares-Aguirre et al., 2018).

The gap between rich and poor does not only exist among different countries but is also becoming increasingly apparent within single, especially wealthy countries (Finkenwirth and Diemand, 2017). Germany has a far-reaching social system and is one of the richest countries in the world. However, almost 20% of people were affected by social exclusion or poverty in 2017 (Statista Research Department, 2020). This is based on the European Union's definition of (relative) poverty, according to which '[p] eople are said to be living in poverty if their income and resources are so inadequate as to preclude them from having a standard of living considered acceptable in the society in which they live' (Lecerf, 2016, p. 4). In this context, they may face disadvantages such as inadequate housing conditions. Problems of marginalisation and social exclusion from activities may also occur. Due to the lack of a globally homogenous definition (Lecerf, 2016) and to the complexity of the poverty concept, a multidimensional indicator has been used to measure it (Rudnicka, 2018). Accordingly, a person is considered poor or affected by social exclusion if he or she fulfils one or more of the following criteria: 'significant material deprivation', 'risk of poverty' and 'belonging to a household with low labour force participation' (Ibid.).

In particular, poor people in wealthy countries are usually still able to satisfy their basic needs, but often lack resources. Problems of social exclusion and imbalance arise, and the concept of *relative poverty* is significant (World Vision Institute, 2018). This understanding of poverty underlies the target group addressed in this study and it may be justified to extend the BOP concept to affluent countries.

As poverty and social exclusion are closely linked, the reduction of inequalities should also be pursued alongside the objective of poverty avoidance in wealthy countries (Arnold, 2018b). The 17 key objectives for sustainable development include the *reduction of inequalities*, *no poverty* as well as *sustainable cities and municipalities*. The concept of sustainability addresses the development of human systems by respecting the environmental limits and social progress within planetary boundaries and carrying capacity (Arnold, 2018a). Progressing BOP products and markets, the triadic dimensions of the triple-bottom line approach, meaning ecological, social and economic dimensions, should be integrated (Gold et al., 2013; Rosca et al., 2016). Thus, housing issues must be addressed in several dimensions. In order to achieve the aim of sustainable development, all three pillars (economic, social and ecological) should be considered (WCED, 1987). Winston and Eastaway (2008) stress the importance of housing in the context of sustainable development and recommend attaching greater importance to it, especially in the context of Sustainable Development Goals.

Against the background of rising rents, especially in large cities, it is to be expected that fewer people will be able to afford 'decent' housing in the future (Reuter, 2017; BAG Wohnungslosenhilfe e.V., 2018). Both homelessness and housing instability have increased for the majority of European countries. In Germany, from 2014 to 2016, and in Ireland, from 2014 to 2017, for example, homelessness has risen by around 150% (Fowler et al., 2019). Until now, there has been no effectively integrated solution to the above-mentioned problems in Germany. Soederberg (2018) points out that challenges of low-income rented housing (such as: over-indebtedness, forced evictions and potential homelessness) have been insufficiently addressed on both an analytical and historical level. It is necessary to recognise the problem and find appropriate solutions, not to leave people to themselves and, at best, to reintegrate them into society.

Tiny Houses are already being used in various forms in connection with homelessness or precarious housing conditions in particular. Tiny Houses already exist in the USA for the homeless as a temporary housing option, and even for long-term living (Green, 2016) despite specific legal hurdles, particularly regarding parking spaces (Osiewacz, 2018/19). Although no definition prevails, most of these are mobile or fixed houses up to 37 square metres in size (Evans, 2017; Tiny Houses Consulting UG, n.d.). Tiny Houses have the potential to work well for BOP markets in Germany, offering several opportunities to enter it. Examples may include their capability to act on different market segments (London and Hart, 2004) and to be adaptable to different user groups (single households, older people, students, etc.) as they can provide a variety of applications (Shearer and Burton, 2019). According to Follman (2012), a focus on national and regional companies could be relevant for operating in the BOP market by having a good understanding of these markets as well as their capabilities and needs (Ibid.). Mostly regional or national Tiny House manufacturers sell their products in their own country, offering a close exchange to the customers (Tiny Houses Consulting UG, n.d.).

It is unclear whether this form of housing represents an innovation for BOP markets and which focal points are to be considered in this context from a sustainability perspective. The latter is not only important in order to achieve the goal of sustainable development but also to identify and avert possible problems. There is a lack of scientific literature dealing with the Tiny House Movement and the associated form of housing on an international level (Shearer and Burton, 2019), especially in Germany. Information is available through various forms of media, such as television reports, blogs, periodical articles and narratives. However, academic reflections are very limited (Ford and Gomez-Lanier, 2017).

The aim of this study is to examine Tiny Houses regarding essential characteristics[1] for innovations in BOP markets. The following questions will be answered: to what extent does this type of housing (the Tiny House) serve as a BOP innovation for Germany? Does it serve as an opportunity against inequalities? Which current challenges and potential for Germany can be identified under the lens of the three sustainability dimensions? Answering these questions, expert interviews were conducted that were evaluated by means of content analysis according to Mayring (2015).

The structure of the paper is as follows: an overview of relevant literature will be followed by the methodological approach. In the next section, the results for all the principles examined will be presented. Following this, resulting potentials and risks at the level of the sustainability dimensions will be discussed and hypotheses will be identified. A short summary with relevant implications is the final part of the study.

BOP innovations and tiny houses

Principles for innovations in BOP markets

Tiny Houses could be a valuable BOP innovation, but are they – and how sustainable would they be? The origin of the BOP concept (BOP 1.0) has been provided by CK Prahalad (Prahalad and Hammond, 2002; Prahalad and Hart, 2002), who, in particular, highlights the benefits that can arise from and for multinational companies (MNCs) when they provide products and services for developing BOP markets (Follman, 2012). From this perspective, the BOP markets are primarily seen as consumer markets (Kuo et al., 2018). In the second generation, the integration of the BOP population into all levels, from the design of products to the local sale of those products and additional services, is of great relevance and the primary view of the BOP population as consumers is dampened (Follman, 2012). Within BOP 2.0, the focus is on the co-creation of values between organisations and

BOP consumers through partnerships (Kuo et al., 2018). Simanis and Hart (2008, p. 2) provide second generation BOP criteria. 'Expand Imagination' and 'Deep Dialogue' appear to be relevant criteria in connection with the analysed type of housing. Neither Simanis and Hart (2008) nor Williams et al. (2012), who later add these criteria to a framework, provide a clear definition of 'Expand Imagination'. The focus should be on 'new business ideas and models that exceed what either partner could imagine or create on their own' (Simanis and Hart, 2008, p. 2). Frugal innovations and BOP innovations are pivotal for the overall development (Arnold, 2018b). Tiny Houses are connected to a social movement that is also related to its specific business models. This concept was taken up and adapted to social thinking patterns. Changes in these patterns might also have an impact on prevailing business models and therefore appear to be highly relevant for the underlying study. 'Deep Dialogue' seems equally important because there is usually a very close exchange between manufacturers and buyers in connection with the type of housing analysed (Tiny Houses Consulting UG, n.d.). BOP 3.0 approaches a focus on the 'active' role of producers for the BOP population (Pedrozo and Sato, 2015). Great importance should be given to the integration of social actors of a corresponding region in all process steps and to the inclusion of the BOP producers' interests (Pedrozo and Sato, 2015). Accordingly, previous points of view in connection with BOP markets can be extended by using the perspective of an inclusive business strategy (Kuo et al., 2018). The target group can take on the role of employees, producers and business owners (Ibid.). It has yet to be examined whether Tiny Houses can cover all three BOP views and represent a corresponding innovation for the BOP.

Therefore, Prahalad (2005) gives a total of 12 principles for innovations in BOP markets as part of the first BOP generation (Prahalad and Hammond, 2002; Prahalad and Hart, 2002). He describes these characteristics (see Figure 5.1) as essential building blocks for BOP markets and creates a very comprehensive framework for the promotion of processes and/or product innovations, which should enable companies to enter BOP markets (Scholl, 2013). Prahalad (2005) points out that not all innovation elements listed need to be relevant to specific projects, but that targeted selection and priority setting should take place. Accordingly, even Tiny Houses do not have to fulfil all principles to be such type of innovation, but need to address targeted settings. Moreover, aspects of BOP 2.0 and 3.0 as addressed by Simanis and Hart (2008) and Kuo et al. (2018) will be included in our investigation and are part of the reference frame (see Figure 5.1).

Tiny Houses and sustainable housing

Tiny Houses have been used for several years in conjunction with the BOP population, especially for homeless people in the USA (Heben, 2014). Examples of Tiny House Villages are Eugene's Collaborative Village or

Prahalad (2005,p. 25 ff)	Simanis and Hart (2008, p. 2)	Kuo et al. (2018, p. 2)
Price Performance	Deep Dialogue	BoP as Employers, Producers and Business Owners
Innovation: Hybrids	Expand Imagination	
Scale of Operations		
Sustainable Development: Eco-Friendly		
Identifying Functionality		
Process Innovation		
Deskilling of Work		
Education of Customers		
Designing for Hostile Infrastructure		
Interfaces		
Distribution: Accessing the Customer		
BoP Markets Essentially Allow Us to Challenge the Conventional Wisdom in Delivery of Products and Services		

Figure 5.1 Principles for innovations in BOP markets and reference frame (author's own source based on Prahalad, 2005; Simanis and Hart, 2008; Kuo et al., 2018).

Portland's Autonomous Village (Ibid.). The question arises whether this would also be feasible for Germany. There are already a few projects in Germany as well as in Austria which are mainly dependent on donations and aim to make small houses usable as an innovative concept and to provide shelter for the homeless. For example, Little Home Köln e.V. (2019) in Germany provides very small dwellings for the homeless. However, central implementation has failed up to now and this is particularly evident in the demolition of individual buildings (Fröhlich, 2019). Tiny Houses are also being used as a tool to help refugees enter the labour market. Another example is the fundraising project KUNA, which allows refugees to build individual houses to give them access to existing networks, German work culture and support in finding a job (Watling, 2018). Therefore, this type of house might be used as a possibility for social integration and poverty reduction, and it implicates a significant contribution to social sustainability. Other advantages concerning social sustainability (Lüdecke, 2019) might be found in the community idea. Pope (2018) shows how community-based learning can serve as a tool for building small houses for the homeless. Additional social significance is also reflected in an alternative lifestyle (Kilman, 2016; Kichanova, 2019).

The previous section highlights the importance of the different dimensions of sustainability for housing and points to opportunities for Tiny Houses to correspond with those dimensions. These small houses have advanced within a few years as a new, environmentally friendly housing alternative to reduce waste in the housing industry (Ford and Gomez-Lanier, 2017). The so called 'Tiny House Movement' or 'small house movement' (Anson, 2014, p. 292) is associated with this form of living. It originates in connection with catchwords such as *clearing out*, *reduction* or *minimisation* in the 19th century and is also supported in the 20th century by the credo 'less is more' (Ford and Gomez-Lanier, 2017, p. 394). According to Shearer and Burton (2019), a distinction should be made between this *movement* and the Tiny House. The two are closely related, but the focus of this study is on the latter.

In addition to various sizes, these houses are differentiated into mobile and fixed houses. For one thing, this lack of standardisation complicates the generalisation of research objects and illustrates the associated diversity. This opens the door to various possible applications (Shearer and Burton, 2019). Likewise, individual concepts can often be flexibly designed and used. While these concepts in the field of design enable adaptability to different environmental influences, excessive flexibility can also result in a barely controllable degree of complexity and increasing resource consumption and waste (Gabe et al., 2009). These potential rebound effects (Greening et al., 2000) must be governed, and this requires awareness and expertise.

Against the background of the potentially adverse effects mentioned above, each (Tiny) housing solution should be examined with regard to its individual potential and challenges in terms of sustainable development. To achieve the goal of sustainable development defined by World Commission on Environment and Development (WCED, 1987), housing should consider all three dimensions of sustainability. Affordable housing solutions play a particularly important role in the economic context and simultaneously have an impact on the social level. Concerning the ecological dimension, high priority should be given to resource-saving solutions in the implementation of housing concepts. Said et al. (2010) state there is an understanding of sustainable concepts in the housing industry, but sustainable approaches have not yet been sufficiently implemented. Grossmann (2019) emphasises the great potential of the housing sector to reduce negative impacts on the environment. The potential of Tiny Houses to reduce the negative impacts of the housing sector can only be realised if all of the various dimensions are taken into account.

In many cases, building materials have targeted ecologically sustainable aspects, and various suppliers have aimed at energy-efficient solutions (e.g. DreamWood GmbH carpentry, GOTINY, WW Wohnwagon). The relevance of energy-efficient concepts in connection with ecological sustainability and the achievement of local and state emission reduction targets has been highlighted by Birck and Pattison (2016). In addition to the high consumption of resources, emissions from the housing sector are a major issue to be considered in the context of potentially more sustainable design (Svane, 2002). This plays a major role for Tiny House self-construction

(Grimble, 2019), particularly when it comes to recycling and upcycling concepts.

Ignoring the social and ecological aspects of housing, for example in rehabilitation programmes, can lead to unsustainable urban development (Winston and Eastaway, 2008). In addition to the above-mentioned social and environmental concerns, Wyatt (2016) emphasises potential *economic benefits*. These housing forms have the potential to be less expensive than standard single-family houses because of their smaller size, which means they could have economic benefits such as lower housing costs (Anson, 2014; Ayoub, 2018). Nevertheless, the actual economic benefits are still unclear, especially due to the variety of Tiny Houses. Possibilities for financial support should be provided in addition to cost-effective concepts. Financial schemes can help make housing more sustainable by providing financial support (e.g. loans) and creating incentives to integrate eco-technologies and to reduce emissions from this sector (Ross et al., 2010; Barbosa et al., 2018). This demonstrates that these effects also influence the other layers of sustainability. According to Ross et al. (2010), user acceptance and user support are also essential elements for increasing sustainability. This kind of support could be essential, particularly in respect to the BOP. Sunikka (2003) emphasises that fiscal instruments are contributing to the slow progress in knowledge and the implementation of guidelines concerning sustainable housing.

Up to now, exactly which sustainability challenges and potentials will arise for the introduction of this type of housing has yet to be explored in Germany, especially in case of BOP markets, although they are of paramount importance.

Methodology

Research design

Since this work deals with a field that has barely been researched thus far (Shearer and Burton, 2019), an exploratory single case study design has been applied (Yin, 1994; Tellis, 1997). This is suitable for generating hypotheses (Döring and Bortz, 2016), which is an essential goal of this study. A deductive approach based on semi-structured expert interviews has primarily been used (Mayring, 2015). Due to the fact that the underlying topic is a field that has received limited research so far, interviews with experts are recommended. The relevant people usually have privileged access to information concerning decision-making processes or specific groups of people (Meuser and Nagel, 2002), and thus possess special knowledge on a specific topic (Gläser and Laudel, 2010). All persons interviewed in this study are highly connected and can draw on correspondingly diverse knowledge of the topic. A qualitative content analysis as proposed by Mayring (2015) has been used to evaluate the material. This method is mainly driven by its systematic approach and its exceptional rule-making (Mayring, 2019). Furthermore, the method is easily applicable if a specific question is asked (Ibid.).

The expert interviews were conducted by telephone in August 2019 and ranged from 50 minutes to 1 hour. All questions were based on a semi-structured guideline. There were 23 questions in total, which were deductively derived based on existing literature with regard to the prescribed reference frame (see Figure 5.1; Prahalad, 2005; Simanis and Hart, 2008; Kuo et al., 2018), and adapted to the studied form of living. The indicators were raised by questions, for example, *Functionality* – To what extent can the functionality of a Tiny House be adapted to the target group? or *Use without electricity and water* – How can Tiny Houses function without external access to electricity and water? After transcribing the complete recorded material, the evaluation was conducted between September and October 2019 using Maxqda18 in order to carry out a structuring content analysis according to Mayring (2015). First and foremost, the entire text material was worked through and essential passages were highlighted. For this purpose, the material was paraphrased, generalised and reduced. In order to increase the research quality, this process was repeated and re-examined. The categories illustrate to what extent the Tiny House can serve as a BOP innovation and form the basis for the sustainability discussion. Possibilities and challenges regarding the three dimensions of sustainability have been analysed with reference to the literature. The deductive category system is shown in Figure 5.2.

As shown in Figure 5.2, the criteria *Interface design*, a principle described by Prahalad (2005), was excluded due to the fact that it has little relevance in this investigation, however, it may be included in later studies with real applications. In addition to the criteria transferred directly from the BOP literature, *application potential* and *financial support* have been included in the deductive category system. The former supports the creation of an idea for specific applications of the (product) Tiny House as a BOP innovation in Germany, as well as the identification of existing projects. This category has been included in the study and thus also in the results section, even though it does not represent a principle in the narrower sense. *Financial support* has been added because it is highly relevant, especially in the context of associations and different levels of poverty. A second (inductive) categorical system was generated and the complete material was coded using the coding guideline (see Appendix). An inductive system was created (Mayring, 2015) in addition to the deductive category system. All inductively generated codes (e.g. *materials*, *circular design, location* etc.) serve to identify relevant topics connected to the investigated characteristics.

The interview questions were tailored to people with specific background knowledge concerning the target group; the focus was placed on the target group in order to obtain the most specific information possible. This approach can be justified by the principle of understanding and the principle of

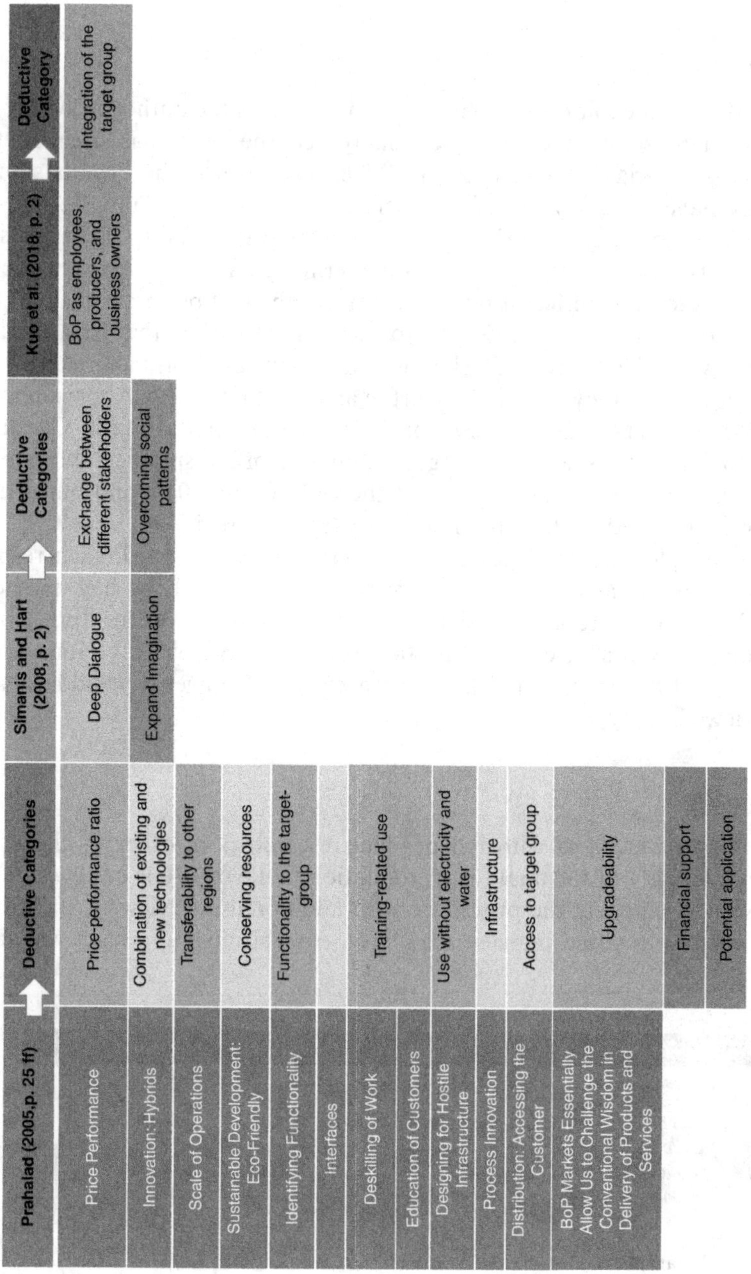

Prahalad (2005,p. 25 ff)	Deductive Categories	Simanis and Hart (2008, p. 2)	Deductive Categories	Kuo et al. (2018, p. 2)	Deductive Category
Price Performance	Price-performance ratio	Deep Dialogue	Exchange between different stakeholders	BoP as employees, producers, and business owners	Integration of the target group
Innovation: Hybrids	Combination of existing and new technologies	Expand Imagination	Overcoming social patterns		
Scale of Operations	Transferability to other regions				
Sustainable Development: Eco-Friendly	Conserving resources				
Identifying Functionality	Functionality to the target-group				
Interfaces					
Deskilling of Work	Training-related use				
Education of Customers					
Designing for Hostile Infrastructure	Use without electricity and water				
Process Innovation	Infrastructure				
Distribution: Accessing the Customer	Access to target group				
BoP Markets Essentially Allow Us to Challenge the Conventional Wisdom in Delivery of Products and Services	Upgradeability				
	Financial support				
	Potential application				

Figure 5.2 Category system of framework (author's own source).

openness (Gläser and Laudel, 2010). Before the actual interviews, pre-tests were carried out to ensure the understanding and quality of the questions. The interviewees (B1–B4) were informed about the recording of the interviews and their consent was obtained. The names of the persons, associations and companies will remain anonymous.

Sampling

Since this is an explorative approach and, as far as the author is aware, no predominant solution exists in Germany yet, the focus has been on the following criteria for the selection of the interviewees: the experts should already have several years of experience in the topic of Tiny Houses, be active in an existing network and have important knowledge in the areas of Tiny House construction, challenges in Germany and possible applications. The aim is to unite different points of view. In the first place, people that are highly connected to the research topic, namely within the Tiny Houses context, were addressed and asked whether they could provide relevant information and if they would take part in an expert interview. Approximately 10–15 respondents knew at most one Tiny House application in Germany that explicitly deals with the target group and offers specific solutions. A letter was sent to the interviewees at the end of July 2019, and out of five persons contacted, four were interviewed (see Figure 5.3).

Two people with management functions were interviewed, each respectively from an association and an NGO. One of them had previous knowledge on the topic of social exclusion and poverty due to his/her own activities as well as a close connection with the topic of Tiny Houses. An employee of a manufacturer and a private person/blogger were additionally interviewed.

Limitations

Discussions were held with independent researchers in order to check the internal validity of the analysis. A limitation is the one-time conduct of the interviews; repeating the procedure with additional interviewers and cross-border analysis could increase reliability. An objective approach was used

Interviewee	Affiliation	Duration
B1	Manufacturer	60 min
B2	Private Person/Blogger	60 min
B3	Association	52 min
B4	NGO	40 min

Figure 5.3 Sample.

when conducting and evaluating the interviews, however, it might be necessary to involve several independent interviewers and evaluators in order to verify this. Finding people who are currently concerned with the target group in Germany and the topic of Tiny Houses is difficult as the community is still operating on a niche level. Therefore, the aim of this investigation was not to draw generalised conclusions, but primarily to identify current possibilities and challenges to the object of investigation (Mayring, 2007).

Results

Table 5.1 provides an overview of the interview results which highlight the social, environmental and economic sustainability issues in connection with the investigated principles for BOP innovations. Selected aspects have been highlighted in the following.

According to the interviewees, there are hardly any ***applications*** in Germany with Tiny Houses as a solution for the target group. One association in Germany was mentioned that offers necessities for the homeless (B3). The primary goal is to provide shelter and to be used as a stepping stone with the objective of helping these people get off the street (B4).

The ***price-performance ratio*** of a Tiny House always depends on how the house is built (B2). From a purely objective point of view, in relation to the area of square metres, it is even disproportionately more expensive than a conventional housing construction (B1). In absolute terms, living in a small house would be cheaper (resource consumption, long-term savings) (B1) compared to the usual 'bigger' homes. A significant potential for savings may be the possibility to acquire leased property and thus significantly save in comparison to larger properties.

Financial support is an essential aspect for achieving the implementation of Tiny House solutions for the BOP. A major challenge is therefore the lending, which is almost to be ruled out, as people with low financial resources generally do not receive loans (B2). One possibility that already serves for financing is combining donations and building events (B4). Companies pay to contribute to this and help build shelter for the homeless. As a further possibility, associations could try to become social carriers in order to receive co-financing by the federal and state governments (B4).

It can be seen that ***new technologies*** are being used for the houses in various areas. Due to the experimental character of small houses it may be easier to implement novelties than in large houses (B2). The potential for water recycling can be realised by integrated circular designs. The so-called shower loop (B2) and specific filter treatment systems (B1) should therefore be mentioned.

The ***infrastructure*** is a particularly critical aspect. It was deliberately undefined in advance in order to see which topics were relevant for the respondents. Above all, communication, a person's financial situation and

Table 5.1 Resulting potentials and challenges under the lens of sustainability (source: interview feedback from B1, B2, B3, and B4)

Principles	*Economic*		*Social*		*Ecological*	
	Potentials	*Challenges*	*Potentials*	*Challenges*	*Potentials*	*Challenges*
Possible applications	Cost savings through integration of target group; Financial advantages compared to other social housing options	Provision of land and financial support by the city	Affordable housing for marginalised people in a scientific/ experimental context; Accommodation and springboard/ reintegration measure to leave streets; Transitional living space, immediate aid; Keeping people in their own environment		Reusable plot of lands	
Price-performance ratio (Prahalad; 2005, **p. 25 No. 1)**	Living in a Tiny House is cheaper (absolutely seen); leasehold properties more available than for conventional	High price per square metre compared to conventional forms of living; scale for assessing costs	Feasible self-construction can reduce individual costs		Low consumption of resources; Use of recycled materials	

	houses; partly improved price-performance ratio for insulating materials; partly use of cost-effective materials (recycling)	questionable; costs depend highly on the individual expansion; weight restrictions; long-term experience missing; frequently high planning and service costs			
Financial support	Combination of donations and building events	Permanent support measures (donations, subsidised loans); co-financing by the federal and state governments; further development of the market		Loans often not granted to persons with low financial resources	
Combination of existing and new technologies (Prahalad, 2005, **p. 25 No. 2)**	Experimental character facilitates implementation (in cities)	Weight restrictions; reach critical mass; possibly high costs for specific techniques	Experience of individuals important to consider a further implementation	Necessary willingness to act in a sustainable manner	Developments for the preservation and lightness of materials; Continuous further development of

(*Continued*)

Table 5.1 (Continued)

Principles	*Economic*		*Social*		*Ecological*	
	Potentials	*Challenges*	*Potentials*	*Challenges*	*Potentials*	*Challenges*
					efficient solutions; Circulation (shower loop) and filter treatment systems; Cold running system for energy and water; Multi-purpose techniques	
Infrastructure (Prahalad; 2005, **p. 26 No. 6)**	Area as a central and critical aspect of dissemination; municipal support relevant; cities as mediators	Make available the area; financial support (donate, sponsor)	Communication to connect people	Challenge for all consumer groups to find a suitable plot of land; finance; central parking space management		
Access to target group (Prahalad; 2005, **p. 27 No. 11)**	Internet for access; charities	Provide location (e.g. by social institutions)	Direct (personal) contact, getting to know each other; existing motivations for implementing project			Presence of the location

Transferability to other regions (Prahalad, 2005, **p. 25 No. 3)**	Utilisation of grey zones; EU or German wide regulations for increasing transferability; Umbrella association; partly at the same time similar efforts in different countries; traditional construction methods in other countries partly comparable	Permanent support by other region; Different rules				Other regional conditions that may influence material use
Conserving resources (Prahalad, 2005**; p. 26 No. 4)**	Definition of specific criteria for construction; introduction of a certificate	Manufacturer reaction	Participants with backgrounds such as minimalism		Predominantly use of domestic materials; low resource consumption during production as target; customers line up on conscious consumption; reduced resource consumption in	

(*Continued*)

Table 5.1 (Continued)

Principles	*Economic*		*Social*		*Ecological*	
	Potentials	*Challenges*	*Potentials*	*Challenges*	*Potentials*	*Challenges*
					the area of use compared to conventional housing; upcycling and recycling (especially for self-building)	
Adaptation of functionality to the target-group (Prahalad, 2005, **p. 26 No. 5)**	Innovative character; Possible long-term savings through efficiency	Additional costs for customer (initial investment); Considerable consulting and planning effort	Needs orientation, Individualisation	Many decisions necessary	Improvement of efficiency and sufficiency	
Upgradeability (Prahalad, 2005, **p. 26 No. 12)**	Domestic companies could act as sponsors	Additional costs for customer; influence on transportability; investment should amortise itself; high cost pressure from foreign companies	The will to have one's own environment beautiful as possibility to address communities	Extensions must be financially viable; may use of more affordable foreign technical products and possibly indirectly support poor working conditions	Co-design of the living environment at a fixed location	Use of cheaper technical, but not regional products

Training-related use (Prahalad, 2005, **p. 26 No. 7/8)**			Relative ease of use			Instruction for special toilet shapes, ventilation or special technical designs (self-sufficient elements); Increase in efficiency is also linked to the state of knowledge among users
Use without electricity and water (Prahalad, 2005, **p. 26, No. 9)**	Grey areas in the power supply area; public support measures for using resource-saving technology; determination of specific criteria that could eliminate the need for compulsory connection;	Cost dependence of power generation; before purchasing technical equipment: considering weighing, durability, costs, amortisation, location, meaningfulness, weight restrictions;	Use of public places for water and electricity; under specific conditions, possible avoidance of compulsory connection	Consumers may have to rely on water tanks, which greatly increases the individual effort involved	Power generation through photovoltaics and storage technology; wastewater treatment plant rarely requires fresh water	Power generation dependents on regional conditions; Efficiency and seasonal constraints; Waste water must be properly disposed of

(*Continued*)

Table 5.1 (Continued)

Principles	*Economic*		*Social*		*Ecological*	
	Potentials	*Challenges*	*Potentials*	*Challenges*	*Potentials*	*Challenges*
	public places for the provision of electricity and water for the target group; offering public places for water and electricity	compulsory connection and high costs; municipalities must ensure proper disposal of waste water; high requirements and special technology necessary				
Integration of the target group (Kuo et al., 2018**, p. 2)**	Integration of the target group; creation of corresponding possibilities (e.g. tutorials, through workshop); reintegration measures	Integration of the long-term unemployed	Target group as workforce; creation of success experiences; appreciation for a project; social value is generated; reintegration into society, ability to live one's own life; be taught how to enjoy work; reduction of criminality; reduction of litter			Reduction of litter

Exchange between different stakeholders (Simanis and Hart, 2008, **p. 2)**	Network with central contact person (e.g. through city)		Reduction of inhibitions and inclusion of critical topics through personal exchange	Currently high manual effort	
Overcoming social patterns (Simanis and Hart, 2008, **p. 2)**	Overcoming classic consumption patterns		Minimalism, downsizing, sustainability lead to questioning of current behaviour patterns; awareness of environmental responsibility on the part of users often plays a role; vision of another society (focus from job to individuality); other ways of dealing with and other relations to the topic of homelessness		Reducing the use of resources and raising awareness; demonstration of the necessity for reduced space utilisation

location are essential aspects from interviewees' point of view. The property on which one places a Tiny House represents a critical and central aspect which, according to B1, also influences how quickly these houses can spread in Germany. This is lacking for both 'normal' buyer groups and for those who are unable to finance such a property (B1). Accordingly, major infrastructural challenges for the integration of a BOP solution lie in providing both financial support and available space.

Access to the target group can take place in person and via the Internet. B4 describes access via Facebook and e-mail (where interested parties contact each other directly), as well as face-to-face contact through the association. In any case, a personal meeting between the association management and potential residents is a relevant starting point (B4).

Transferability of specific solutions ***to other regions*** is generally conceivable from the perspective of the interviewees. B1 sees no reason for them not being transferable, even if regulations are different. It can be assumed that the regulations in other countries are not as strict as they are in Germany (B1). One way to facilitate transfer to other regions might be to establish EU-wide schemes (B2).

The ***conservation of resources*** seems to have high relevance, especially for the production of Tiny Houses. Manufacturers in Germany pay attention to the lowest possible consumption of resources in order to produce the least possible negative consequences for residents and the environment (B2). Upcycling and recycling potential is also highly relevant, especially in the area of self-construction (B1).

Almost all manufacturers build to individual customer requirements, which means that almost 100% customisation is possible (B1). Even series or standard models can be individualised using additional equipment (B1, B4). Accordingly, these houses can be adapted to their individual purpose and thus be designed in a ***functional*** way. Nevertheless, size and weight restrictions must be respected (B1).

In general, there are several ***upgrading*** possibilities for Tiny Houses. In this context, care should be taken to maintain the transportability, especially for mobile versions (B1). Highlighting how residents help to positively shape their environment (B1) might be one way of making communities approvingly aware of the issue and of integrating this form of housing in Germany.

It turns out that there seem to be only a few areas in which ***training*** or instruction ***for use*** may be necessary. This mainly depends on the corresponding technical design, for example in the area of self-sufficient elements (B1, B3). Use of a special toilet (e.g. a dry toilet or compost toilet) might require a certain amount of instruction (B1, B2, B4).

Theoretically, a considerable amount is feasible in the area of self-sufficiency (***use without external access for electricity and water***) depending on regional conditions and costs (B2, B3). Nevertheless, certain points should be weighed up, such as the durability, costs, amortisation, location and usefulness of such a system (B2). Weight restrictions must often be considered (B1). Water and electricity can be obtained from public places for BOP use (B4).

It is conceivable to involve the target group as labourers with several options (B1). Workshops can be one way and might be implemented as re***integration*** measures for homeless people (B4). There could be potential in showing the homeless that work and a stable social structure can be enjoyable. This must often be relearned (B4). Nevertheless, it can be a major challenge to integrate a long-term unemployed person into the construction process repeatedly in order to give him a job (B4).

From a social point of view, significant potential exists in the changed perceptions of the BOP population. B4 describes potentials of change in dealing with the homeless in our society as another important reason: the residents become visible to society in a different way due to the fact that blinders disappear because of their accommodation. When talking to each other, it often becomes clear that homelessness can happen to anyone (B4). Thus, existing ***social*** (thinking) ***patterns*** could be ***overcome***.

The ***exchange between different stakeholders*** can be considered highly relevant. An exchange via networks (B1) plays a particularly important role. One potential may be to set up a network in which there would be a central contact person such as the city. So far, this effort is still very manual (B3).

In summary, the results indicate the high relevance of the examined principles and make clear that Tiny Houses can be seen as an innovation for BOP markets. Depending on their application, individual potentials and challenges arise for each principle in order to integrate a sustainable Germany-wide solution. The results also suggest that Tiny Houses in Germany can help to reduce existing inequalities if the BOP population is integrated into existing processes.

Discussion

In the following section, specific potentials, challenges and further research as well as practical implications will be highlighted within an economic, social and ecological setting. It should be noted that individual factors cannot always be captured in only one concept and that effects may also be present in other areas.

Economic aspects

The interviews reveal that there are hardly any existing innovative solutions from Tiny Houses with the focus on the target group, or if present, they are not available in the form of nationwide integrated concepts. In Germany, there is currently one association that is specifically concerned with providing homeless people with permanent accommodation (in the form of very small private dwellings) and aims to reintegrate people into society (Little Home Köln e.V., 2019). A partial lack of support from the state or municipalities becomes clear, which can notably be seen in the problem of parking spaces, also reflected in media reports (Osiewacz, 2018/19). The desire for a Tiny House often goes hand in hand with the idea of being able to build small and save costs. Finding suitable sites (also smaller than usual) or parking spaces which must also be located on private ground is often difficult (Osiewacz, 2019).

Usually, available sites are designed for large houses, and there is a lack of small ones with suitable construction possibilities (Tiny Houses Consulting UG, n.d.). According to discussions with Tiny House owners and manufacturers, dependencies on the support of local authorities determine possible sites and clarify the permitted form of construction. Persons belonging to the target group generally do not possess private sites or corresponding alternative physical or financial access enabling them to place such housing solutions. This makes them even more dependent on external support options. There is already a lack of locations for normal buyer groups, and this component may be much more difficult to obtain for people in precarious life situations. It once repeatedly becomes clear in practice if one would like to forgo an expensive building plot.

This problem dominates the Tiny House Movement on an international level (Evans, 2017) and thus hinders the use of various possibilities, because the necessary parking space is continuously cited as the starting point. Findings of this study show that the association's work occasionally helps more people get off the streets than seems to be the case with social institutions (B4). These statements are based only on the interview data and are difficult to verify as there is currently a lack of accurate data (Hansen, 2012). Further investigations should be carried out in this respect.

Due to the wide variety of Tiny Houses (Shearer and Burton, 2019), no generalised statements should be made concerning the actual price–performance ratio. The costs are very individual and depend on many factors: size, technical design, self-construction or external construction, origin of materials, etc. B1 stated that it is questionable which standards should be applied in the case at hand, and whether absolute costs or other factors are not more decisive. The quality of life should not only be defined by the size of the house, because life in and within a Tiny House is often quite different, and people tend to live need-oriented and in harmony with their environment (Kilman, 2016). Reports show that Millennials already define their quality of life differently than their predecessors. Instead of housing size, factors such as proximity to the workplace and good accessibility play a greater role (Kichanova, 2019). Mobile homes would have advantages in this respect. Results of this study and previous applications show that it is nevertheless possible to keep costs very low if it is only a question of establishing a shelter (Ayoub, 2018).

If self-financing is excluded or only partially possible, this study points to necessary *financial support*. The literature shows that microloans have already been used for BOP markets in the past and created entrepreneurs in this way (Follman, 2012). A differentiation of poverty levels may also be relevant. If a regular income can be proven, loans to finance a house could possibly be considered, depending on the level of income. Further research is needed in this respect. Additionally, donations or companies paying for their work on a specific project may be appropriate for financing (B4). In line with the BOP literature, B4 states that in order to be able to work on a long-term and sustainable basis, co-financing by the federal and state governments would be necessary for associations already active in this field. Pedrozo and Sato (2015) emphasise the state's role as a catalyst for the sustainable progress of global actors and local development. First and foremost, incentives should be created to involve the BOP population, in particular by promoting business types that support local skills and knowledge, as well as production based on natural resources. Results of this study indicate that the already mentioned workshops for the Tiny House production could be very suitable in this context. In addition to the *financial requirements* and *location*, *communication* is an essential *infrastructural requirement* from the respondents' point of view.

Communication plays an important role because integrated solutions can only be promoted if people with the necessary motivation and similar interests come together. A central administrative unit, for example, in the form of an association, was often considered desirable and has meanwhile been established (Schleyer, 2019). This demonstrates the rapid progress of the topic in Germany at the moment. The association can play a mediating role and take up topics such as the allocation of parking spaces, financing, development, etc. In addition to the possibility for centralising all topics and having a mutual contact person, an association has further options for approaching cities compared to private individuals; it might help to counteract the currently described fragmentation of the topic in Germany. In times of digitalisation, importance should be given to the Internet in establishing contacts. If no personal access is available, public access can be used in this particular case. Nevertheless, personal contact with the target group is important in order to learn about the background and goals of the people, because the motivation is relevant to implementing assistance.

Environmental aspects

In the respondents' view, the conservation of resources has been given high priority, which once again makes this form of housing socially attractive. The housing sector offers great potential for conserving resources and reducing emissions (Grossmann, 2019). Current manufacturers of the Tiny House Movement are primarily trying to use regional materials, pay attention to the low consumption of resources, and would like to generate the fewest negative consequences possible (B2). Simultaneously, users are coming from areas such as minimalism and are striving for a conscious lifestyle. Recycling and upcycling also play a role, especially in self-construction. This corresponds to the existing literature (Grimble, 2019). Manufacturers and users therefore often complement each other. Actual implementation of such measures could be supported by clearly defined regulations and certificates (B3).

The self-sufficient use of Tiny Houses could be relevant, especially in precarious life situations, as there might be no water or electricity available. The results point to various possible solutions depending on the degree of technological design, associated costs, regional and financial conditions, weather conditions, and building regulations (Pieńkowski and Zbaraszewski, 2019). A compulsory connection is necessary, but does not fit completely with these concepts. The study points to cost comparisons and control instances in order to make it possible to avoid a compulsory connection.

If it is only a matter of providing people with shelter, the interviews show that it can be done relatively well, as there are public places for getting electricity and water. However, a basic requirement is the necessary parking space, which is again one of the biggest hurdles. Therefore, cooperation with the respective cities is essential. Unused areas could possibly be made available for this purpose. Other studies on sustainable housing also emphasise the importance of fallow areas that offer the possibility of fulfilling valuable ecological as well as social functions (Korsunsky, 2019). An advantage in this context may be the experimental character of these small forms of housing, which makes it easier to implement and try new developments (B2). As a test, homeless villages whose role models already exist in other countries (Heben, 2014) could also be analysed in terms of their transferability to Germany.

Another advantage is that the property can usually be reused, which is hardly possible in the case of large construction projects. Thus, Tiny Houses may be made usable for a certain period for the target group and the property could be repurposed later. The houses can also often be adapted, extended or reduced for specific-use purposes (hotel rooms, apartments, etc.). This means that they can be used in a needs-oriented and thus resource-saving manner.

Social aspects

It can be assumed that Tiny Houses, as potential innovations for the BOP, can generate social, individual and environmental value and contribute to overcoming current social patterns. It would be conceivable to integrate the target group into the value creation process, thus creating jobs, training places or the opportunity to learn certain skills. This would facilitate entry into workplaces and creates a sense of success, giving people hope for their lives. Miller and Happell (2006) emphasise the importance of hope, particularly in relation to people marginalised by diseases or other social conditions.

Since the working time is a particularly costly part of production, the results point to the possibility of saving costs depending on the form of the integration concept (e.g. workshops). This could in turn have a positive effect on the overall price and affordability of the product, making it more attractive for people with lower incomes. The highest priority should be to enable people to regain an independent life. This would also enable them to pay taxes and thus give something back to state and society (B4). Recent application examples for homeless people point to positive developments in terms of the reduction of litter (B4) and crime (Lüdecke, 2019) at corresponding locations, which in turn would benefit not only society, but the environment as well.

There is the potential that current social patterns can be broken thanks to this form of housing. Existing consumer behaviour should be mentioned here. Since backgrounds such as minimalism, downsizing or a sustainable lifestyle are often relevant for users and manufacturers, consumption could be questioned more strongly and become more needs-oriented. Accordingly, the results complement existing studies that highlight the increasing awareness of consumption and the environment (Kilman, 2016). Regarding the target group, there is the potential to put people in a different light and above all to make them visible to society (B4); things can only be changed if the problem is seen and recognised.

Transferability to other regions could be particularly important against the background of an increasing number of homeless eastern European people (Fokken, 2017) in order to give them potential in their own countries. This may contribute to the objective of reducing inequalities between countries. Importantly, transferring concepts from Germany to other regions requires permanent support from these countries (B4). Obstacles could arise due to legal requirements or different climate conditions. Since the made usable as Tiny House Movement already exists in other countries, it could also be easier to integrate national concepts on an international level. Based on this investigation, the following hypotheses can be formulated:

- The better and clearer cities and municipalities in Germany strengthen the availability of suitable parking spaces for Tiny Houses the greater market expansion is for this form of housing in Germany.
- The more the BOP population is integrated into workshops for the construction of Tiny Houses the lower the costs become for the production of a house.
- The more Tiny Houses are made usable as BOP innovations the stronger improvement results will be for social integration compared to previously established concepts.

Conclusion

Due to a variety of causes, the threat of housing loss and related poverty, homelessness and social exclusion continue to represent increasing problems in Germany. Existing measures seem to have reached their limits or do not function sufficiently. Against this background, it may make sense to consider alternative concepts, such as those of Tiny House living, in order to address these problems in a sustainable manner.

Tiny Houses can be seen as an innovation for BOP markets, fulfilling essential criteria of all three BOP approaches. The underlying study demonstrates the extent to which the Tiny House can be adapted as a BOP innovation for the German market. According to Prahalad (2005), not all principles described need to be adaptable to a case. Nevertheless, criteria must be chosen according to the priority for the given situation. This means that for each situation, it is necessary to look carefully which principles can be useful in the individual case. In the context of homelessness, for example, a house does not necessarily have to be self-sufficient, because public facilities can also be used.

Based on the principles examined, individual potentials and challenges for Germany have been derived and discussed under the lenses of ecological, social and economic issues. Further research, practical implications and hypotheses have been identified. A particularly critical aspect is the placement of the house due to the fact that it represents one of the most essential access requirements for users and is simultaneously a central obstacle for integrating this form of housing nationwide, both for normal user groups and for socially disadvantaged people. Specifically, from a societal perspective, the results show that even existing social patterns can be overcome with Tiny Houses. Furthermore, the results suggest the possibility in the reduction of existing inequalities by reintegrating people into society and make them visible in a new way. Accordingly, there is a need for urban and community support, especially in terms of finance and the provision of the necessary locations.

The derived practical and research implications of this study are the following:

- Further studies are necessary to determine whether suitable concepts for integrating the target group would result in price reductions and to analyse the effects on people with lower incomes.
- Further analyses of the various factors and pilot projects would be conceivable in order to see what impact specific solutions would have, for example, on domestic homelessness.
- In addition, more research should be carried out to determine which benchmarks should be used to assess the price-performance ratio of Tiny Houses.
- It is necessary to investigate whether there is a lack of state reintegration measures and if so, why this is the case.
- In order to find cross-national solutions, it is also necessary for the respective countries to support each other.
- The experimental character of the houses can serve to verify the implementation of new concepts and developments. This could also

serve to test the implementation of international exemplary projects in Germany.
- State or municipal support should be expanded in order to make full use of the potential in this area, especially to find and arrange suitable locations for the Tiny Houses. These represent the necessary starting points for implementing appropriate concepts.
- Further progress should be made in strengthening ecologically sustainable construction methods by clearly defining regulations and certification. This could lead to uniform standards.

The views of cities and social institutions should also be integrated within the scope of further research. In addition, a review of the applicability of international projects such as Tiny House villages could be relevant for Germany in connection with homelessness. The aim should not be to understand Tiny Houses as an all-encompassing solution or fashion trend, but to accept them as an innovative way to address current social problems and to accept them in co-existence with other alternative forms of housing.

Note

1 Principles and characteristics are synonymously used in this work.

References

Anson, A (2014). "'The world is my backyard': romanticization, thoreauvian rhetoric, and constructive confrontation in the Tiny House Movement", in William G. Holt (Ed.), *From Sustainable to Resilient Cities: Global Concerns and Urban Efforts*. Bingley, United Kingdom: Emerald Group Publishing Limited, pp. 289–313

Arnold, M (2018a). Inclusive value creation for sustainability of frugal innovations in the base of the pyramid low-income contexts. *Journal of Contemporary Management. 15*, Special Edition (1), 218–244.

Arnold, M (2018b). Sustainability Value Creation in Frugal Contexts to Foster Sustainable Development Goals. Business Strategy and Development. https://doi.org/10.1002/bsd2.36.

Ayoub, N (November 5, 2018). Schon 63 Stück: Dieser Verein verschenkt Mini-Wohnboxen an Obdachlose. Retrieved from https://utopia.de/little-home-obdachlose-holz-haus-72505/ (accessed on 14 November 2019).

BAG Wohnungslosenhilfe e.V. (September 19, 2018). Bezahlbarer Wohnraum für alle - statt Rendite für wenige. Retrieved from https://www.bagw.de/de/presse/index~158.html (accessed on 30 April 2020).

Barbosa, EI, Hernández, A, Castillo, C, & Triay, JC (2018). The role of development banks in financing sustainable and affordable housing: The EcoCasa program. *Housing Finance International*, Summer 34–47.

Birck, N, & Pattison, A (2016). The importance of sustainable affordable housing: A story from San Buenaventura. *Journal of Housing & Community Development, 73*(3), 18–23.

Dembek, K, York, J, & Singh, PJ (2018). Creating value for multiple stakeholders: Sustainable business models at the Base of the Pyramid. *Journal of Cleaner Production, 196*, 1600–1612.

Döring, N, & Bortz, J (2016). *Forschungsmethoden und Evaluation in den Sozial- und Humanwissenschaften* (5., vollst. überarb., akt. u. erw. Aufl. 2016.). Berlin, Heidelberg: Springer.

Evans, K (2017). Integrating Tiny Houses into the American urban fabric: A comparative case study of land use policy change in the Carolinas (Doctoral dissertation, Clemson University).

Finkenwirth, A, & Diemand, S (March 2, 2017). Armutsbericht 2017. Wie arm sind die Deutschen? Retrieved from https://www.zeit.de/wirtschaft/2017-03/armutsbericht-2017-deutschland-paritaetischer-wohlfahrtsverband-faq (accessed on 30 April 2020).

Fokken, S (December 21, 2017). Obdachlosigkeit in Deutschland "Wir haben ein Riesenproblem". Retrieved from https://www.spiegel.de/panorama/gesellschaft/obdachlosigkeit-in-deutschland-wir-haben-ein-riesenproblem-a-1184255.html (accessed on 30 April 2020).

Follman, J (2012). BoP at ten: Evolution and a new lens. *South Asian Journal of Global Business Research, 1*(2), 293–310.

Ford, J, & Gomez-Lanier, L (2017). Are tiny homes here to stay? A review of literature on the tiny house movement. *Family and Consumer Sciences Research Journal, 45*(4), 394–405.

Fowler, PJ, Hovmand, PS, Marcal, KE, & Das, S (2019). Solving homelessness from a complex systems perspective: Insights for prevention responses. *Annual Review of Public Health, 40*, 465–486.

Fröhlich, A (May 2, 2019). "Das war nicht der Auftrag" Ermittlungen nach Abriss von "Little Homes," in Kreuzberg. Retrieved from https://www.tagesspiegel.de/berlin/das-war-nicht-der-auftrag-ermittlungen-nach-abriss-von-little-homes-in-kreuzberg/24281502.html (accessed on 30 April 2020).

Gabe, J, Vale, R, & Vale, B (2009). Trompe l'œil: architects, consumers, and the need to rediscover technical function for ecologically sustainable housing. *International Journal of Consumer Studies, 33*(5), 604–610.

Gläser, J, & Laudel, G (2010). *Experteninterviews und qualitative Inhaltsanalyse. Als Instrumente rekonstruierender Untersuchungen* (Lehrbuch, 4. Aufl.). Wiesbaden: VS Verlag.

Gold S, Hahn, R, & Seuring, S (2013). Sustainable supply chain management in "Base of the Pyramid" food projects-A path to triple bottom line approaches for multinationals? *International Business 22*, 784–799.

Green, MH (January 30, 2016). In a Tiny House Village, Portland's Homeless Find Dignity. Retrieved from http://peopledemandingaction.org/the-people-s-budget/item/499-in-a-tiny-house-village-portland-s-homeless-find-dignity (accessed on 30 April 2020).

Greening, LA, Greene, DL, & Difiglio, C (2000). Energy efficiency and consumption—The rebound effect—A survey. *Energy Policy, 28*(6–7), 389–401.

Grimble, J (June 25, 2019). Tiny Upcycled Homes Made from Trash. Retrieved from https://www.msn.com/en-us/money/realestate/tiny-upcycled-homes-made-from-trash/ss-AACcex7(accessed on 14 October 2019).

Grossmann, K (2019). Using conflicts to uncover injustices in energy transitions: The case of social impacts of energy efficiency policies in the housing sector in Germany. *Global Transitions*, *1*, 148–156.

Hansen, ET (2012). Gibt es echte Obdachlosigkeit in Deutschland? Retrieved from https://www.zeit.de/politik/ausland/2012-11/usa-obdachlosigkeit-armut (accessed on 14 October 2019).

Heben, A (2014). *Tent City Urbanism: From Self-Organized Camps to Tiny House Villages*. Eugene, Oregon: Village Collaborative.

Kichanova, V (2019). Size doesn‘t matter. Giving a green light to micro-homes, Retrieved October 14, 2019, from http://thinkhouse.org.uk/2019/micro.pdf (accessed on November 3, 2019).

Kilman, C. (2016). Small house, big impact: The effect of tiny houses on community and environment. *Undergraduate Journal of Humanistic Studies*, *2*(Winter 2016), 1–12.

Korsunsky, A (2019). From vacant land to urban fallows: A permacultural approach to wasted land in cities and suburbs. *Journal of Political Ecology*, *26*(1), 282–304.

Kuo, T, Shiang, WJ, Hanafi, J, & Chen, S (2018). Co-development of supply chain in the BOP markets. *Sustainability*, *10*(4), 963.

Lecerf, M (2016). *Poverty in the European Union. The Crisis and Its Aftermath*. Brussels: European Parlament.

Little Home Köln e.V. (2019). Retrieved from https://web.archive.org/web/20190118073318/https://little-home.eu/ (accessed on 3 November 2019).

London, T, & Hart, SL (2004). Reinventing strategies for emerging markets: Beyond the transnational model. *Journal of International Business Studies*, *35*(5), 350–370.

Lüdecke, S (September 10, 2019): Stellplatz gegen Präsenz. Retrieved from https://www.facebook.com/Sven.Luedecke (accessed on 7 August 2019).

Mayring, P (September 2007). On generalization in qualitatively oriented research. *Forum Qualitative Sozialforschung/Forum: Qualitative Social Research*, *8*(3) 1–9

Mayring, P (2015). *Qualitative Inhaltsanalyse: Grundlagen und Techniken* (12, überarb. Aufl.). Weinheim: Beltz.

Mayring, P (September, 2019). Qualitative content analysis: Demarcation, varieties, developments. *Forum Qualitative Sozialforschung/Forum: Qualitative Social Research*, *20*(3), 1–15

Meuser, M, & Nagel, U (2002). “ExpertInneninterviews—vielfach erprobt, wenig bedacht”, in Alexander Bogner, Beate Littig, and Wolfgang Menz (Eds.), *Das Experteninterview*, Wiesbaden: VS Verlag für Sozialwissenschaften, pp. 71–93

Miller G, & Happell B (2006). Talking about hope: The use of participant photography. *Issues in Mental Health Nursing*, *27*(10), 1051–1065. doi: 10.1080/01612840600943697.

Osiewacz, F (December 1, 2018). Mini-Holzhaus trotzt bislang hauptsächlich der Witterung. Standortsuche für “Little Home” stockt - Nicht mehr als Symbol? Retrieved from https://www.wa.de/hamm/hamm-mitte-ort370531/schwierige-standortsuche-little-home-hamm-agneskirche-9520654.html (accessed on 07 August 2020).

Osiewacz, F (2019). Zukunft war lange ungewiss Geheimnisvoll: “Little Home” hat ersten Bewohner. Retrieved from https://www.wa.de/hamm/obdachlosen-holzhaeuschen-little-home-hamm-ersten-bewohner-12186129.html (accessed on 14 October 2019).

Palomares-Aguirre, I, Barnett, M, Layrisse, F, & Husted, BW (2018). Built to scale? How sustainable business models can better serve the base of the pyramid. *Journal of Cleaner Production*, *172*, 4506–4513.

Pedrozo, EA, & Sato, SAS (2015). Proposition of BOP 3.0 as an Alternative Model of Business for BOP (Base of Pyramid) Producers: Case Study in Amazonia, in Marcela Rebeca Contreras Loera and Andrzej Marjanski (Eds.), *The Challenges of Management in Turbulent Times: Global Issues From Local Perspective*. Los Mochis, Mexico: Universidad de Occidente..

Pieńkowski, D, & Zbaraszewski, W (2019). Sustainable energy autarky and the evolution of German bioenergy villages. *Sustainability*, *11*(18), 4996.

Pope, L (2018). Community-based learning: An amazing tool used by college students to build tiny houses for the homeless. *Journal of Sustainability Education*, *1*, 1–20.

Prahalad, CL, & Hammond, A (2002). Serving the world's poor, profitably. Harvard Business Review, *80*(9), 4–11.

Prahalad, CL, & Hart, SL (2002). The fortune at the bottom of the pyramid. *Strategy and Business*, *26*(26), 1–14.

Prahalad, CK (2005). *The Fortune at the Bottom of the Pyramid: Eradicating Poverty through Profits*. New Delhi: Pearson Education/Wharton School Publishing.

Reuter, T (November 22, 2017). Die meisten leben nicht auf der Straße. Retrieved from http://www.faz.net/aktuell/gesellschaft/menschen/wohnungslose-warum-die-wenigsten-auf-der-strasse-leben-15297200.html (accessed on 30 April 2020).

Rosca, E, Arnold, M, & Bendul, J (2016). Business models for sustainable innovation – An empirical analysis of frugal products and services. *Journal of Cleaner Production*, *162*, 133–145.

Ross, N, Bowen, P, & Lincoln, D (2010). Sustainable housing for low-income communities: Lessons for South Africa in local and other developing world cases. *Construction Management & Economics*, *28*(5), 433–449.

Rudnicka J (November 6, 2018). Von Armut oder sozialer Ausgrenzung betroffene Bevölkerung in Deutschland 2017. Retrieved from https://de.statista.com/statistik/daten/studie/244865/umfrage/von-armut-oder-sozialer-ausgrenzung-betroffene-bevoelkerung-in-deutschland/ (accessed on 23 April 2020).

Said, I, Shafiei, MWM, Razak, AA, Osman, O, & Kamaruddeen, AM (2010). Sustainable housing development: Defining the project team roles and responsibilities. *International Journal of Organizational Innovation*, *2*(3), 287.

Schleyer, R (October 30, 2019). Überregionaler Tiny House Verband ist gegründet! Retrieved from https://www.tiny-houses-karlsruhe.de/ueberregionaler-tiny-house-verband-ist-gegruendet/ (accessed on 14 October 2019).

Scholl, J (2013). "Inclusive business models as a key driver for social innovation", in Thomas Osburg and René Schmidpeter (Eds.), *Social Innovation*. Berlin, Heidelberg: Springer, pp. 99–109.

Shearer, H, & Burton, P (2019). Towards a typology of Tiny Houses. *Housing, Theory and Society*, doi: 10.1080/14036096.2018.1487879.

Simanis, E, & Hart, S (2008). The base of the pyramid protocol: Toward next generation BoP strategy. *Cornell University*, *2*, 1–57.

Soederberg, S (2018). The rental housing question: Exploitation, eviction and erasures. *Geoforum*, *89*, 114–123.

Statista Research Department (2020). Statistiken zur Armut in Deutschland. Retrieved from https://de.statista.com/themen/120/armut-in-deutschland/ (accessed on 30 April 2020).

Sunikka, M (2003). Fiscal instruments in sustainable housing policies in the EU and the accession countries. *European Environment*, *13*(4), 227–239.

Svane, Ö (2002). Nordic consumers and the challenge for sustainable housing. *Sustainable Development*, *10*(1), 51–62.

Tellis, WM (1997). Application of a case study methodology. *The Qualitative Report*, *3*(3), 1–19. Retrieved from http://nsuworks.nova.edu/tqr/vol3/iss3/1 (accessed on 30 April 2020).

Tiny Houses Consulting UG (n.d.). Tiny Houses, Wohnen auf kleinem Raum. Retrieved from http://tiny-houses.de/was-sind-tiny-houses/ (accessed on 26 September 2019).

Watling, M (October 30, 2018). Tiny House und die Flüchtlinge. Retrieved from https://siyach.wordpress.com/2018/10/30/tiny-house-und-die-fluechtlinge/ (accessed on 12 June 2019).

Williams, RL, Omar, M, & Rajadhyaksha, U (2012). "The value flame at the base of the pyramid (VFBOP): Identifying and creating a valuable market", in *Interdisciplinary Approaches to Product Design, Innovation, and Branding in International Marketing.* Bingley: Emerald Group Publishing Limited, pp. 267–279.

Winston, N, & Eastaway, MP (2008). Sustainable housing in the urban context: International sustainable development indicator sets and housing. *Social Indicators Research*, *87*(2), 211–221.

World Commission on Environment and Development (WCED) (1987). *Our Common Future.* Oxford: Oxford University Press.

World Data Lab (2018, October). World Poverty Clock. Retrieved from https://worldpoverty.io/ (accessed on 25 October 2019).

World Vision Institute (2018). Armut in Deutschland. Retrieved from http://www.armut.de/definition-von-armut_relative-armut.php (accessed on 17 October 2019).

Wyatt, A (2016). Tiny houses: Niche or noteworthy? *Planning*, *82*(2), 39–42.

Yin, R (1994). *Case Study Research: Design and Methods* (2nd ed.). Thousand Oaks, CA: Sage Publishing.

Appendix

Table 5.2 Coding guide (source: B1–B4)

Code	*Description*	*Anchor quote*
Possible applications	Statements referring to existing or potential use of Tiny Houses with the target group in Germany	'I can imagine them quite well in the form of a village'.
Price-performance ratio	Respondents' statements on the price/performance ratio of a Tiny House	'Price-performance is of course difficult, because it depends on how you build the house'.
Financial support	Respondents' statements relating to financial support to the target group	'That would certainly make sense to create such supportive measures in the long term'.
Combination of new and existing technologies	Statements referring to technological novelties in the field of Tiny Houses	
Materials		'Insulation materials are certainly still an exciting field in the context of the Tiny House'.
Electricity generation and self-sufficiency		'Filter treatment techniques … But that wouldn't be completely new to me'.
Circular design		'Then the water is briefly filtered and comes out of the shower again, so that you can use the water 2 or 3 times'.
Infrastructure	All statements which are mentioned by the person as relevant with regard to infrastructural conditions	
Communication		'I think that infrastructure is especially the communication and the gathering of people'.
Financial precondition of a person		'Then there is the missing money. I need a third party who then contributes a lot of money to lease land or to buy or finance. That is then again an additional hurdle'.
Location		'The property is simply the central infrastructure. This is simply still lacking'.
Access to target group	Statements about parallel possibilities to achieve access to the target group	'We have a registration list of over 17,000 who have registered with us via

(*Continued*)

Table 5.2 (Continued)

Code	*Description*	*Anchor quote*
		Facebook, e-mail or volunteers, but at the same time we are out on the street directly advertising to people'.
Actual application		'I take over conversations and go there, chat with people, have a coffee, get to know them that way'.
Internet access		'We have our internet presence, everyone who googles 'Tiny House' on the internet can find our website, many are on Facebook and there are Facebook groups on the topics'.
Condition of social support		'The right people come together and that's motivation to do something like that'.
Condition of location		'If a municipality does not support the project, it immediately becomes much more difficult, because just the area is the topic again and again'.
Transferability to other regions	All statements referring to potential transferability of Tiny Houses to other regions	
Existing application		'In other countries it must be ensured that they support us permanently'.
Movement in other countries		'If you follow this in other countries as a movement, it is relatively similar to what is happening here'.
Regulations		'And then it's something like how high the bridges are in these countries and that one can also see whether it is possible to drive under them'.
Materials		'You'd certainly have to look at specific materials'.
Conserving resources	Statements relating to the potential of Tiny Houses to conserve resources	

(*Continued*)

Table 5.2 (Continued)

Code	*Description*	*Anchor quote*
Use of materials during use		'When using Tiny Houses, you have a significantly lower consumption of resources, which goes hand in hand with living in a Tiny House'.
Use of materials during production		'Already started building with wood, a renewable raw material. Most manufacturers also take wood from domestic production'.
Adaptation of functionality to the target-group	Statements on the adaptability of Tiny Houses for corresponding applications	
Efficiency		'I'm now thinking about energy supply, but so specifically what you have to adapt overall, because of course the idea is always to make it as efficient as possible'.
Needs orientation		'I think that's exactly what the people who choose a Tiny House want. A house that is exactly tailored to their needs and a Tiny House can be individualised almost indefinitely'.
Adaptability		'Actually, 100%. Virtually all manufacturers have designed their products in such a way that they can be individually tailored to the customer's wishes, so every house is unique'.
Upgradeability	Statements that refer to the upgrade potential of Tiny Houses	
Costs		'Considering batteries and inverters, these are things that are expensive again'.
Fixed location		'Most people then live very close to nature outside and spend a lot of time there and always adapt their environment to the environment'.

(*Continued*)

Table 5.2 (Continued)

Code	*Description*	*Anchor quote*
Mobile use		'Yeah, it's just a question of definition. It can be said that it is easy to integrate, but it goes hand in hand with the need to reschedule, so anything is feasible. As long as the requirements, such as the 3.5 tonnes etc., are met, because it is just a requirement'.
Training-related use	Statements relating to the training of users for the application of a Tiny House	
Ventilation		'In any case, I think that's good, concerning ventilation, if you have a pallet oven, it certainly requires a briefing'.
Efficiency		'Yes, I think that in principle, if you are interested in efficiency, you have to be clear as a user what that means and where I can limit the consumption of goods, the consumption of water, the consumption of electricity'.
Self-sufficiency		'If, of course, I go in the direction of self-sufficiency and photovoltaics and storage and water treatment, then it becomes very technical and therefore necessary of explanation'.
Toilet		'A certain amount of instruction is always gladly given, particularly with the topic toilet technology'.
Use without electricity and water	Statements on the options to use Tiny Houses without electricity and water	
Example of use		'So, the homeless people take showers at Caritas, SKM, at the train station or in cafés, there is also the possibility to recharge their mobile phones or to recharge their powerbank'.

(*Continued*)

Table 5.2 (Continued)

Code	*Description*	*Anchor quote*
Role of government		'It should actually be rewarded from the public side'.
Compulsory connection		'I don't have to use that, but I'm subject to the compulsion to connect'.
Electricity		'Yeah, it works. I can get a photovoltaic system on the roof with appropriate storage technology'.
Water		'I can install a water treatment plant and put a small septic tank on my roof. Technically, it all works'.
Integration of the target group	Statements related to integrating the target groups into Tiny Houses value and/or supply chain	
Create value		'Yes, the value for society is that at some point a person can return to leading an independent life and then become part of society and pay taxes again'.
Integration as labour		'We are also working very hard to get a repair shop or various repair shops at locations in Germany, where we are implementing reintegration measures with the homeless'.
Exchange between different stakeholders	Statements on how the exchange between stakeholders usually takes place	
Networks		'Everyone uses these networks to connect partners, but also to ask customers and authorities to talk to each other'.
Personal exchange		'What I always find stimulating at the festival is that there are always individual parties coming together'.
Internet		'There is social media and many forums and platforms on the Internet'.
Obstacles to exchange		'That is, of course, the most difficult part, because everyone always makes their own soup'.

(*Continued*)

Table 5.2 (Continued)

Code	*Description*	*Anchor quote*
Overcoming social patterns	Statements about the possibilities of Tiny House to change social patterns	
Visions		'Theoretically, there would be quite a lot of crazy things possible, but that the focus is no longer on this Nine To Five system …'
Taking up major trends		'They integrate mega trends such as minimalism, downsizing and sustainability'.
Changed use of resources		'Then there is also always such a topic in the direction of sensitisation and environmental protection thought. If I live in a Tiny House, I reduce my use of resources'. 'Yeah, I think what you break through is this classic consumption pattern'.
Relation to the topic of homelessness		'The woman died and so people lost the ground under their feet. It's not always that I'm an addicted person and therefore landed on the street, but that the trigger was a completely different one'.
Change of perspective on homelessness		'It makes people visible to society in a different way and also reduces inhibition thresholds'.

6 Far from clean: Labour exploitation in the UK's hand car wash sector

Akilah Jardine, Alexander Trautrims, and Alison Gardner

Introduction

Hand car washing, the process of washing a vehicle by hand, is a relatively new business activity in the United Kingdom (UK). Prior to 2004, hand car washes (HCWs) were virtually non-existent (Clark and Colling, 2018). However, it is estimated that between 10,000 and 20,000 HCW operations exist in the UK today, making up 70% of the share of the car wash market and inhibiting the growth of the automated car wash (ACW) industry (Petrol Retailers Association, 2018). Many have sprung up on the side of the road, in petrol stations, disused forecourts, supermarket car parks and former public car parks, offering a low cost and conveniently accessible car wash service (Jardine et al., 2018). In an age of technological advances, such labour intensive operations are fuelled largely by an abundant low-skilled workforce. They are often described as operations run by migrants for migrants, allowing low-skilled migrant workers the opportunity to earn an income to improve their livelihood opportunities (Clark and Colling, 2018). However, reports on this sector suggest that workers are left economically and socially vulnerable. They work long hours, are paid below the national minimum wage (NMW), and operate under poor working conditions, such as without adequate protective safety gear and equipment (Jardine et al., 2018). Reportedly, while some workers are victims of labour and employment violations, others are exploited and forced into modern slavery (Jardine et al., 2018). At present, the UK does not have a system to register and licence HCWs and thus such businesses have been able to flourish without almost any regulatory overview. These activities are also not captured by the UK's Standard Industrial Classification code which categorises and describes business activities and therefore there is a lack of visibility across the sector.

Despite offering a popular service and operating in plain sight, there is a lack of data available on this sector. This makes it difficult to assess the number and locations of HCWs in the UK, their business operations and the incidence rate of labour exploitation. Although considerable research has touched on high-risk sectors for labour exploitation and modern slavery in the UK, such as the food industry, construction and care (Scott et al., 2012; Crates, 2018; Phillips and Trautrims, 2018; Emberson and Trautrims, 2019), not much attention has been paid to exploitation in the less formalised HCW sector. To date, few studies have been published on this increasingly common phenomenon. Our research, therefore, asks (a) to what extent does labour exploitation in HCWs constitute 'modern slavery' or lower levels of exploitation such as underpayment of wages? (b) Why are exploitative HCWs widespread in the UK? (c) What are the ways in which exploitative practices could be addressed? Using the HCW sector in the UK as a case study, this chapter illustrates how such a high-risk area for labour exploitation and modern slavery is able to flourish almost without any regulatory overview in an affluent country. In the absence of data on this sector, the chapter primarily draws on prior joint-research conducted by the Rights Lab at the University of Nottingham and the Office of the UK's Independent Anti-Slavery Commissioner (IASC) on labour exploitation in the sector (Jardine et al., 2018), and existing academic and grey literature on this area. We interviewed relevant stakeholders including law enforcement officials and industry practitioners, and distributed a survey to all police forces in the UK. The chapter will begin by outlining the research methods used in our research with IASC. It will then provide a background of the HCW sector, exploring its growth in the UK and the business model. The following section will discuss the nature and prevalence of labour exploitation in car wash activities to establish the linkages between the bottom of the pyramid (BOP) and slavery. Subsequently, it will explore the current state of regulation in the UK and the challenges in addressing exploitative labour practices. It will then briefly touch on some of the costs to the UK of HCWs operating using exploitative labour. In highlighting the potential linkage between the enforcement of environmental regulation and labour standards, the following section then looks to Germany and France to explain why such comparable economies do not share the same experience or challenges of HCWs as the UK. To conclude, the chapter will discuss ways in which exploitative practices could be addressed to safeguard workers' rights and prevent the exploitation of vulnerable individuals. This chapter concludes that the current state of the HCW sector gives rise to vulnerability and precarious labour and therefore stricter enforcement of regulations is critical to improve compliance and protect vulnerable individuals at the BOP.

Researching labour exploitation in hand car washes

As aforementioned, little academic literature about labour exploitation in HCWs is available. In addition to our research, very few other researchers have researched this area (e.g. Clark and Colling, 2016, 2018; Clark, 2018). Subsequently, the qualitative approach adopted by the research involved gathering data and information from a range of sources.

Our data collection involved two stages. The first stage was a review of literature and unstructured interviews with different stakeholders. The purpose of this stage was to familiarise ourselves with the problem of HCWs. We reviewed existing published work relating to labour exploitation and modern slavery in car washes. This included academic and grey literature such as scholarly articles, online press reports and work published by law enforcement, industry bodies and other agencies. We also reviewed evidence submitted to the UK parliament's Environmental Audit Committee who at the time of the research, conducted an enquiry into the social and environmental impact of HCWs. Following the review of existing literature, we carried out nine unstructured interviews with representatives from law enforcement agencies, car wash associations, and a HCW provider. The literature review and unstructured interviews provided us with a broad overview of problems associated with the sector, the impact on the wider car wash sector in the UK, and the current state of regulation. We recognised that HCWs would be a difficult area to investigate as the topic raises ethical and practical challenges, particularly when engaging with vulnerable workers (Clark and Colling, 2018). Subsequently, during unstructured interviews, we were able to identify the sort of information that law enforcement officials would be able to share with the research team. This enabled us to refine the scope of the study and gave us a useful insight into how we could go about collecting further data.

The second stage of our data collection focussed on obtaining new data and information to fill gaps. We recognised that there was a lack of in-depth information on the nature and prevalence of the problem. During the second stage of data collection, we carried out four semi-structured interviews and surveys with law enforcement. Our questions were designed from interesting aspects that emerged from the data collected during stage one. For instance, we explored the characteristics and vulnerabilities of workers operating in HCWs, the nature of exploitative practices, and the challenges of addressing labour exploitation in the sector. Interviews were conducted by telephone with four police officials from different forces (Greater Manchester Police, Police Scotland, Gwent Police and the Police Service of Northern Ireland). The aim of the interviews was to understand whether different areas of the UK have different experiences with regards to HCWs. The interviews lasted approximately one hour each and were recorded by note-taking. Separately, survey questions were distributed via email by IASC to 43 police forces' modern slavery single point of contacts (SPOCs). Seventeen (17) SPOCs completed and returned the surveys. The survey questions asked SPOCs about specific information on employer and worker characteristics, working and living conditions, and issues concerning modern slavery. The recording and storage of police data vary significantly among forces, as a result, the time period of information referred to in the responses varied. Table 6.1 illustrates the data sources consulted.

The data was prepared and analysed using Microsoft Word and Excel. The semi-structured interview notes were uploaded into Microsoft Word.

Table 6.1 Data sources

Data sources		
Stage 1	Newspapers	• Online press reports of exploitation and criminal activity relating to labour issues at car washes from 26 March 2015 to March 2018
	Literature	• Academic articles (Clark and Colling, 2016, 2018; Clark, 2018) • Written evidence submitted to the Environmental Audit Committee and final report on the social and environmental impact of HCWs (Cockbain, 2018; Environment Agency, 2018; Environmental Audit Committee, 2018; Gangmasters and Labour Abuse Authority, 2018b; Health and Safety Executive, 2018; Jardine et al., 2018; Petrol Retailers Association & Car Wash Association, 2018; Downstream Fuel Association, 2018) • Reports from anti-slavery organisation Unseen on car washes (Unseen, 2018) • Petrol Retailers Association 2018 Market Review (Petrol Retailers Association, 2018) • Report published by the Gangmasters and Labour Abuse Authority on labour exploitation within UK sectors (Gangmasters and Labour Abuse Authority, 2018a) • International Car Wash Association 2017 European Car Wash Consumer Study (International Car Wash Association, 2017)
	Unstructured Interviews	Nine (9) stakeholders • Gangmasters and Labour Abuse Authority (2018) • National Crime Agency (2018) • Petrol Retailers Association (2018) • Car Wash Association (2018) • Belgian Association Vehicle Cleaners ((Belgische Beroepsvereniging Reiniging Voertuigen – BBRV) (2018) • International Car Wash Association (2018) • Waves car wash ltd (2018) • Sussex Police (2018) • East Midlands Modern Slavery Police Transformation Coordination Unit (2018)
Stage 2	Semi-Structured Interviews	• Four (4) police forces: Greater Manchester Police; Police Scotland; Gwent Police; and the Police Service of Northern Ireland (2018)
	Surveys	• Seventeen (17) police forces' modern slavery single point of contacts (2018)

Survey responses were all returned in Word format. Interview notes and survey responses were then transferred into Excel. The text was categorised according to key areas of enquiry to make the data more manageable.

An inductive approach was adopted in the process of qualitative data analysis to capture respondents' perspectives and experiences. Working systematically through the text, we familiarised ourselves with the data and identified key aspects that emerged. We then collated extracts from the responses and matched them to specific codes. Following this, we reviewed the codes to identify significant themes. This process involved refining and collating codes and reviewing themes and extracts to ensure they accurately represented the data set as a whole.

Themes were then analysed in detail to elaborate and draw conclusions on the nature and prevalence of labour exploitation in the HCW sector. For instance, key conclusions were drawn around the prevalence of the issue across the UK, the spectrum of exploitative practices and the difficulty of addressing violations. Separately, we also identified approaches adopted by law enforcement agencies and industry bodies to investigate abuses and improve compliance.

The main limitation to this study was the absence of data and information on this sector and the difficulties of obtaining HCW workers' perspectives. Whilst the lack of this information has limited the scope of the research, the analysis provides a more in-depth understanding of the nature and prevalence of this problem. This includes information on business practices, employer and worker characteristics and working conditions. It also highlights certain areas worthy of further exploration, such as improved understanding of workers' consent to exploitation and how that interacts with policing and support mechanisms. Finally, it identifies several ways forward to improve compliance and protect workers in HCWs from abuse. These include: increased enforcement of regulations; educating workers and employers; implementing licensing schemes; undertaking multi-agency collaborations and improving public engagement.

History of hand car washes

There is no one definitive reason to explain the growth of HCWs in the UK. Clark and Colling (2018) suggest that the growth of operations is largely due to the result of economic restructuring in petrol retailing and the change in regulation around alcohol and smoking. They maintain that in the 1990s supermarkets began dispersing on retail parks and, due to the de-regulation of licensing restrictions in these areas, were able to expand their operations to include the sale of alcohol and petrol. Their expansion into alcohol retailing allowed consumers to buy large quantities of alcohol at affordable prices. Subsequently, with the change in regulation that banned smoking in public places in 2007, consumers began staying at home to drink. This greatly affected pubs, roadside public houses and other establishments which were forced to close (Clark, 2018). The closure of these businesses led to an abundant availability of spaces where HCWs were able to locate their businesses.

Separately, the closure of mechanical car washes also led to the establishment of HCWs on former forecourt sites. Prior to HCWs, the predominant forms of car washes were rollover and drive through jet washes which operated mostly on forecourt sites by fuel retailers and supermarkets. However, the price of operating these services led retailers to seek cheaper alternative services, and in some cases rent spaces on their forecourt to independent operators (Clark, 2018). The HCW services began to flourish on these sites because of the ease in setting up establishments and the competitive advantage it afforded over its mechanical counterparts.

Business model

HCW businesses provide a largely commoditised service that competes predominantly on costs and convenience of access (Jardine et al., 2018). In comparison to ACWs, HCWs are easier to establish, conveniently accessible and could offer a competitively cheaper alternative to other car wash services. Though a labour-intensive business activity, they have the commercial advantage of a cheap and abundant workforce. As aforementioned, they are often described as being run by migrants for migrants. Clark and Colling's (2018) research identified different categories of migrant labour employed in HCWs. For instance, they identified a category of workers who worked in HCWs to improve their English and viewed HCWs as an opportunity to develop their skills to move them up the job ladder. Additionally, their research identified workers who relied on agents and networks to secure work, because they spoke limited English and lacked qualifications and skills.

Evidently, similar to migrant workers in other low-skilled sectors, individuals often take up work in HCWs to improve their socio-economic circumstances. For many workers, the wages and conditions of work, though poor, are a better opportunity in subjective comparison to alternative employment options (Jardine et al., 2018). Car wash owners may then take advantage of workers' desperation to improve their circumstances and their limited options for employment.

Our research findings revealed that there is a high proportion of Albanian and Romanian owners/managers and workers in HCWs (Jardine et al., 2018). The presence of Romanians might be attributed to the UK's rules on accessing its labour market for citizens from A2 nations – Romania and Bulgaria – that joined the European Union (EU) in 2007. Up until 2013, citizens coming to work in the UK from these countries had to apply for and be granted a worker's authorisation document before starting work, unless they were self-employed (UK Government, 2016a, 2016b). This may have encouraged self-employment and entrepreneurship via HCWs. Regarding Albanian workers and car wash owners/managers, the visa schemes differ as

Albania is not in the EU. To work in the UK, Albanian nationals must apply for a work visa, which may be granted via different categories, if the necessary requirements are met (UK Government, 2019b). An assessment of available work visa schemes suggests that HCW work is unlikely to satisfy the requirements of the current visa routes. In addition, following Brexit the government is tightening immigration requirements, with a compulsory registration scheme for EU migrants until December 2020, and a points-based immigration system planned from January 2021, which explicitly cuts the migration options open to low-skilled workers (Home Office, 2020). This could increase the risk of exploitation and abuse for workers who may not qualify for the right to work in the UK.

Operations and investigations on HCW activities have described multiple forms of abuse concerning the working and living conditions of workers. Our research sought to develop a better understanding of these conditions. Regarding their wages and employment, survey responses and interviews reflected existing HCW concerns identified by the press, academic literature and law enforcement. For example, research by Clark and Colling 'found widespread denial of employment status, avoidance of the minimum wage, and working time regulations' (2018). Similarly, police respondents reported workers that were employed without a contract or on a zero-hour contract, paid cash in hand and not given a payslip, paid below the NMW, or not paid at all. Survey responses from police forces' SPOCs indicate that some workers were aware of the NMW but content with being paid below it, while others were unaware that there was a minimum wage.

An assessment of current research and reporting in this area also highlighted potential concerns for the health and safety of workers. Substances such as hydrochloric acid, detergents and other cleaning chemicals can be hazardous to workers, particularly if they do not have the proper gear to handle chemical substances or adequate training (Environmental Audit Committee, 2018). In one case, media coverage referred to an investigation that discovered workers with leprosy-like damage to their skin, due to exposure to chemicals (Rose, 2017). Our research findings indicated that some employees were found working without proper health and safety gear such as waterproof boots, gloves and goggles. A police respondent noted: 'Most car washes did not provide adequate protection equipment and uniforms for staff. On some visits, the Health and Safety personnel who accompanied our team have closed down the car washes due to safety concerns'. Another commented that 'a few premises had the electric metres bypassed, one premise had no toilet facilities, most staff worked long hours over a short number of days'. Regarding rest breaks, some workers were not allowed breaks, had limited access to basic facilities and were operating in potentially hazardous environments.

Whilst HCWs are not illegitimate businesses, there is a commercial rationale for the violation of labour, employment, health and safety and environmental regulations. Subsequently, the practice of undercutting such standards is sufficiently systemically dominant to be leading to widespread labour and employment violations (Jardine et al., 2018).

Labour exploitation in hand car washes: A continuum of abuse

As part of the United Nations 2030 sustainable development agenda, the UK has made a commitment to promote sustained, inclusive, and sustainable economic growth, full and productive employment and decent work for all. This also includes the commitment to take immediate and effective measures to eradicate forced labour and end modern slavery and human trafficking. Our research found that HCWs and labour violations committed within them are widespread across the UK. Police officials interviewed acknowledged a rise in HCW businesses in their localities and reported that workers were most often likely to be subject to some form of labour violation. This included working excessive hours or being paid below the NMW. The lack of data on the sector makes it difficult to assess the extent to which labour abuse within these operations constitutes modern slavery or lower-level forms of abuse. There is a lack of evidence on the number of workers referred to the National Referral Mechanism (NRM), the UK's system for identifying and supporting victims of modern slavery and human trafficking, and subsequently positively identified as victims. This is partly due to the NRM system aggregating all labour and criminal exploitation into one category, rather than breaking it down by sector.

Research by Clark and Colling (2018) found no evidence to indicate that workers were victims of modern slavery. However, an assessment of reports, interviews and surveys with police officials, suggest that labour exploitation in HCWs does not rigidly fit into a specific category of labour abuse. Rather, evidence points to a continuum of exploitation which includes modern slavery. Not all workers experiencing abusive labour practices in HCWs are technically 'enslaved'. Article 1 of the United Nations Slavery Convention 1926 defines slavery as 'the status or condition of a person over whom any or all of the powers attaching to the right of ownership are exercised'. Thus, modern slavery encompasses the extreme end of the spectrum of labour exploitation and requires the restriction of freedom to be present, via mechanisms such as coercion, threat, debt and intimidation. An assessment of intelligence on HCWs indicates that labour exploitation does not always satisfy this threshold. However, even where it does satisfy it, and workers are restricted in their freedoms, potential victims may still not be identified. This is due to victims themselves accepting their situation due to the lack of viable economic alternatives. Their wages and working conditions, though poor, allow them the opportunity to make a better income than possible at home or in other informal sectors in the UK. Thus, they are more likely to accept coercive, violent or deceptive arrangements. This makes it difficult to get a full picture on the scale of modern slavery. Potential victims may never enter the NRM whether through their own lack of self-identification as a victim or due to police accepting their reported contentment with their working conditions.

Separately, an assessment of media coverage, investigative and operative reports suggest that car wash owners use a number of methods to control their workers. This includes financial coercion, withholding of workers' identification documents and in some instances, physical abuse (Jardine et al., 2018). Our research found that the use and methods of control also vary among HCWs. In addition, interviews with police officials indicate that not all HCW workers are restricted in their freedom. While some police forces surveyed did not report on methods used to control workers, 24% of responses described various methods of control such as withholding of workers' passport or identification documents, debt bondage, physical abuse and withholding or non-payment of wages. One respondent reported that in four locations, car wash staff 'were subject to physical assaults and threats… in one location staff had their entire routine dictated to them… when they should eat and when they had to go to bed'. Another police respondent commented that 'assaults [were] common if workers disagreed with the rules. Bondage against those that broke the rules if they wanted to continue working at location, this could be money or passport being taken from them'. Subsequently, other workers were found living in accommodation that was imposed on them and the rent was taken directly from their wages.

Police authorities' perspectives varied on whether labour exploitation in HCWs in their localities met the threshold for modern slavery. For instance, an official from one police force voiced that within their vicinity, though some workers were subject to labour abuse, they were content with their working conditions. The official suggested that it was 'more of an HMRC (Her Majesty's Revenue and Customs) national minimum wage or tax evasion issue', as opposed to the more serious offence of modern slavery. Moreover, they referred to the Her Majesty's Inspectorate of Constabulary and Fire & Rescue Service report on policing response to modern slavery and human trafficking which highlighted that 'exploitation in which an individual chooses to work for less than the NMW or to live in undesirable conditions, without being forced or deceived into doing so, would not constitute modern slavery' (HMICFRS, 2017). This view was also echoed by other respondents who suggested that though some workers have been referred into the NRM, evidence shows that the majority of workers interviewed may not meet the threshold for modern slavery. This is because workers voluntarily chose to work in HCWs under poor circumstances and had the choice to leave. Contrarily, some officials suggested that in their locality labour exploitation in HCWs mainly satisfies the threshold for modern slavery. They reported that many workers are forced into debt bondage to pay for costs such as transportation or accommodation. One respondent held, 'next to sexual exploitation, HCW is the second most prominent type of exploitation'. Further, there were cases where workers were positively identified as victims and were repatriated back to their country of origin upon their request.

The variances of police perspectives could indicate different recruitment channels for workers to specific regions that may affect the level of abuse, inconsistencies in the identification of abuse and exploitation, engagement with workers, and how workers are viewed. For instance, while some police respondents referred to workers as 'victims' regardless of whether they were positively identified as such, others referred to workers as 'illegal workers'. In particular, one police respondent appeared to emphasise the workers' potential status in the UK by referring to them solely as 'illegal workers' though acknowledging that they came across workers who 'worked long hours over a short number of days', did not know the UK had a NMW, and were 'surprised how high the rate was'. This recalled an observation within the HMICFRS' (2017) report that 'victims who come into contact with the police are not always recognised as such and therefore remain in the hands of those who are exploiting them. Others are arrested as offenders or illegal immigrants. While law enforcement has a duty to refer individuals to immigration and enforcement, the vulnerability of victims must be considered in parallel' (HMICFRS, 2017). Further, disregarding exploitation in HCWs because it is of a lower-level form of abuse or because workers appear 'content with conditions' risks subjecting workers to further and escalating victimisation.

Regarding corporate complicity in modern slavery, HCW activities may not be adequately captured by the UK's antislavery frameworks. For instance, in 2015 the UK established the Modern Slavery Act (MSA) to aid its efforts in the eradication of slavery. Section 54 of the legislation requires companies with an annual turnover of £36 million or more to report on the steps that they have taken, or have not taken, to tackle slavery in their supply chains and operations. By requiring only large companies to report, the MSA fails to acknowledge that smaller-scale operations like car washes can also be complicit in related human rights abuses and violate labour standards. With increasing scrutiny of business activities, a number of voluntary initiatives have been established to promote best practice with suggestions on the steps businesses can take to address slavery. This includes Corporate Social Responsibility (CSR) activities such as establishing anti-slavery policies and conducting a risk assessment to comply with legislation and protect a company's brand image (New, 2015). Whilst a company's engagement with the antislavery agenda may affect their reputation, there is no evidence that this will have an implication for business behaviour. New (2015) for instance, notes that Krispy Kreme Doughnuts, though acknowledging that they do not '...engage in verification of product supply chains to evaluate and address risks of human trafficking and slavery, nor conduct audits of suppliers to evaluate supplier compliance with company standards against trafficking and slavery in supply chains', have not experienced any negative effect. As companies with the benefits of a greater turnover and incentive of legislation may show little effort to mitigate modern slavery risks, it is questionable what impact anti-slavery policy and

CSR initiatives can have on smaller businesses without the resources or same incentives. Accordingly, the proposition that HCWs might improve conditions based on brand reputation considerations is not likely for independent HCWs (Jardine et al., 2018).

Hand car wash workers and the bottom of the pyramid

According to the World Bank, four billion people, a majority of the world's population make up the base or bottom of the economic pyramid (BOP) (Hammond et al., 2007). These individuals are in relative poverty, with annual incomes less than US $3000. Absolute poverty reflects the amount of purchasing power of household income required to meeting basic living standards such as food, shelter and healthcare (United Nations Development Programme, 1997). Relative poverty relates to income distribution and describes a household income that is less than the average or median income within a country. Subsequently, individuals in relative poverty often fall behind most others in their community (United Nations Development Programme, 1997). Sengupta (2010) defines extreme poverty as a combination of income poverty, human development poverty and social exclusion. He maintains that income poverty is economic deprivation, creating an inability to meet basic needs, whether relative or absolute. Additionally, he argues that human development poverty is a social, cultural and political form of poverty where there exists a lack of access to resources such as food, health and education that is essential for human development. Subsequently, social inclusion goes beyond having the necessary income to purchase goods and services, and rather concerns situations where individuals lack social capital for various reasons such as being marginalised, discriminated or excluded from social relations.

Whilst modern slavery and labour exploitation is not synonymous to poverty, such deprivation of basic necessities and opportunities to improve one's socio-economic circumstances may increase individuals vulnerability to exploitation. Exploitation can involve a degree of fraud, force or coercion to lure, abuse and in some cases enslave individuals. Subsequently, while factors such as discrimination, conflict and low worker protection can make an individual vulnerable to exploitation (Gold et al., 2015), poverty itself is also a means of coercion as it gives individuals only a selected few options to improve their livelihood (Zwolinski, 2007). Many workers may have no alternative options to earn an income and therefore accept precarious work. Though allowing individuals to earn some form of an income, others may be left economically vulnerable as income generated is for self-preservation as opposed to economic advancement. Therefore, individuals may be unable to elevate themselves from a cycle of poverty and exploitation.

Regarding the wages paid, the average wage reported via surveys was £40 for a day's work which ranged between 8 and 12 hours a day. As one police respondent noted: 'generally we found workers to be very happy to engage with police and tell us how much they were earning, which tended to be around £40 to £60 per day, working between 8 and 10 hours. They were aware of the minimum wage and were content with their conditions'. More significantly low wages included £10 for a day's work. Two police forces reported that in some cases, cigarettes and food were used as payment. A police official also reported that individuals from Romania were often trafficked to their locality via bus, costing individuals roughly a £150 debt for the journey. The official stated that HCW jobs are advertised in Romania, promising workers £35 a day, which workers deemed a good wage. However, on arrival in the UK, workers were placed in dilapidated and cramped accommodation, with a lack of basic facilities such as electricity or water. The official also reported that individuals were then forced to work for two weeks and only paid £10 for their labour. As a result, some survived by vacuuming coins from the cars they washed. Joint-research by the University College London and the National Crime Agency (NCA) on labour trafficking into, within and from the UK, recognised that workers identified as victims in some cases were found to be underfed and surviving on a nutritionally limited diet (e.g. bread, jam and beans), and though working long hours with few or no breaks during the day, were often provided with very little food or money to buy food (Cockbain, 2018). In one case the traffickers provided 15 victims housed in a single property with a total of £25 per day for food.

Separately, the circumstances of workers may prevent them from meeting basic living standards, such as shelter. An analysis of literature on labour abuse in car washes, suggests that in some cases workers were living on either the car wash site or off-site in cramped and dilapidated accommodation. This was sometimes provided by car wash owners. A notable case is the death of Romanian national Sandu Laurentiu-Sava who was electrocuted in August 2015 while showering in squalid accommodation adjacent to the car wash where he worked. This was as a result of his employer bypassing the electricity metre (Gillett, 2017). Survey responses and interviews further indicated other potential accommodation styles and conditions identified during law enforcement investigations. The most common categories of accommodation included workers who lived on-site at the car wash, workers living in a house of multiple occupancy (HMO) off-site, and workers living off-site in makeshift accommodation such as caravans. Several responses suggest that it is common for workers to be housed in HMOs, provided by HCW owners. In this situation, it is usual for workers to pay the owners for the accommodation or for a portion of their salary to be deducted. A police respondent noted: 'across our visits there is some commonality in regard to the reduction in pay against minimum wage, offset by accommodation provision. In the majority of cases however the view is that the workers are more than happy with that (usually declared at £5 per hour) – even when minimum wage is discussed there is a clear lack of interest and that generally there is satisfaction with the conditions'. In the UK, when calculating the NMW or national living wage (NLW), accommodation provided to workers can be taken into account. As of April 2019, an employer cannot charge their worker more than £7.55 per day for providing daily accommodation, and more than £52.85 per week when weekly accommodation is provided (UK Government, 2019a). This is known as the 'offset' rate, and charges above this will need to be taken into consideration when calculating NMW. If the accommodation is provided free of charge, the offset rate will be added to the worker's wages and then calculated to determine whether the worker's wages are below the NMW.

In line with existing research, some respondents described workers living in cramped housing with mattresses on the floor, limited facilities, and health and safety issues. While responses to our survey indicate varied accommodation styles, 41% commented on the condition of the accommodation available to workers. Fifty-seven percent (57%) described accommodation as poor, 14% said it was acceptable, and 29% acknowledged that conditions varied, as some were 'generally in good condition and clean' while others were 'far from ideal'.

Though HCW activities are at risk of exploitative labour and employment practices, police officials acknowledged that some workers, though operating in poor conditions and paid below the NMW, did not self-identify as victims of labour abuse or modern slavery and were accepting of their working conditions. One respondent highlighted a case where workers were positively identified as victims of modern slavery and human trafficking but nevertheless returned to work in exploitative car washes: 'workers entered the NRM and are placed into safe accommodation; many workers left the safe house and went back to work for traffickers after they got positive conclusive grounds decision as they wanted to earn money'.

Whilst low-wage work does not equate to poverty (Filandri and Struffolino, 2019), the nature of HCW work risks economically and socially depriving individuals of a sustainable livelihood. This is further exacerbated by low-skilled migrant workers operating in the UK's current 'hostile environment' to immigration (Grierson, 2018). Responses from law enforcement officials acknowledge the difficulty of engaging with car wash workers as they may be distrusting of the police and immigration officials. Separately, though operating in plain sight, a challenge with combatting exploitation in car washes is the acceptance and normalisation of informal labour and employment practices by the general and often unsuspecting public. Unregulated and potentially illegal HCWs continue to be utilised because of their low-cost and easily accessible car wash service.

The cost of labour exploitation in hand car washes to the UK

There are several costs to the UK of HCWs operating with exploitative labour practices. Such activities have resulted in the loss of tax payments, such as business rates, corporation tax and value-added tax (VAT).

Additionally, national insurance (NI) contributions are likely to have been missed. Some have been non-compliant by accepting only cash as a form of payment for service and not declaring these payments for tax purposes and, as noted above, paying their workers significantly below the NMW.

In 2018, the Clewer Initiative, the Church of England's modern slavery initiative, launched the Safe Car Wash mobile application to provide a community intelligence-led approach to identify slavery at car washes in the UK. The app found that 80% of car wash visits reported had a cash-only policy, 41% of users had to pay the manager directly, and 87% of users were not offered a receipt (Jardine and Gardner, 2019). Car wash prices that are unfeasibly cheap could also indicate that labour and employment obligations are not being met (Chesney et al., 2017). HCW provider Waves' assessment of the industry suggests that the breakeven cost, including VAT, is £6.88 for an outside wash and £11.10 for an in and outside wash. As demonstrated in Table 6.2, these figures take into consideration expenses such as labour costs and the price of materials and resources used such as electricity, water, chemicals and equipment, business rates, insurance, amongst other costs. Though this figure will vary to some extent throughout the UK, HCWs that charge significantly below this cost could indicate that they are evading tax, NI, and NMW obligations, resulting in loss of revenue for the public purse. According to the Petrol Retailers Association and the Car Wash Association, with an anecdotal estimate of between 10,000 and 20,000 HCWs in the UK, the cost to the public purse could fall between £700,000,000 and £1 billion annually in unpaid taxes (Petrol Retailers Association & Car Wash Association, 2018).

The cost of investigating labour exploitation in HCWs is also relatively high. The visibility of HCWs on the high street and increased press coverage around potential illegalities has heightened investigations into this sector. However, the growth of HCWs in the UK, coupled with a degree of invisibility have made it difficult for law enforcement bodies to investigate operations to ensure that they comply with the relevant regulations. Investigations, where they do occur, appear to be costly. This is evident from the GLAA's investigations into labour abuse in this sector. According to GLAA, 25 investigations into HCWs took a total of 1384 days to be completed (average 55.36 days per investigation) and amounted to a cost of £286,685 (£11,467 per investigation) (Gangmasters and Labour Abuse Authority, 2018b). The cost and time of conducting investigations has resulted in enforcement and regulatory bodies allocating resources to cases where substantial evidence of labour abuses have been provided based on prioritisation methods. By adopting intelligence-led risk-rated approaches, agencies are then able to prioritise high-risk cases. However, it is important to note that this risks neglecting lower-level forms of labour abuse that may escalate into modern slavery (FLEX Labour Exploitation Advisory Group, 2016). This, coupled with the aforementioned fact that many HCW workers may not self-report as victims, means it is important to consider whether the

Table 6.2 Cost of car wash: Extracted from evidence submitted by the Downstream Fuel Association to the Environmental Audit Committee enquiry on the environmental and social impact of hand car washes (Downstream Fuel Association, 2018)

	Outside only wash	*In and out wash (mini valet/Gold)*
	Wash, TFR, shampoo, rinse, leather	*As outside, plus vacuum, inside glass and wipe dashboards*
Average time to complete (total minutes)	*18*	*39*
	£ Apr-18	£ Apr-18
Direct costs		
Labour cost inc. hourly rate, pensions etc. (no vehicle movement)	2.81	6.09
Water	0.06	0.06
Electricity	0.08	0.16
Chemicals	0.16	0.21
Consumables	0.01	0.02
Maintenance	0.06	0.08
Rent (highly variable, average amount assumed)	0.9	0.9
Sub-total	4.08	7.52
Other (hidden) costs		
Rates (based on £15K RV and small business rates relief)	0.45	0.45
Insurance	0.17	0.17
Supervisor/manager	0.75	0.8
Trade effluent	0.03	0.03
Uniforms	0.02	0.03
Internet	0.03	0.03
Mobile phone	0.01	0.01
Credit card charges	0.03	0.04
Bank charges	0.04	0.05
Accountancy/payroll/legal	0.12	0.12
Sub-total	1.65	1.73
Total costs	5.73	9.25
Cost plus vat	**6.88**	**11.10**

Based on 200 cars per week cleaned, 35 hours per worker at NLW, 25+ years old plus statutory pension. No vehicle movements or productivity calculations. Regional variations may apply.

GLAA is resourced sufficiently to be able to prevent slavery in HCWs. If resourcing restricts it to investigating only those with the most severe risk attached or with the most intelligence provided, it is evident that alternative or complementary approaches are needed. An alternative model to funding investigations is found at the Health and Safety Executive (HSE) which has a Fee for Intervention (FFI) off-setting its investigation costs as those found to be in breach of health and safety legislation are held responsible for paying investigative and enforcement costs (Health and Safety Executive, 2018).

Hand car washes are often described as unregulated operations, however, like other businesses operating in the UK, there are regulations to which they should adhere. These include planning permission, paying business rates, environmental policies – including permission to dispose of liquid waste, paying national insurance, corporate tax, NMW and health and safety. Though an increasingly common phenomenon in the UK, HCWs as a business activity barely exist in comparable economies such as Germany and France. Research by the International Car Wash Association found that HCWs were the least popular form of car wash service in Germany, as only 6% of motorists interviewed use HCWs (International Car Wash Association, 2017). In France, this figure drops to 4%.

Interestingly, the scarcity of HCWs in Germany and France could be attributed to the enforcement of environmental practices as opposed to labour and employment regulations. Incorrect handling and disposal of wastewater, chemicals used to wash cars, oil residues and debris washed off cars, can result in the discharge of trade effluent into surface water drains and pollute the environment. Similar to the UK, Germany has a number of environmental policies, particularly influenced by European Union law, to regulate wastewater. For instance, under Germany's Federal Water Act (Wasserhaushaltsgesetz, WHG) a permit is required to discharge wastewater and to discharge substances into groundwater (Irmer et al., 2013). A person washing a car must then have the relevant permit to discharge wastewater or utilise designated establishments that have been authorised to do so. Generally, environmental policies in Germany are often strictly enforced by environmental bodies (Elshorst, 2013).

Likewise, in France, there are several regulations pertaining to the protection of the environment. Similar to Germany, France's regulations around environment and wastewater management places some restrictions on the washing of cars. For instance, in Paris, article 99-3 of the Departmental Health Regulations for Paris, forbids the discharge of wastewater on public roads and directly prohibits the washing of cars on public roads, private roads open to public traffic, banks, ports and wharves, as well as in parks (The Departmental Health Regulations, 1979). Like Germany, persons discharging wastewater must have the relevant permissions to do so.

The UK has several comparable regulations to protect the environment and a number of regulatory bodies to ensure compliance. Though environment policy is devolved in the UK, like Germany and France, permits are also required from relevant environmental agencies to discharge trade effluent. There is no evidence to suggest that environmental policies are more strictly enforced in Germany and France than in the UK. However, the phenomena of HCWs in the UK suggests that environmental policies may need to be more strictly enforced to better regulate car wash activities, particularly as many have been established on sites that do not have the appropriate drainage systems in place to dispose and recycle wastewater, thus posing a threat to the environment. In England, the Environment Agency (EA) operates by a 'risk based and proportionate' response approach, meaning assessing the severe impact of operations on the environment (Environment Agency, 2018). Such an approach heavily relies on sufficient evidence that an activity poses a significant risk to the environment, thus allocating resources to more severe incidents. HCWs tend not to be considered the most severe incidents and therefore are usually addressed through 'advice and guidance to correct any problems or warning letters'. Contrarily, under Scotland's General Binding Rules (GBR), a set of compulsory rules which cover certain low-risk activities, the prosecution is based on a more observable threshold, as it only needs to be proved that trade effluent was disposed into surface water drainage systems (Scottish Environment Protection Agency, 2011). Lack of data on the HCW sector makes it a challenge in comparing the impact of environmental policies in England and Scotland.

To encourage good practice in the prevention of pollution to the environment, Natural Resources Wales, the Northern Ireland Environment Agency and the Scottish Environment Protection Agency, established the Guidance for Pollution Prevention Vehicle Washing and Cleaning (GPP13). GPP13 educates car wash businesses on the relevant environmental regulations and outlines measures they should take to prevent their operations from harming the environment (Natural Resources Wales, Northern Ireland Environment Agency, & Scottish Environment Protection Agency, 2017). The advantage of such a document is that it sifts through environmental regulations, drawing on those that are specifically relevant to car washing. This provides businesses with a comprehensive understanding of the measures that they should adopt to ensure that they are complying with the law.[1]

There is no definitive reason to explain the proliferation of HCWs in the UK compared to other countries such as France and Germany. However, inadequate enforcement of regulations and in effect turning a 'blind-eye' to the impact of HCWs on the environment may have contributed to the growth of such operations in the UK, opening the floodgates to non-compliancy in other areas such as labour and employment practices. As aforementioned, inadequate training in the correct handling and disposal of potentially hazardous chemicals and waste not only damages and pollutes the environment but also threatens the health and safety of the workers. Whilst it may be difficult to investigate unlawful labour conditions, particularly where workers do not self-identify as victims, enforcement of environmental policies potentially provide an alternative avenue for identifying and investigating unregulated operations.

Separately, it is important to note that though stricter enforcement of environmental policies may reduce unlawful operations, exploitation of BOP individuals would remain a concern due to their vulnerability. Vulnerable workers may be compelled to seek alternative options for work.

Consequently, cleaning up the sector may leave workers with no better option than entering an exploitative labour relationship or forced to work in other high-risk sectors such as construction and agriculture. In addition to addressing exploitative conduct, policies need to consider the root causes and vulnerabilities that give rise to abusive practices.

In contrast to sectors such as agriculture, for example, not only are HCWs not categorised in their own separate industry code but they also do not require a licence to operate from the GLAA. In November 2018, the Environmental Audit Committee proposed that the UK government compel HCWs to require licences to operate to prevent exploitation of workers and environmental pollution. The Committee recommended that the government trial a licensing scheme that collates key compliance requirements to strengthen enforcement (Environmental Audit Committee, 2018). However, the government has instead endorsed voluntary industry-led initiatives in favour of piloting a licensing scheme. In the absence of adequate enforcement of labour standards and environmental policies, there are a number of proposed solutions to preventing exploitation and safeguarding the rights of vulnerable workers employed in HCWs.

Educate hand car wash owners/managers

In his 2018–19 strategy, the UK's Director of Labour Market Enforcement (DLME), highlighted that effective labour market enforcement should consist of a mix of compliance and deterrence approaches (Metcalf, 2018). According to DLME, '[t]he compliance approach is premised on the idea that violations of employment regulations are the result of employer ignorance and incompetence'. Thus, while regulations must be strictly enforced to drive compliance, it is also vital to educate employers on labour and employment policies they must adhere to. An assessment of research on HCWs suggests that some are legitimate businesses that have planning or leasing permission but breach other relevant regulations. Some HCW employers may lack a comprehensive understanding of the policies around establishing and running a business. Employers should, therefore, be educated on labour and employment standards, and their responsibilities to prevent exploitative labour practices. Such an approach will ensure that employers are not simply punished for non-compliance, but rather demonstrate what compliance looks like, and work with businesses to continuously improve practices. The GLAA also adopt a preventative and educative approach to improve compliance, allowing the allocation of resources to high-risk cases of labour exploitation (Gangmasters and Labour Abuse Authority, 2018b). The GLAA is currently working in collaboration with Waves, Tesco supermarket's largest HCW provider and a consortium of stakeholders to pilot an industry code of practice for the car wash sector, which forms the basis of the Responsible Car Wash Scheme (RCWS). The scheme aims to accredit car washes that comply with the code.[2] The code's ethos is to, 'bring legitimacy to the sector, promoting compliance and raising standards through the dissemination of best practice' and 'be a positive force for improving the working conditions of employees'. Such a code not only ensures that car washes are compliant, but it could also educate entrepreneurs, particularly migrant employers. Some may be unaware of the necessary regulations they should abide by to establish and operate a business in the UK, and thus are inadvertently complicit in violations.

Engagement with workers

In line with promoting a compliance approach, the DLME acknowledges the importance of promoting worker rights, supporting awareness and access to enforcement. To improve engagement with workers, authorities can ensure workers are also educated on labour and employment policies, such as the NMW, NLW, health and safety policies and working time regulations. There also needs to be effective channels to allow workers to enforce such rights.

Authorities might wish to consider educating workers about the risks of labour abusive practices and slavery, and how to report abuses. Reports from police officials interviewed show that though some workers were unwilling to disclose any, or accurate, information of their working conditions, all forces ensured that workers were aware of any support available to them. All officials interviewed reported distributing leaflets translated in different languages to educate workers on their labour and employment rights. Separately, to improve engagement with workers, some police forces have begun using officers and community actors from the same national or ethnic background as workers.

Evidently, a number of factors may hinder engagement with workers. Workers may not self-identify as victims of labour abuse or may be accepting of their working conditions. Thus, confusion around the relevance of consent in identifying cases of labour abuse or modern slavery may result in law enforcement officials choosing not to engage with workers further than initial or early-stage contact. Separately, officials reported the difficulty in engaging with workers, as some feared retaliation from their employers or denouncement to immigration officials if they were from outside of the EU. As we noted above, HMICFRS' (2017) report acknowledged the failure of some forces to adequately identify potential victims as they were ultimately treated as illegal immigrants. Recognising that law enforcement has a duty to report cases of illegal immigration, it is equally obligatory that officials recognise and address the vulnerability of exploited workers. Another issue highlighted by respondents is that some workers do not want to be referred into the NRM, as their focus is on securing employment to support themselves and their families. One official suggested that measures should be adopted to prevent workers from being drawn towards unregulated and exploitative employment practices such as support in applying for a NI number, developing their skills and applying for other job opportunities.

Public engagement

A challenge highlighted by officials was the lack of resources to investigate all HCWs for potential labour abuse violations. As a result, some officials reported the importance of adopting a prevention approach by raising awareness among the public to be vigilant to the signs of labour exploitation in HCWs. There have been a number of campaigns and press coverage to raise awareness of exploitative practices, and how to 'spot the signs' of modern slavery in car washes. Most notably, the Safe Car Wash app allows individuals to pinpoint their geographical location when at a car wash, and enables users to anonymously answer a series of questions such as whether the workers have access to suitable clothing, if there is evidence of workers living on-site and the cost of the car wash service. Data entered is then fed back to the NCA and GLAA. Such data has the potential to draw a better picture of the size of the HCW sector, geographical locations of operations, and provide an improved insight into the prevalence of labour exploitation in these operations. HCWs are widespread and operate in plain sight, and educating the public on the signs of labour exploitation and modern slavery can help shed light on abusive practices. Anti-slavery organisation Unseen's assessment of calls made to its Modern Slavery Helpline concerning car washes illustrate that the public has an important role to play as the majority of reports were made by members of the public (Unseen, 2018).

However, it is also important to protect the public from spaces where criminality may be occurring and to avoid encouraging citizen vigilantism. Sometimes reports from members of the public may not be sufficiently detailed: the GLAA has reported that the majority (62%) of referrals it receives regarding HCWs are often vague and relate to workers not looking happy or engaging in conversation with customers (Gangmasters and Labour Abuse Authority, 2018b). Research from Birks and Gardner (2019) also found that members of the public were reticent about reporting potential instances of labour abuse, as they found widely shared 'signs' of modern slavery to be too vague, and were sometimes concerned about worsening workers' situations, particularly in relation to potential immigration violations. Awareness-raising activities about labour exploitation in HCWs, therefore, need to focus on promoting awareness and reporting by members of the public in a way that safely collates useful information whilst discourages racial profiling and discrimination.

Conclusion

The conventional approach to the base of the pyramid concept focusses on finding or creating fortune at the BOP (Gupta and Khilji, 2013). Prahalad et al. (2012), for instance, argue that business participation in BOP markets and innovation allows them to generate profit. By targeting the purchasing power of poor people as customers through the production of goods and services, businesses are said to create a win–win relationship for eradicating poverty.

Arguably, this is often achieved by targeting poor people as consumers or empowering them as suppliers, producers, and employees (Agnihotri, 2013). Whilst there are innovative approaches businesses can adopt to help eradicate poverty (Polak and Warwick, 2013), such methods are not viable in addressing the exploitation of BOP workers in independent HCWs. Extracting profits from car wash workers will not improve their conditions or reduce poverty. Not all car wash workers are 'free consumers' as some do not have the free will to choose the goods and services they want to consume. Access to basic necessities such as food and shelter in some cases are provided by employers to exercise control over their workers. In this case, HCW owners/managers are able to further extract profit from forced consumption, compelling workers to remain at the BOP.

The lack of visibility questions the extent to which the government can regulate a sector that essentially does not exist in policy. Reducing poverty and improving the labour and employment conditions of workers heavily relies on licensing and registering HCW activities and improving the enforcement of existing regulations to ensure that car washes are compliant. However, the lack of enforcement of regulations and the structure of the sector increases workers vulnerability to exploitative practices, particularly as they already work predominantly in the informal sector. This has resulted in an environment that is undercutting legitimate businesses in the formal economy, and shifting low-wage and precarious labour towards the bottom of the pyramid.

Moreover, activities such as HCWs are largely not captured by anti-slavery legislation and therefore do not have to report on the steps they are taking to ensure compliance in tackling slavery. Their operations are also not picked up by corporate risk management systems of companies that are in-scope of the MSA as the spent on HCW is a relatively minor expense. Further, no formal relationships are usually established with the service providers of HCWs (Jardine et al., 2018). Whilst voluntary CSR initiatives may fill the gap in the absence of inadequate legislation, such principles alone are incapable of addressing exploitation in car washes as they do not deal with the underlying causes that contribute to vulnerability and precarious labour. Further, unlawful operations will continue to flourish in the UK if consumers continue to utilise their services, as opposed to more regulated operations – such as those run by supermarkets – because of the considerably lower prices offered (Jardine et al., 2018).

HCWs are not illegitimate business activities, but unregulated operations threaten workers' rights, pollute the environment, and pose a significant risk to the public purse. Much more should be done to clean up the sector: licensing and registering car washes; enforcing labour, employment, health and safety and environmental standards; improving engagement with car wash owners/managers and workers; and educating the public on unlawful operations so that they can make more informed decisions when choosing a car wash provider. Moreover, further research on the impact and effectiveness of interventions is required. In particular, research on the comparison of regulations and enforcement mechanisms across countries would be desirable. Additionally, further research is needed on the correlation between environmental regulations and the social impact of HCWs to progress understanding of the growth of HCWs in the UK in comparison to other economies. Like other sectors in the UK, HCWs can be commercially viable and economically sustainable for workers while operating in an ethical, legal and responsible manner. However, government intervention is critical to strengthening enforcement, ensuring compliance and protecting society's most vulnerable individuals.

Notes

1 The Environmental Agency for England has not endorsed GPP13.
2 www.rcws.org.uk

References

Agnihotri, A (2013). Doing good and doing business at the bottom of the pyramid. *Business Horizons*, *56*, 591–599. https://doi.org/10.1016/j.bushor.2013.05.009.

Birks, J, & Gardner, A (2019). Introducing the slave next door: Local media and public perceptions of modern slavery. *Anti-Trafficking Review*, *13*, 66–81. https://doi.org/10.14197/atr.201219135.

Chesney, T, Gold, S, & Trautrims, A (2017). Agent based modelling as a decision support system for shadow accounting. *Decision Support Systems*, *95*(C), 110–116. https://doi.org/10.1016/j.dss.2017.01.004

Clark, I (2018). Abandoned spaces and technology displacement by labour: The case of hand car washes. *New Technology, Work and Employment*, *33*(3), 234–249. https://doi.org/10.1111/ntwe.12123

Clark, I, & Colling, T (2016). New insights into informal migrant employment: Hand car washes in a mid-sized English city. *Economic and Industrial Democracy*, *40*(3), 755–775. https://doi.org/10.1177/0143831x16669840

Clark, I, & Colling, T (2018). Work in Britain's informal economy: Learning from road-side hand car washes. *British Journal of Industrial Relations*, *56*(2), 320–341. https://doi.org/10.1111/bjir.12286

Cockbain, E (2018). *Written Evidence Submitted to the Environmental Audit Committee Hand Car Washes Inquiry by Dr Ella Cockbain, Lecturer in Security and Crime Science, UCL.* http://data.parliament.uk/writtenevidence/committeeevidence.svc/evidencedocument/environmental-audit-committee/hand-car-washes/written/83094.pdf

Crates, E (2018). *Construction and the Modern Slavery Act: Tackling Exploitation in the UK.* https://www.ciob.org/sites/default/files/CIOBReport on UK Construction and the Modern Slavery Act_0.pdf

Downstream Fuel Association (2018). *Written Evidence Submitted to the Environmental Audit Committee Hand Car Wash Inquiry by Downstream Fuel Association.* http://data.parliament.uk/writtenevidence/committeeevidence.svc/evidencedocument/environmental-audit-committee/hand-car-washes/written/84031.pdf

Elshorst, D (2013). *Enviromental Law in Germany.* https://www.cliffordchance.com/briefings/2013/10/q_a_on_environmentallawingermany.html

Emberson, C, & Trautrims, A (2019). "Public procurement and modern slavery risks in the English adult social care sector", in O Martin-Ortega, & CM O'Brien (Eds.), *Public Procurement and Human Rights: Opportunities, Risks and Dilemmas for the State as Buyer*, Edgar Online, pp. 180–191. https://doi.org/https://doi.org/10.4337/9781788116312

Environment Agency (2018). *Written Evidence Submitted to the Environmental Audit Committee Hand Car Wash Inquiry by the Environment Agency.* http://data.parliament.uk/writtenevidence/committeeevidence.svc/evidencedocument/environmental-audit-committee/hand-car-washes/written/85913.pdf

Environmental Audit Committee (2018). *Hand Car Washes Tenth Report of Session 2017-19 Report, together with Formal Minutes Relating to the Report.* https://publications.parliament.uk/pa/cm201719/cmselect/cmenvaud/981/981.pdf

Filandri, M, & Struffolino, E (2019). Individual and household in-work poverty in Europe: Understanding the role of labor market characteristics. *European Societies, 21*(1), 130–157. https://doi.org/10.1080/14616696.2018.1536800

FLEX Labour Exploitation Advisory Group (2016). *Labour Compliance to Exploitation and the Abuses In-Between.* labourexploitation.org/sites/default/ files/publications/LEAG position paper 01.pdf

Gangmasters and Labour Abuse Authority (2018a). *The Nature and Scale of Labour Exploitation across All Sectors within the United Kingdom.* https://www.gla.gov.uk/media/3537/external-nature-and-scale-of-labour-exploitation-report-final-version-may-2018.pdf

Gangmasters and Labour Abuse Authority (2018b). *Written Evidence Submitted to the Environmental Audit Committee hand car washes inquiry by Gangmasters and Labour Abuse Authority.* http://data.parliament.uk/writtenevidence/committeeevidence.svc/evidencedocument/environmental-audit-committee/hand-car-washes/written/83129.pdf

Gillett, F (2017, January 18). Man jailed after worker is electrocuted in shower at Bethnal Green "bed in shed" flat. *Evening Standard.* https://www.standard.co.uk/news/crime/man-jailed-after-worker-is-electrocuted-in-shower-at-bethnal-green-bed-in-shed-flat-a3443246.html

Gold, S, Trautrims, A, & Trodd, Z (2015). Modern slavery challenges to supply chain management. *Supply Chain Management, 20*(5), 485–494. https://doi.org/10.1108/SCM-02-2015-0046

Grierson, J (2018, August 27). Hostile environment: Anatomy of a policy disaster. *The Guardian.* https://www.theguardian.com/uk-news/2018/aug/27/hostile-environment-anatomy-of-a-policy-disaster

Gupta, V, & Khilji, SE (2013). Revisiting fortune at base of the pyramid (BoP). *South Asian Journal of Global Business Research, 2*(1), 8–26. https://doi.org/10.1108/20454451311303257

Hammond, AL, Kramer, WJ, Katz, RS, Tran, JT, & Walker, C (2007). *The Next Four Billion.* World Resources Institute and International Finance Corporation. https://www.wri.org/publication/next-4-billion

Health and Safety Executive (2018). *Written Evidence Submitted to the Environmental Audit Committee Hand Car Washes Inquiry by the Health and Safety Executive.* http://data.parliament.uk/writtenevidence/committeeevidence.svc/evidencedocument/environmental-audit-committee/hand-car-washes/written/85519.pdf

HMICFRS (2017). *Stolen Freedom: The Policing Response to Modern Slavery and Human Trafficking.* www.justiceinspectorates.gov.uk/hmicfrs

Home Office (2020). *The UK's Points-based Immigration System: Policy Statement.* https://www.gov.uk/government/publications/the-uks-points-based-immigration-system-policy-statement/the-uks-points-based-immigration-system-policy-statement

International Car Wash Association (2017). *2017 European Car Wash Consumer Study.* http://www.prowash.fi/wp-content/uploads/2017/11/ICA-European-Consumer-Study-2017.pdf

Irmer, U, Huber, D, & Walter, A (2013). *Water Resource Management in Germany.* https://www.umweltbundesamt.de/sites/default/files/medien/378/publikationen/wawi_teil_01_englisch_barrierefrei.pdf

Jardine, A, & Gardner, A (2019). *Safe Car Wash App Report.* https://static1.squarespace.com/static/58f723af1b631bc0c1e17415/t/5ca1f6a1ec212d250eb89ee5/1554118348298/Safe+Car+Wash+App+FINAL+%28March+2019%29.pdf

Jardine, A, Trautrims, A, & Gardner, A (2018). *Written Evidence Submitted to the Environmental Audit Committee Hand Car Washes Inquiry by the Rights Lab, University of Nottingham.* http://data.parliament.uk/writtenevidence/committeeevidence.svc/evidencedocument/environmental-audit-committee/hand-car-washes/written/83103.pdf

Jardine, A, Trautrims, A, & Kenway, E (2018). *Labour Exploitation in Hand Car Washes.* http://www.antislaverycommissioner.co.uk/media/1238/labour-exploitation-in-hand-car-washes.pdf

Metcalf, D (2018). *United Kingdom Labour Market Enforcement Strategy 2018/19.* https://assets.publishing.service.gov.uk/government/uploads/system/uploads/attachment_data/file/705503/labour-market-enforcement-strategy-2018–2019-full-report.pdf

Natural Resources Wales, Northern Ireland Environment Agency, & Scottish Environment Protection Agency (2017). *GPP 13: Vehicle Washing and Cleaning.* http://www.netregs.org.uk/media/1414/gpp-13-v2-plussepa-plusniea-plusnrw.pdf

New, S (2015). Modern slavery and the supply chain: the limits of corporate social responsibility? *Supply Chain Management, 20*(697–707). https://doi.org/10.1108/SCM-06-2015-0201.

Petrol Retailers Association (2018). *Market Review 2018.* https://www.ukpra.co.uk/assets/documents/market-review-pra-2018.pdf

Petrol Retailers Association, & Car Wash Association (2018). *Written Evidence Submitted to the Environmental Audit Committee Hand Car Washes Inquiry by the Petrol Retailers Association and the Car Wash Association.* http://data.parliament.uk/writtenevidence/committeeevidence.svc/evidencedocument/environmental-audit-committee/hand-car-washes/written/83130.pdf

Phillips, A, & Trautrims, A (2018). *Agriculture and Modern Slavery Act Reporting: Poor Performance Despite High Risks.* https://www.antislaverycommissioner.co.uk/media/1220/modern-slavery-act-and-agriculture-poor-performance-briefing.pdf

Polak, P, & Warwick, M (2013). *The Business Solution to Poverty: Designing Products and Services for Three Billion New Customers* (1st ed.). San Francisco, California: Berrett-Koehler Publishers.

Prahalad, CK, Di Benedetto, A, & Nakata, C (2012). Bottom of the pyramid as a source of breakthrough innovations. *Journal of Product Innovation Management, 29*(1), 6–12. https://doi.org/10.1111/j.1540-5885.2011.00874.x

Rose, E (2017, October 11). Acid-burned hands and sleeping four to a room: The horrors of your local car wash. *Evening Standard.* https://www.standard.co.uk/news/

modern-slavery/acidburned-hands-and-sleeping-four-to-a-room-exploitation-is-rife-in-car-washes-a3656091.html

Scott, S, Craig, G, & Geddes, A (2012). *Experiences of Forced Labour in the UK Food Industry.* https://www.jrf.org.uk/file/41944/download?token=MhqtahpQ&filetype=full-report

Scottish Environment Protection Agency (2011). *The Water Environment (Controlled Activities) (Scotland) Regulations 2011 (as amended).*

Sengupta, A (2010). Human rights and extreme poverty. *Economic and Political Weekly, 45*(17), 85–93. https://www.jstor.org/stable/pdf/25664389.pdf?refreqid=excelsior%3A547f7da3e75a5c62f30c4f5cf292ef86

The Departmental Health Regulations (1979). *Order of 23 November 1979 on Health Regulations of the Department of Paris.*

UK Government (2016a). *Entitlement: Residence Rules - Right to Reside: Right to Reside for Nationals of Bulgaria and Romania (A2 nationals).* Retrieved from https://www.gov.uk/hmrc-internal-manuals/tax-credits-technical-manual/tctm02087 (accessed on 12 July 2019).

UK Government (2016b). *Migrant Workers: A2 Worker Authorisation Scheme.* Retrieved from https://www.gov.uk/hmrc-internal-manuals/claimant-compliance-manual/ccm20140 (accessed on 12 July 2019).

UK Government (2019a). *National Minimum Wage and Living Wage: accommodation.* Retrieved from https://www.gov.uk/national-minimum-wage-accommodation (accessed on 12 July 2019).

UK Government (2019b). *Work in the UK.* Retrieved from https://www.gov.uk/browse/visas-immigration/work-visas (accessed on 12 July 2019).

United Nations Development Programme (1997). *Human Development Report 1997.* http://hdr.undp.org/sites/default/files/reports/258/hdr_1997_en_complete_nostats.pdf

Unseen (2018). *Annual Assessment 2017.* https://www.unseenuk.org/uploads/20180413150810356.pdf

Zwolinski, M (2007). Sweatshops, choice, and exploitation. *Business Ethics Quarterly, 17*(4), 689–727. https://doi.org/10.5840/beq20071745

Index

Note: Page numbers in italics refer to figures. Page numbers in bold refer to tables.

Printed in the United States
by Baker & Taylor Publisher Services